INDIAN FIGHTS
New Facts on Seven Encounters

INDIAN FIGHTS

New Facts on Seven Encounters

By J. W. Vaughn

University of Oklahoma Press : Norman

By J. W. Vaughn

With Crook at the Rosebud (Harrisburg, Pa., 1956)
The Reynolds Campaign on Powder River (Norman, 1961)
The Battle of Platte Bridge (Norman, 1963)
Indian Fights: New Facts on Seven Encounters (Norman, 1966)

Library of Congress Catalog Card Number: 66–13416

Copyright 1966 by the University of Oklahoma Press, Publishing Division of the University. Composed and printed at Norman, Oklahoma, U.S.A., by the University of Oklahoma Press. First edition.

To My Wife
FLORENCE L. VAUGHN

Preface

Ꮮ Ꮮ Ꮮ Ꮮ Ꮮ Ꮮ

FOR MANY YEARS it has been my hobby to visit and study the battlefields of the Indian Wars in Wyoming and Montana, where the soldiers met the Sioux, Cheyennes, and Arapahos in bloody conflict. In addition to the complete coverage of each field with a metal detector, extensive research has uncovered new material and primary sources of information not theretofore used. Knowledge of the terrain and eyewitness accounts have made possible the faithful reconstruction of various campaigns and battles which have been published from time to time. My purpose has been to develop and record all the factual details concerning each battle together with convincing proof of its exact location before these sites are lost forever before the relentless onslaught of time and modern civilization. This work contains a critical analysis of seven such encounters between the white man and the Indians from 1864 to 1877.

During the Civil War the Bozeman Trail, which lay along the eastern slopes of the Big Horn Mountains, was the best route to the gold fields of Montana. Since the Indians occupied the territory north of the North Platte River, the Trail was extremely hazardous, and Chapter I covers a series of incidents which took place at Brown Springs, one of the most popular campsites, near present-day Douglas, Wyoming.

In 1866, the army's establishment of posts along the Bozeman Trail to protect the emigrants and supply trains resulted in attacks by the Indians upon soldiers from the garrisons. Chapter II contains highly detailed accounts of the fight of December 6, 1866, between soldiers from Fort Phil Kearny and the hostile Indians, and the well-known and so-called Fetterman Massacre of December 21, 1866, in which Captain William J. Fetterman, Brevet Lieutenant Colonel, and his entire detachment of eighty-two officers, enlisted men, and civilians were killed out of sight of the fort. New material from the National Archives and the Sheridan, Wyoming, Public Library are included, together with physical findings on the field pinpointing the several battle sites, which are located between Buffalo and Sheridan in northern Wyoming. The action of the twenty-first is highly controversial, and the important portions of Colonel Henry B. Carrington's manuscript and writings are printed in full in the Appendix to assist the reader in drawing his own conclusions.

The Hayfield Fight of August 1, 1867, near Fort C. F. Smith, forty-five miles southwest of present-day Hardin, Montana, is covered in Chapter III. With the aid of official reports and records from the National Archives, the complete story of the stand made by a handful of soldiers and hay cutters against overwhelming numbers of the attacking Indians, can be pieced together.

Since the Battle of the Rosebud of June 17, 1876, was one of the largest and most intricate actions between the soldiers and hostiles in Western United States history, a condensed version of the campaign and battle is included as Chapter IV for the benefit of those who lack the patience to follow the fortunes or misfortunes of numerous detachments of soldiers scattered over rough country along a six-mile front. The troop movements and battle areas have been ascertained by extensive use of a metal detector and contemporary sketches by participants.

One of the numerous side lights of the battle of the Little Big Horn in which General George A. Custer and five troops of the

Seventh Cavalry were annihilated is discussed in Chapter V. The action was commenced by Major Marcus A. Reno and three companies attacking the Indian village on the west side of the river. Because of extensive changes in the terrain and river courses, students have been unable to agree upon the location of Reno's skirmish lines. The writer definitely found one of the lines and with the descriptions of returning soldiers and testimony from the Reno Court of Inquiry is able to locate the first line and also the route Major Reno took in his retreat to the river.

In August, 1876, a small supply train from Camp Carlin, near Cheyenne, Wyoming, bound for Fort Fetterman with government supplies destined for General George Crook's army, was attacked near Elkhorn Creek, ten miles west of present Glendo, Wyoming, resulting in the death of the wagon boss. This incident is set forth in Chapter VI, and although some historians may consider small incidents such as this one relatively unimportant, they have a relevance in any close study of frontier history, and they are more difficult to reconstruct because of lack of material. A local dispute concerning the exact location of the wagon-train encounter was settled by using the detector.

During the Starvation March of General Crook's forces in September, 1876, an Indian village was attacked and captured by a detachment under Captain Anson Mills near Slim Buttes in what is now South Dakota. In celebration of the victory, the officers who led the charge had their pictures taken by the well-known Western photographer, Stanley J. Morrow, before an Indian tipi draped with one of Custer's guidons. Since these men were prominent figures in the military actions of the period, a short sketch is given of the life of each together with their chief accomplishments, in Chapter VII.

It is my pleasure to acknowledge the assistance of George G. Osten and Kenneth F. Roahen, of Billings, Montana, in the reconnaissance on the Reno and Hayfield areas. Mr. Roahen, a prominent photographer, has furnished photographs of various points of interest.

The late L. C. Bishop, of Cheyenne, Wyoming, collaborated in the field work on the Fetterman Massacre and is entitled to nearly all the credit for the research involved in the Heck Reel Wagon Train incident.

Brigadier General Charles D. Roberts, U.S. Army, Retired, has furnished professional help and advice on the Fetterman Massacre, concurring in my reconstruction of the action.

Colonel Arcadi Gluckman, U.S. Army, Retired, and Colonel B. R. Lewis, U.S. Army, Retired, have initiated me into the mysteries of the Spencer carbine and ammunition.

Lieutenant Colonel Elwood L. Nye, U.S. Army, Retired, has aided in identifying various articles of cavalry equipment found on many fields.

Mrs. Elsa Spear Byron, Ed Kopac, and Emil Kopac have offered valuable suggestions in the research on the Hayfield Fight.

Mrs. M. C. Helms, librarian of the Sheridan, Wyoming, Public Library, has graciously consented to the inclusion of portions of the manuscript and writings of Colonel Henry B. Carrington, now in the custody of the Library.

Eddie Smith and Stevie Smith, of Banner, Wyoming, assisted with research on the areas around Fort Phil Kearny.

Acknowledgment is gratefully extended to the New York Posse of the Westerners, in whose *Brand Book* earlier appeared a version of Chapter VII, "The Buckskin Lodge at Slim Buttes," here revised and enhanced.

Sam Denny, of Garryowen, Montana, has assisted in many ways in locating the Reno skirmish lines and identifying various portions of the field.

Ray C. Davis, Roy Nayumatsu, and Roy Nagashima have furnished information leading to a more complete understanding of the scenes of action on the Reno field.

My appreciation is extended to all other persons who have aided in these projects.

J. W. VAUGHN

Windsor, Colorado
February 16, 1966

Contents

Illustrations

┌┐┌┐┌┐┌┐┌┐┌┐

Burial Site of Lieutenant Brown   *following page* 80
Fort Phil Kearny, 1867
View from Fort Phil Kearny
Death Site of Lieutenant Grummond and Cavalry
Wheatley-Fisher Rocks
Site of the Hayfield Fight
General George Crook, 1875
Fort Fetterman
Issuing Arms and Supplies

Crook's Forces Crossing Goose Creek   *following page* 160
Crook's Infantry in the Black Hills
Ravine from Calhoun Hill to Little Big Horn River
Reno's Second Line
View Northeast towards Custer Monument
The Little Big Horn Battlefield
The Buckskin Lodge at Slim Buttes
Casualties of Battle of Slim Buttes

Maps

INDIAN FIGHTS
New Facts on Seven Encounters

1
Death at Cheyenne Fork
⊓⊔⊓⊔⊓⊔⊓⊔⊓⊔⊓⊔⊓⊔⊓⊔⊓

CHEYENNE FORK, situated forty miles northwest of present-day Douglas, Wyoming, was one of the most popular camping places on the Bozeman Trail during the mid and late 1800's. Brown Springs, for which the stopping-off place was later named, produced so much water that pools stood along the little stream which ran from the spring northeasterly three or four miles to its junction with the Dry Fork of the Cheyenne River. Grass grew waist high about the spring, so there was excellent grazing for the stock.

The Bozeman Trail, also known as the Montana Road, ran northwesterly from its intersection with the Oregon Trail along the eastern slopes of the Big Horn Mountains, forming the shortest route to Virginia City, Montana. The Trail had been followed by Father Jean De Smet in 1851, and the Raynolds Expedition went over it with heavily laden wagons in the fall of 1859. John Bozeman, for whom the route was named, conducted civilian wagon trains over it in 1862 and 1863. Because the road ran through the heart of Indian country, it was a hazardous route, the hostile Sioux and Cheyenne Indians bitterly resenting the intrusions into their territory. As the traffic over the Trail increased, the army in 1866–67 established Fort Reno, Fort Phil Kearny, Fort C. F. Smith, and Fort Fetterman at intervals along the road to protect the emigrants, supply trains, and miners traveling to the gold fields of Montana. Cheyenne Fork, or Brown

3

Springs, was thirty miles northwest of Fort Fetterman, while Fort Reno was fifty miles farther on. Fort Phil Kearny and Fort C. F. Smith lay farther to the northwest.[1]

Travelers along the road gauged each day's march so that in the evening they would arrive at a suitable campsite. Wagon trains and infantry troops going north from Fort Fetterman often spent the first night at Sage Creek, thirteen miles distant, arriving at Brown Springs on the second day. Cavalry troops and other horsemen often reached Brown Springs on the first day. During winter weather, large outfits would follow the little stream down to the Dry Fork where more water was available.[2]

The old Bozeman Trail, which is followed closely by the present narrow, country road, crosses low ranges of hills called "divides" spaced every four or five miles, and near the center of each valley is a small stream. From the divides there are gentle slopes leading down to the trough of the valleys where the ground rises to the crest of the next ridge. Brown Springs lies in one of these valleys and originates several miles southwest of the road, and the stream is augmented by numerous other springs along its course to the Dry Fork. One-half mile south of the crossing and lying west of the road is a rocky butte which commands the surrounding area. During the early days the threat of Indian attacks made it dangerous to stop in the valley, so camp was made on the butte where a good lookout could be maintained for any signs of hostility. Five hundred yards north of the crossing is a rocky ridge which extends northward along the west side of the road, overlooking the lush pastureland to the east and south.

The springs were named after Lieutenant John Brown of Company E, Eleventh Ohio Cavalry, who was killed there by Indians on July 21, 1864. Brown was twenty-two years of age

---

[1] See Grace Raymond Hebard and E. A. Brininstool, *The Bozeman Trail*; and Robert W. Frazer, *Forts of the West*.
[2] J. W. Vaughn, *The Reynolds Campaign on Powder River*, 44.

when he left his wife and child to go to Cincinnati, Ohio, where he enlisted as first sergeant in Company E on June 1, 1863. One week later he was mustered into the U.S. Army at Camp Denison, Ohio, and on September 4 he was promoted to second lieutenant, serving initially under Captain Levi G. Marshall. He came West with his company in the fall of 1863 and spent part of the winter at Platte Bridge Station guarding the Oregon Trail. In March and April, 1864, Brown was on detached service at the post at South Pass which is now known as the "Burnt Ranch."[3] His company contained many "galvanized Yankees," captive southern soldiers who were permitted to serve in the army out West instead of remaining in federal prisons. Although most of these men were good soldiers, a few of them were not, and some even conspired to mutiny against their officers. One incident involving these soldiers occurred when three of them refused to obey an order at Platte Bridge Station on May 12, 1864. Lieutenant Brown and the loyal troops shot and killed Patrick Grey and two men, both named "John Sullivan," who were southern sympathizers.[4] The muster roll for May and June, 1864, shows that Brown was again on detached service, and one might surmise that he was stationed at various points along the Oregon Trail. Shortly before his death he adopted the name of "John R. Brown," possibly to distinguish him from Lieutenant John A. Brown of Company K of the same regiment.[5] In July, Brown was serving with his company at Fort Laramie when he was caught up in the series of events which led to his death.

In the summer of 1864 the Indians were in a turmoil. Those at the Upper Platte Agency were dissatisfied by the Treaty of Fort Wise, whereby the Southern Cheyennes lost their country

[3] Records of the Adjutant General's Office of the United States; and Records of the Adjutant General's Office of the State of Ohio.

[4] Lewis F. Crawford, *Rekindling Campfires*, 62–66.

[5] Muster Roll of Company E, Eleventh Ohio Volunteer Cavalry, for July and August, 1864.

5

without their consent. Unscrupulous squaw men from Canada fomented hatred against the United States government, furnishing the Indians with whisky and other presents. Northern bands of three hundred to four hundred Sioux each were committing depredations, and there were frequent conflicts with the soldiers and emigrants. On July 3, the situation had become so bad that Lieutenant Colonel W. O. Collins, commandant of Fort Laramie, requested Indian Agent John Loree, of the Upper Platte Agency, to identify the hostile Indians who were stealing stock on the north side of the Platte River from careless emigrants. On July 13, Loree replied that he had learned from Swift Bear, chief of the Brulés, that one hundred Indians intended to attack Fort Laramie and another one hundred to attack Bordeaux ranch, while a third band of one hundred would take possession of the road in the vicinity of Scott's Bluffs in order to steal government and civilian horses. The attacking parties consisted of the Minneconjous and Two Kettle's band. The day after receiving this information, Colonel Collins issued a circular to all persons near Fort Laramie:

> The recent attacks made and threatened by the Missouri Indians along the Platte River make it necessary that every precaution should be taken for defence against them. It is, therefore, recommended that all mountaineers and other citizens and settlers in the vicinity of Fort Laramie who may be exposed to danger should immediately collect at some proper point, with their families and stock, and prepare themselves to defend their persons and property, and be in a situation to give prompt notice to the commander of the post in case of danger. Some place between the stations of Bearrais and Burdeau [*sic*] would be sufficiently near.[6]

On July 13, the same day Loree's message was received, Collins ordered two companies of the Eleventh Ohio Cavalry com-

---

[6] U.S. Department of the Interior, *Report of the Commissioner of Indian Affairs for the Year 1864* (Washington, Government Printing Office, 1865), 386–90.

manded by Captain Jacob S. Shuman and Captain Levi G. Marshall to pursue a group of Indians, with Frank Ecoffey as guide for the expedition. Although it has been claimed that the troops were ordered out to recoup stock stolen from the emigrants,[7] it is possible that they were sent to find Fanny Kelly, a white woman seized by the band of Indians attacking the Larimer party on the Little Box Elder the previous day. Four men were killed defending the Larimer wagon train, and Mrs. Kelly's adopted daughter was missing, to be found dead a few days later. Mr. Kelly managed to escape, and when he reached Deer Creek Station he telegraphed to Fort Laramie, telling of the outbreak of the Indians and of his wife's capture. Mrs. Kelly herself later claimed that the two units had been sent to rescue her and to chastise the Indians if they resisted.[8]

Whatever the immediate cause of the expedition, the troops arrived too late to rescue the woman. Pursuing the Indians northward, the two cavalry units arrived at Cheyenne Fork, later known as Brown Springs, on July 19, where they made camp on the butte south of the stream.

Mrs. Kelly, later ransomed from the Indians by a payment equivalent to nineteen horses, told about the encounter at Brown Springs, presumably as related to her by her husband:

> Sad to relate, a young and daring officer, Lieutenant Brown, of the Eleventh Ohio Volunteers, fell a victim to savage cruelty in my behalf, for with a view of prospecting the neighborhood, he, with Mr. Kelly, left the main body with a small squad of men in quest of the Indians.
>
> Coming suddenly upon a band of warriors, in their encampment, the brave Lieutenant indiscreetly ordered an attack,

[7] C. G. Coutant, *History of Wyoming*, 709; *Annals of Wyoming*, Vol. III, No. 2 (October, 1925), 147; and Fanny Kelly, *Narrative of My Captivity Among the Sioux Indians*, 223.

[8] Kelly, *ibid.*, 19, 223.

but the men, seeing the futility of opposing such numbers, fled, and left Mr. Kelly and the officer.

Becoming conscious of his dangerous situation, he feigned friendship, addressing them in the usual way, "How Koda [Kola]?" which means, "How do you do, friend?"

But they were not to be deceived, and sent an arrow, causing him to fall from his horse, and the effects of which caused his death a few hours afterward.

He was immediately reported dead, and with all the speed the men could command they pursued his murderers; but the fresher horses of the savages carried them off beyond their reach, and the soldiers were compelled to return in disappointment.

Brave young man! The ardent friend of Mr. Kelly, and the husband and father of an affectionate wife and child, stricken down in his early manhood, we would humbly lay the wreath of "Immortelles" upon thy lonely grave.[9]

Lieutenant Brown was wounded in the evening and was believed to be dead. The next morning a party was sent out to bring in his body and, much to their astonishment, found him alive but dangerously wounded. Brown was brought into camp, but he died on the twenty-first and was was buried at the springs. The company muster roll dated August 31, 1864, at La Bonte Station, states: "The company left Fort Laramie, I.T. July 13th, 1864, in pursuit of hostile Indians. Marched 600 miles returning to Fort Laramie July 29/64 having had three severe skirmishes with Sioux Indians killing and wounding near 40 of them and having Second Lieut. J. R. Brown mortally wounded on 19th died on 21st." Opposite Brown's name on the muster roll appeared the notation, "Mortally wounded in action on Cheyenne Fork, I.T. July 19th, 1864, died 21st July."

The young bugler Mike Henry, who may have been with the

[9] *Ibid.*, 223.

soldiers, in later years described the fight in this manner. The men, encamped on the butte with their arms stacked, were unaware of the presence of Indians. When Lieutenant Brown and thirteen men went down to the spring to get water, they were ambushed by Indians hiding in the tall grass. An eighteen-year-old boy who was herding horses and mules east of the road was killed and scalped. His awful screams were plainly heard. A running fight which ensued lasted for three days. The Indians were driven north past the Dry Fork towards Sand Creek but returned at night to retrieve their dead and wounded. Since there is no record of any other Indian fights between July 13 and July 29, the "three severe skirmishes" mentioned by Captain Marshall probably refer to the three days' fight north of Brown Springs.

Lieutenant Brown was buried in a rocky cairn on the brow of the ridge north of the springs, and for many years there was a high mound which has since been leveled off. The soldiers chiseled his initials "J R B" in the sandstone on the east side of the cairn. The initials were visible for many years but have now eroded from the rock. The names of all the dead were chiseled on the rocks on the butte south of the springs but are now illegible. The muster roll of Company E, dated August 31, 1864, does not give the name of any other soldier in the company as killed or wounded during the two months' period, although three were named as deserters. The boy herding the horses, and other civilians who may have been killed, were undoubtedly buried in the meadow east of the road. According to the army records, Lieutenant Brown was the only soldier killed in the fight. The muster roll of Captain Shuman's Company H does not even mention this skirmish and makes no mention of any of the company's being killed or wounded during the period.

Two years later, on July 29, 1866, a civilian train was attacked at Brown Springs, and eight men were killed and two wounded, one of whom died. Colonel Henry B. Carrington, who was in command of Fort Phil Kearny at the time, described the incident as it had been reported to him:

> One fact in this skirmish requires record, viz, that while the men were well armed with Henry and other special arms, they were killed although the force of Indians was small, viz, less than 80. The Indians professed friendship, and 1 man killed was killed by an Indian, who, just after shaking hands with him and accepting tobacco, shot him in the back. Some of the party were in pursuit of game and some in pursuit of Indians on the hill. Two were in advance and were shot while parleying, and a mile from the camp.[10]

Margaret Irvin Carrington, wife of Colonel Carrington, also referred to this encounter:

> Their grave is still memorial of the confidence with which they left [Fort] Laramie, assured that all was peace. These men, though too few in numbers, were well armed, but were deceived by a show of friendship; and one Indian shot a white man in the back just after shaking hands and receiving a present.[11]

These men were probably buried in the Henry meadow east of where the Henry ranch house later stood, for it is unlikely that they would have been carried fifty miles northward to Fort Reno, even had wagons been available for transportation.

On August 21, 1866, Caspar H. Walsh, a soldier, was killed on the Dry Fork of the Cheyenne River, while W. R. Pettis and A. G. Overholt, civilians, were wounded.[12]

In the summer of 1866 the long wagon train of Hugh Kirkendall, loaded with merchandise bound for Montana, was attacked

[10] "History of Indian Operations on the Plains, furnished by Col. Henry B. Carrington to a special commission which met at Fort McPherson, Nebr., in the spring of 1867," 50 Cong., 1 sess., *Sen. Exec. Doc. 33,* 12.

[11] Margaret Irvin Carrington, *Ab-Sa-Ra-Ka, Land of Massacre,* 124.

[12] Coutant, *History of Wyoming,* I, 558.

at Brown Springs. A running fight ensued, and although the number of Indians increased, the train was able to push through without casualties.[13]

On April 2, 1867, "Major" Van Volzah, the mail carrier, and two other civilians were ambushed and killed north of Brown Springs, in the vicinity of the head of the Dry Fork of Powder River. The mail was being carried in an army ambulance, while two pack mules laden with onions were bound for Fort Phil Kearny where the men were suffering from scurvy. The three bodies were found amid evidence of the most desperate fighting. From the wrecked ambulance a trail led eastward to the small safe which had been dragged into a draw. The Indians had been unable to open the safe, and it was retrieved and taken on to Fort Reno. Several days later, A. B. Ostrander, returning from Fort Phil Kearny, found some of the mail scattered about on the mesa south of the descent into the Dry Fork.[14]

Margaret Irvin Carrington referred to this incident: "Such men as . . . Van Zolzpah [*sic*], with his experience and quiet coolness, who, after a life in Oregon and Washington Territories, and many successful trips to [Fort] Laramie, was butchered at last, with his whole party."[15]

The three dead men likely were buried at Brown Springs, which was closer than Fort Reno. In the Record of Events in the regimental return of the Twenty-seventh Infantry for April, 1867, appears the following notation: "A mail from the east was lost near the Dry Fork of Powder River on or about the 2nd day of April, and the mail carrier Mr Van Volzah, and two other citizens were killed by Indians but little of the mail was recovered."

In 1878, Mike Henry, impressed by the excellent grazing in the area, settled at Brown Springs with a small spread of cattle

[13] Hebard and Brininstool, *Bozeman Trail*, I, 227–28.

[14] Robert B. David, *Finn Burnett, Frontiersman*, 151; A. B. Ostrander, *An Army Boy of the Sixties*, 217; and Hebard and Brininstool, *ibid.*, II, 108.

[15] Carrington, *Narrative*, 137.

bearing the "88" brand. An enlistee as a bugler in the Union Army during the Civil War at the age of thirteen, Henry was returning to an area with which he had become acquainted during his years of service. After the war Henry had married and lived several years on a farm in Kansas, where his son, John F., and four other children were born. When he returned to Brown Springs, his family remained at Fort Laramie, where another son, Will M., was born. Mike Henry was joined by his wife, Catherine, and their six children when construction of a ranch house was completed on the west side of the road near the springs.

Soon after the Henrys arrived, they discovered a number of mounds in the meadow east of the house, marking the burial sites of thirty soldiers and emigrants. Although the identities of those buried in the unmarked graves were unknown to her, Mrs. Henry found time to fashion headboards for the mounds. At a later date the soldiers were disinterred and reburied in a national cemetery, but the bodies of the civilians remained.

After Mike Henry settled there, Brown Springs became a stage stop on the Bozeman Trail, while emigrants, miners, and soldiers made camp in the valley west of the house. Many herds of Texas longhorn cattle were driven past on their way to Montana. The Indians had been herded onto their reservations, so it was no longer necessary to camp on the butte a half mile away. The Henry boys grew up hearing tales about the early history of the area around the campfires at night. Frank Grouard, the famous scout, camped here on many occasions, while Colonel Guy V. Henry (no relation to Mike Henry) often camped near the springs with some of his Ninth Cavalry troopers.[16]

With the advent of the railroads, the Bozeman Trail was no

[16] Information concerning the Henry family has been furnished by the late John F. Henry, the late Will M. Henry, and Maude W. Henry, the widow of Will. For a more detailed account of the family life at Brown Springs, the reader is referred to the article by Mrs. Will M. Henry, "Brown Springs Station," *Annals of Wyoming*, Vol. 36, No. 1 (April, 1964).

longer used, and the Henry place became just another cattle ranch with a good spring. There is no traffic over the lonely road now except for an occasional rancher in a pickup truck. The grass is no longer waist high because cattle keep it grazed closely. The old pioneer, Mike Henry, died years ago, while recently his sons, van." The burial mounds have been leveled by cattle and the headboards disintegrated so that there is little trace of the graves except eight or ten sunken places and and several partially filled excavations where the soldiers were disinterred. The ranch house which once welcomed the weary traveler has been removed, leaving only the skeleton timbers of the barn, corral, and out-buildings. Soon, these too will be gone, and there will be nothing left at this historic spot except the lonely cairn of Lieutenant Brown overlooking the unmarked graves in the pasture.

2
A New Look at the Fetterman Disaster

ⴰⴰⴰⴰⴰⴰⴰⴰⴰⴰⴰⴰⴰⴰⴰⴰⴰⴰⴰⴰⴰ

ONE OF THE MOST FAMOUS BATTLE SITES of the Indian Wars is situated along a ridge near Highway 87 midway between the cities of Buffalo and Sheridan, Wyoming. Here, nearly one century ago, a band of soldiers under the command of Brevet Lieutenant Colonel William J. Fetterman, Captain, Eighteenth U.S. Infantry, was wiped out by the combined forces of Cheyenne, Arapaho, and Sioux warriors. Tourists today riding along the paved highway can look up to a ridge on the east and see the three battle locations where the soldiers were overwhelmed by superior numbers. On the west side of the highway may be seen the broken slopes leading down to Peno Creek, the sites of other skirmishes with the tribes.

The story has often been told how Colonel Henry B. Carrington led his troops of the Eighteenth Infantry to the Big Horn country and established Fort Phil Kearny between the forks of the Piney in July, 1866.[1] Here the fort was built of pine timber hauled from the mountains five or six miles distant, and by December the construction was almost completed.

The hostile Sioux and Cheyennes bitterly resented this intrusion into their domain, and there was constant harrassment of the garrison and its wood parties and of the supply trains travel-

[1] See Dee Brown, *Fort Phil Kearny: An American Saga*; Carrington, *Ab-Sa-Ra-Ka*; Frances C. Carrington, *My Army Life*; and Hebard and Brininstool, *Bozeman Trail*. A convincing fictionalized version appears in Michael Straight, *Carrington*.

14

ing along the Bozeman Trail northward to the gold fields of Montana. By December 21, 1866, ninety-one enlisted men, five officers, and fifty-eight civilians had been killed and twenty more wounded, while the enemy had captured 306 oxen and cows, 304 mules, and 161 horses. The troops were poorly armed, the infantry using the old Civil War .58-caliber muzzle-loading Springfield rifles, while the cavalry, having no revolvers, were armed with the Springfield rifles and Starr carbines, single-shot breech-loading weapons using the same copper cartridges as the Spencer carbine. The Regimental Band had the seven-shot repeating Spencer carbines which had proved so effective during the Civil War. The requisition of November 6 for revolvers for the cavalry companies had not been received, and the new Spencers which had left Fort Leavenworth on September 15 had not yet arrived. Although the supply of ammunition had been reduced to forty-five rounds per man, there was a standing order at the post for the soldiers to keep forty rounds of ammunition in their cartridge boxes.[2]

While the fort was being built, the never-ending controversy between the army and the Indian Bureau received new impetus in the form of an order by Brevet Brigadier General P. St. George Cooke, commander of the Department of the Platte. Dated July 31, 1866, the order prohibited traders from selling arms and ammunition to the Indians and enjoined all commanders of troops within the Department to co-operate in enforcing the prohibition. The intent of the order was to prevent weapons from falling into the hands of hostile Indians and, of course, to forestall the use of such arms against soldiers and settlers. Indian Commissioner Lewis V. Bogy objected to Cooke's ban, however, claiming that the Indians needed guns to hunt game for their subsistence. The Commissioner criticized Colonel Carrington for not treating with the Indians, who he claimed were starving, alleging that the

[2] Testimony of Captain William H. Bisbee before the Sanborn Commission.

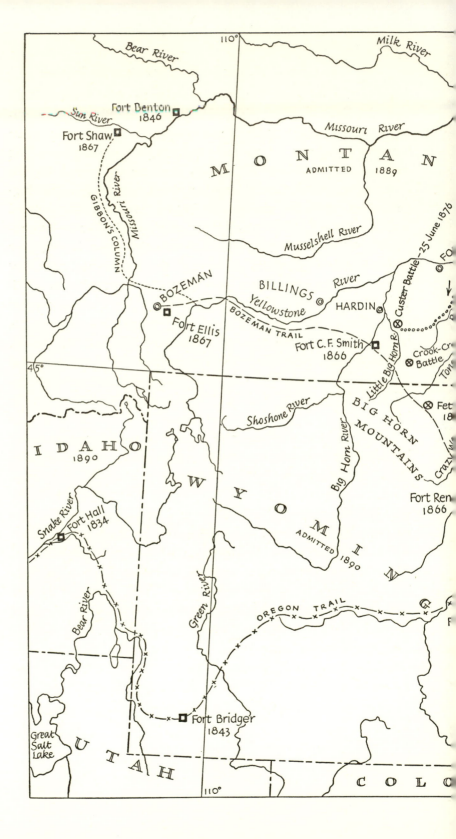

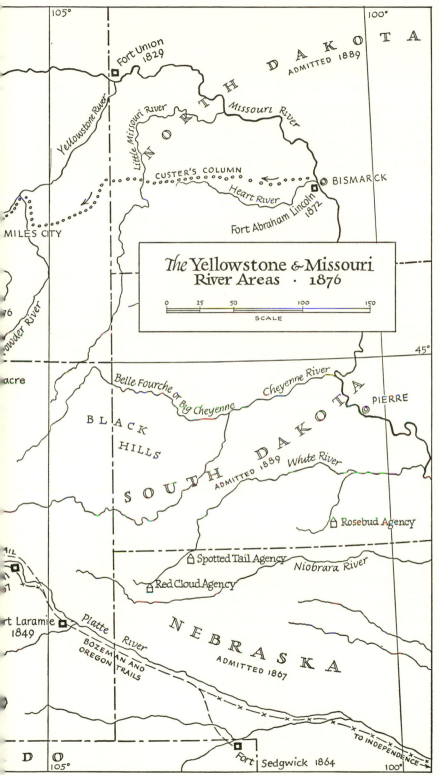

Indians had attacked the fort because they were unable to shoot game. Carrington was thus between two fires, the Indian Bureau on the one side, and his superiors, who underestimated the strength of the Indian resistance, on the other.

As early as September 27, General Cooke had suggested that Carrington take the offensive against the Indians and surprise them in their winter camps, while on November 25 a positive order was received, instructing Carrington to avenge the Indian attacks by striking them as soon as all the troop quarters were built. The army high command believed that the best results could be obtained by attacking the Indians, who wintered in small bands, during the cold weather when their ponies were weak from lack of forage. In accordance with these instructions, Carrington turned his attention from construction activities to making plans for attacking the hostiles. The post return for November, 1866, shows a total of 427 officers and men, consisting of troops of the Eighteenth Infantry together with Company C, Second Cavalry, which numbered 63 men. The cavalry had arrived in November under the command of Lieutenant Horatio S. Bingham, armed with Springfield rifles and Starr carbines. There were about seventy-five men at the post for whom no arms had been obtained, although a requisition had been made five months earlier, and the weapons had been shipped because invoices on them had been received at least two months prior to the engagement of December 21.[3]

While there have been many excellent accounts of the events around Fort Phil Kearny, there have been no satisfactory reconstructions of the battles with the Indians which occurred on December 6 and 21. On the latter date occurred the engagement in which Fetterman with his entire command of eighty men perished a short distance out of sight of the post. There being no survivors to tell what really happened, history has labeled him a

[3] Testimony of Lieutenant Alfred H. Wands before the Sanborn Commission.

reckless and headstrong officer who led his men into the enemy trap in disregard of specific orders from his superior.

In response to the public indignation arising from the defeat, the President appointed the Sanborn Commission "to visit the Indian country in the neighborhood of Fort Phil Kearny, for the purpose of ascertaining the facts."[4] The records and testimony obtained by this body contains valuable and detailed information concerning both the December 6 and the December 21 fights and the circumstances surrounding them. The Commission was composed of Generals Alfred Sully, J. B. Sanborn, and N. B. Buford, Colonel E. S. Parker, G. P. Beauvais, a trader who had lived among the Sioux for many years, and Jefferson T. Kinney, who had been post sutler at Fort Phil Kearny. On March 2, 1867, the members of the Commission met at the Herndon House in Omaha, Nebraska, and organized. The testimony of First Lieutenant Alfred H. Wands, Eighteenth Infantry, was heard on March 4. The next two days were occupied with hearing the testimony of Brevet Captain W. F. Arnold, First Lieutenant, Twenty-seventh Infantry. On March 7, the Commission heard the testimony of Brevet Captain William H. Bisbee, First Lieutenant, Twenty-seventh Infantry, aide-de-camp on the staff of General P. St. George Cooke. The General's testimony was heard, but it was necessary to recall him for supplemental testimony on March 11. The Commission heard Private George B. Mackey, Company E, Eighteenth Infantry, on March 9, while on March 11, Dr. C. M. Hines, a contract surgeon twenty-eight years of age while at Fort Phil Kearny, was called to testify.

When the weather permitted, the Commission moved to Fort McPherson, Nebraska, where Colonel Henry B. Carrington was post commander. Here, from March 20 to March 27, Carrington told of his experiences at and around Fort Phil Kearny and offered official messages, reports, letters sent and received, and all testi-

---

[4] 40 Cong., 1 sess., *Sen. Exec. Doc. 13*, 55.

mony and documents having the slightest bearing on the affairs at the fort.[5] Most of the Commission seemed satisfied with Carrington's presentation of his evidence, and they did not call any other witnesses at Fort McPherson, which must have displeased Carrington for he complained that his orderly, Archibald Sample, three other enlisted men, and William Bailey, a civilian guide who had come with Carrington from Fort Phil Kearny, were not called. Carrington's testimony and supporting documents were hidden away in the files of the Department of the Interior for twenty years, while the Senate Committee on Indian Affairs published derogatory statements by the commissioner of Indian affairs and letters from personal enemies of Carrington, including Dr. Hines and General Cooke. It was not until 1887 that Carrington persuaded the U.S. Senate to make public his official report and the testimony given before the Commission at Fort McPherson.

From Fort McPherson the Commission moved to Fort Laramie, Fort Sedgewick, and various frontier settlements to take the testimony of the hostile Indian tribes. In order to contact the Indians, Todd Randall and Leon F. Pallardy were employed as interpreters, and since a large area had to be covered, the Commission was divided into three branches: General Sully and Colonel Parker were to travel to the Upper Missouri and interview the Missouri Sioux; General Sanford, General Buford, and Mr. Beauvais were to remain at Fort Laramie to interview the Indians who could be induced by an offer of presents to come in; while J. T. Kinney was authorized to represent the Commission at Fort Phil Kearny in taking testimony there and meeting with the "Mountain Crows." General Sully was not in favor of any of the members going to Fort Phil Kearny because he thought sufficient evidence had already been obtained, but Mr. Kinney felt the record would be incomplete without such testimony. The

[5] 40 Cong., 1 sess., *Sen. Exec. Doc. 13.*

20

Commission separated at Fort Laramie on May 8 with the understanding that the members would meet on the first Monday in September, 1867, at the National Hotel in Washington, D.C., to make the final report. This meeting, however, was never held, and most of the members made their own separate reports.

Commissioner J. T. Kinney had made arrangements with Brevet Brigadier General Henry W. Wessels, Lieutenant Colonel, Eighteenth Infantry, in command of Fort Phil Kearny, to have the Mountain Crows at the fort for the interviews, so he left Fort Laramie on May 13 with an escort of 150 troopers of the Second Cavalry under the command of Major John Green, Brevet Lieutenant Colonel, Second Cavalry. The road was under constant attack by hostile Indians so that supply trains overtaken on the road could not move. When Kinney finally arrived at the fort on May 31, most of the Crows were out on a hunting trip along the Tongue River, and it was necessary to send for them. The hunting party returned on June 21, and three days later Kinney delivered a speech to the assembled council of friendly Indians, probably consisting of about five hundred warriors or eighteen hundred men, women, and children.

J. T. Kinney then sat as a commission of one and on July 5 heard the testimony of Captain Tenodor Ten Eyck, Eighteenth Infantry; on July 24, he heard Brevet Major James Powell, Captain, Twenty-seventh Infantry; on July 25, Brevet Major Samuel L. Horton, assistant surgeon at the post, testified; on July 27, Michael Boyer, post guide and interpreter was heard; while on July 29, J. B. Weston, a lawyer and civilian at the post, was the last witness to testify.[6]

---

[6] While the other two branches of the Sanborn Commission were far away conducting hearings at Fort Phil Kearny and on the Upper Missouri, Commissioners Sanborn, Buford, and Beauvais were meeting with the Indian chiefs around Fort Laramie. At a council on June 8, the hostile Indians demanded that all their territory, including the Bozeman Trail and the forts guarding it, be vacated because the soldiers and settlers were driving away the wild game and

Meanwhile, upon learning of the testimony taken by the Commission at Omaha in early March, General Ulysses S. Grant, by the direction of the President, appointed a Court of Inquiry to consist of Brevet Major General John Gibbon, Lieutenant Colonel L. P. Bradley, Major James Van Voast, and Brevet Colonel Alexander Chambers, the last serving as recorder. By Special Order No. 128, dated March 13, 1867, the Court was ordered to assemble at Fort Phil Kearny, on the first day of April, 1867, or as soon thereafter as practicable, to inquire into the facts attending

---

interfering with the Indians' way of life. On June 12, Sanborn and Beauvais had a meeting with the Oglala and Brulé chiefs at Fort Laramie and became satisfied that all the hostile Indians had agreed to make peace with the whites and planned to abandon all hostilities. On the strength of this meeting, General Sanborn made his report of July 8, believing there would be no more trouble with the Indians. General Buford had already made his report on June 6, and it was similar to that of Sanborn, both men absolving Colonel Carrington of all blame for the Fetterman disaster because of his shortages of troops and supplies. Both reports were printed in 40 Cong., 1 sess., *Sen. Exec. Doc. 13*, and both recommended that the Bozeman Trail and its forts be abandoned since the Indians intended to remain at peace. While the meetings at Fort Laramie were in progress, Commissioner J. T. Kinney and an escort of 150 cavalrymen were fighting their way through these same bands of Indians along the Bozeman Trail on the way to Fort Phil Kearny. During the two-month period that Kinney sat as a commissioner at Fort Phil Kearny, none of the hostile Indians appeared at Fort Laramie. On August 1 and 2, 1867, the same tribes who had protested their peaceful intentions towards the government made a strong attack on the Hayfield Corral near Fort C. F. Smith and on the Wagon Box Corral five miles northwest of Fort Phil Kearny. During the time Kinney was sitting as a commissioner, the hostile Indians made almost daily raids on the herds and parties around the vicinity of the fort.

On October 7, J. T. Kinney made his report to the Honorable O. H. Browning, secretary of the interior, in which he stated that under the Treaty of 1851 all this territory had been awarded to the Crows but that the Sioux and Cheyennes now occupied it. He recommended that the territory be restored to the Crows and that the hostile Indians be driven onto reservations by the War Department. In a strongly worded document he contended that the Indians should not be allowed to stand in the way of progress and the building of settlements which were springing up in Montana. No further action or reports were made by the Sanborn Commission, although the government followed the advice of Commissioners Sanborn, Buford, and Beauvais and abandoned the Bozeman Trail and its forts in accordance with their suggestions.

and preceding the Fetterman disaster and to report whether they felt any disciplinary measures were necessary.

Dated April 8, Supplementary Order No. 176 directed the Court of Inquiry to organize at Omaha, Nebraska, then to adjourn to Fort McPherson, Nebraska, and Fort Phil Kearny. The Court met at Omaha on May 9 and after moving to Fort McPherson heard the testimony of Colonel Carrington, who gave them all the documentary evidence which he had already presented to the Sanborn Commission, including the complete itinerary of his march from Fort Kearny, Nebraska, on May 14, 1866, until he turned over the command of Fort Phil Kearny to Brevet Brigadier General Henry W. Wessels.

Colonel Carrington testified before the Court that the orders delivered by him to Colonel Fetterman on December 21 were not obeyed and that his orders to Captain Ten Eyck in going to the relief of Fetterman also were not obeyed. Captain Ten Eyck, Carrington said, had been ordered to take the most direct course towards the supposed point of contest and had been advised to follow the Lodge Trail Ridge and join Colonel Fetterman at all hazards. Just as the advance party of Ten Eyck's command had reached the crest of the hill on the opposite side of the road from Lodge Trail Ridge, two couriers had broken from his command on horseback and reported back to Carrington. Captain Ten Eyck had not taken the most direct course, but in the opinion of Carrington even if Captain Ten Eyck had obeyed orders and taken the advice the destruction of Fetterman's command would still have occurred.

While giving his testimony, Carrington called the attention of the Court to the fact that Lieutenant A. H. Wands, Orderly Archibald Sample, and other responsible witnesses familiar with the facts connected with the tragedy were present at the fort awaiting summonses from the Court. However, the Court declined to call any of them, deciding their testimony was not needed, but requested Colonel Carrington to turn over to the Judge Advocate the original books and instruments which had been introduced in evidence. The documentary evidence as well as the personal testimony of Colonel Carrington was similar in general terms to that given before the Sanborn Commission which had already met at the same place.

After hearing testimony and inspecting the pertinent records, the military Court of Inquiry, finding no one to blame but the dead Fetterman, adjourned sine die.

The testimony heard by the Sanborn Commission was taken down by a reporter and is now in Record Group 75 of the records of the Bureau of Indian Affairs in the files of the National Archives in Washington, D.C. Until this material came to light recently, there was no authentic source material on the Fetterman disaster except the testimony, reports, and maps of Colonel Carrington. This new material calls for a complete reappraisal of the background situation at the post and a careful analysis of all the circumstances surrounding the various engagements.

In the first place, regimental morale appears to have been at a low ebb. Colonel Carrington had not been a combat officer during the Civil War, while most of his younger officers had distinguished war records. These officers found fault with Carrington for not immediately mounting an expedition against the Indians, and were contemptuous of his failure to act according to the instructions of General Cooke. It seems clear from the testimony before the Commission that there was ill feeling between Colonel Carrington on the one side, and Major Powell, Captain Bisbee, Dr. Hines, and Colonel Fetterman on the other. Private George B. Mackey of Company E, Eighteenth Infantry, said, "The ill feeling was jealousy, partly towards the commanding officers. There was not that harmony that should be in a regiment." Lieutenant W. F. Arnold put it this way, "Some of the officers were not on the most friendly terms, but never clashed at all. The feeling was not harmonious but there was no open rupture." Captain Bisbee stated that there was a general feeling of disgust towards Colonel Carrington, while Major Powell, Carrington's bitterest critic, never missed an opportunity to downgrade him. Carrington, in turn, claimed that when Major Powell and Colonel Fetterman arrived at Fort Phil Kearny, knowing that the Second Battalion of the Eighteenth Infantry had become the Twenty-seventh Infantry, they expected to be placed in command of Fort C. F. Smith and Fort Phil Kearny respectively, and they were disappointed when they did not receive the assignments.

Evidence is overwhelming that discipline at the fort was poor, and many of the soldiers were recruits who had never been drilled. There was much testimony on this point by witnesses before the Sanborn Commission. General Cooke testified that he had intended to relieve Carrington because of the latter's maintenance of poor discipline at the fort. Cooke had received letters from an officer at the post (probably Major Powell) complaining of the poor state of discipline. Major Powell, in his testimony before the Commission, criticized Carrington extensively for the prevailing lack of discipline:

> Q: During the period last mentioned from November 5 through December 21, 1866, what was the discipline at the Post?
>
> A: With the Company Officers it was good, with an effort on their part to discharge their duties to the best of their abilities. With the enlisted men it was chaotic.
>
> Q: In using the word chaotic do you mean to be understood that there was no discipline at the Post, among the enlisted men?
>
> A: I do.
>
> Q: What was the cause of the want of discipline at Fort Philip Kearny, during the time mentioned?

A: A want of proper support, officially and personally . . . from the Commanding Officer.

Q: During the time, how did the enlisted men employ their time?

A: In answering the question I shall have to answer it in various ways, as there was paroled prisoners from the Guard House in the garrison, and who had the liberty of such, and there was a detachment of mounted men belonging to the Post from different Companies, which detachment had no direct or immediate commander. The first party spoken of, the paroled prisoners, being without guard, seemed to exercise their pleasure, if such it should be called, of breaking into the Sutlers Store, which facts came under my official notice. The mounted Detachment amused themselves principally with card playing, horseracing and getting drunk. The rest of the garrison performed their accustomed details in a very loose manner.

Q: What were these details?

A: Guard duties, fatigue duties in the Quarter Master and Company Departments and guard to the wood-train.

Q: During the time you have mentioned . . . did any hostile Indians make their appearance about the Post, and if so, how frequently and in what numbers?

A: From the date of my arrival, up to the 21st of December 1866, Indians were seen nearly every day, and causing a great deal of trouble to the herds, from the number of twenty up to one hundred; three days previous to the battle on the 21st of December, they appeared in large force, seemingly for the purpose of attack.

Q: On the occasion of the appearance of these Indians, were officers and men sent in pursuit of them?

A: In answering the question, I must say that there seemed to be a system of volunteering, Officers going out in charge of men from the number of about 40 to 60, which custom seemed to have been tolerated by the Post Commander.

Q: How far were these Indians usually pursued?

A: Seldom exceeding eight or ten miles.

Q: . . . were any additional measures adopted at the Post to provide against Indians?

A: Not that I observed.

Q: During the time you have mentioned . . . which party was the most successful, the Indians in killing people and running off stock or the soldiers in chasing them?

A: The Indians.

Q: What effect did the success of the Indians produce upon them?

A: It seemed to have emboldened them, and to encourage a great contempt for the men of the garrison.

Although most of these charges are corroborated by other sources, some of them were denied by Lieutenant Wands and other soldiers in letters written to Colonel Carrington years after the disaster.[7] However, in his testimony before the Sanborn Commission, Lieutenant Wands said, "I do not consider the troops at Fort Phil Kearny at that time in the state of discipline and drill, then existing, as at all fitted to fight Indians, for the reason mainly that they had no drill, and had seen little or no service, being mostly recruits." This opinion was shared by Lieutenant W. F. Arnold, who had come to the fort on December 2, when he stated, "The men sent out were generally raw recruits who had not been drilled as busy building the post." Captain Bisbee, a friend of Colonel Fetterman who blamed Carrington for the disaster, testified as follows:

Q: What was the state of discipline in the Post?

A: Very poor.

Q: Were the orders issued by the commanding officer of the Post and District generally enforced?

[7] See Michael Straight, "The Strange Testimony of Major Powell in the Fetterman Massacre Inquiry," New York *Westerners Brand Book*, Vol. VII, No. 1 (1960).

A: They were not.

Q: In what order did the parties or troops move out, when going out to attack Indians?

A: On the 6th of December they were gotten together as speedily as possible, and moved out in a body. Before this, troops were in the habit of dashing helter skelter over the stockade whenever an Indian appeared, without regard to orders, and generally before the Commanding Officer knew there were Indians about, or had issued any orders. Frequently bodies of twenty or thirty mounted men would dash out without orders, on receipt of reports that Indians were driving off herds.

Q: Were matters conducted there in an orderly manner, or in a disorderly and irregular manner?

A: Irregular and disorderly generally.

As far as is known, Colonel Carrington was the only person to deny the lack of discipline, but it is difficult to blame him for the laxity when he was devoting all his energies to building the fort before winter set in. With his command engaged in wood-cutting, construction work, guard duty, and escort duty, it is small wonder that no time was found for drill. The severe shortage of arms and ammunition did not permit target practice.

In accordance with General Cooke's instructions, the first offensive movement by the troops was ordered on December 6, when an attempt was made to entrap a party of Indians between two forces, but the movement was unsuccessful. It is difficult to ascertain whether the encounter in which Fetterman and his command were killed was a planned offensive in keeping with the new policy or whether it was intended purely as a defensive gesture to protect the wood train which had been besieged by Indians. Regardless of the original plan, the movement at some point became offensive because an attack was launched against the Indians north of Lodge Trail Ridge and out of sight of the post, although the wagon corral had been relieved and was on its way to the pinery.

The main battle position where Fetterman's body and those of his infantry troops were found on the ridge north of the post is well known and is marked with a large rock monument, but the other two battle sites were unknown until the late L. C. Bishop and the writer found them with a metal detector farther north along the ridge at points corresponding with the sketch map drawn by Colonel Carrington shortly after the engagement. By use of modern aerial photographs of the area, the exact distances of each position from the fort were determined, while the nature of the terrain was ascertained by trips over the field. There was one detachment of cavalry and a larger contingent of infantry, and it is but a problem of logistics to determine where each party was at specific times, taking into consideration the circumstances brought out in testimony before the Sanborn Commission. When the position of the units at a given time are known, the actions of each force can be reconstructed in the light of military standards of conduct under similar circumstances.

The main difficulty in understanding the military maneuvers near the fort lies in the extremely rugged character of the terrain. No understanding has been possible in the past because of the absence of reliable maps and photographs of the area. Colonel Carrington made a number of sketches, but they are confusing because Lodge Trail Ridge has been foreshortened, the west one-half of it being omitted. On his sketch made before the battle and on the one illustrating the action of December 6, the directions are wrong, due north being northeast on the maps, whereas Massacre Ridge is actually only twenty degrees west of north of the fort.

Fort Phil Kearny was built on a plateau between the forks of Piney Creek, out of rifle range of the bluffs which overlooked it on three sides. To the west and about six miles away lay the Big

Horn Mountains. One-half mile north of the post was the sloping east shoulder of the Sullivant Hills, a ridge four miles long extending towards the west and separated from the mountains by a narrow valley. North of Sullivant was the north fork of Piney Creek, called the Big Piney, flowing southeasterly through the valley bounded on the north by the southern edge of Lodge Trail Ridge, which was actually two ridges coming together in the shape of a triangle. Lodge Trail Ridge commences north of the post at the point where the Bozeman Trail crosses the Big Piney, then extends northward along the road for one and four-tenths miles, where it meets the other ridge, two miles long, coming in from the west, the latter ridge being separated from the mountains by a small valley. The south end of Lodge Trail Ridge is curved towards the northwest parallel with Big Piney Creek, forming a plateau which ascends gradually towards the north, terminating at a crest forming a small peak about four hundred yards west of the road. Only the very top of this peak is visible from the fort because the view of the rest of the north ridge is shut off by the southern edge of Lodge Trail Ridge. The writer has many times walked along the north ridge and was unable to see the present reconstruction of the fort except from this peak, but the fort is plainly visible from the ridge east of the road. From the fort, only the south edge of Lodge Trail Ridge is visible with the high peak in the distance rising behind it.

The north slope of Lodge Trail Ridge descends abruptly over broken hills and ravines for one mile to Peno Creek, which flows through a valley extending at right angles across the Bozeman Trail. The creek heads on the slopes of the Big Horns west of Lodge Trail Ridge where, after flowing northward, it soon turns towards the east. Peno Creek is actually the headwaters of Prairie Dog Creek and runs a short distance east of the road and then angles towards the northeast, eventually joining Tongue River. The Bozeman Trail runs east of the fort and northward along the valley on the east side of Lodge Trail Ridge, passing down the crest of a spur or hogback from the ridge which descends for one and one-fourth miles to Peno Creek by a series of slopes. The hogback is known as Massacre Hill because it is the place where the Fetterman tragedy occurred. The ruts of the old road are still visible, in some places being two or three feet deep. Approaching the creek, the road angles down a small ravine northwesterly to the stream near the present highway. In the valley of Peno Creek west of the road are two dry creeks or ravines, about one-half mile apart, which rise near the summit of Lodge Trail Ridge and extend northerly to the creek. Most of the action on December 6 took place in this broken area west of the road, while the fight on the twenty-first occurred wholly along Massacre Hill to the east.

The hostile Indians had their camps on Tongue River and along Prairie Dog Creek and approached the fort by riding up Peno Creek westward past the Bozeman Trail. By circling around in the valley between the mountains and Lodge Trail Ridge, past Sullivant Hills, they arrived in the vicinity of the fort from the west. Although this was a roundabout way, the Indians used it because they were concealed from the fort and there were no hills for their ponies to climb. They could also make surprise attacks on parties from the fort by swooping down over the Sullivant Hills from the north.

The wood road ran westward from the fort south of the Sullivant Hills to the pinery about five miles away, where wood was cut by the woodchoppers and hauled to the post in wagons. The wood trains were attacked so often that they developed the system of traveling in two parallel lines about one hundred yards apart. If war parties appeared, the leading and rear wagons in each column would come together forming a square corral from which a stout defense could be made on short notice. Since there were no block houses on Sullivant or on Lodge Trail Ridge, pickets were stationed on Pilot Hill, one mile southeast of the fort; they could see a long distance in every direction and could send messages to the fort by a system of signals.

On previous occasions when the wood train had been attacked, the cavalry or mounted infantry rode directly westward to the corral and drove the hostiles away. Pursuit was found to be futile because the fleet little Indian ponies could always outrun the cavalry horses after the larger animals had been winded by the gallop to the scene of action. Part of the new offensive program, therefore, involved forcing the Indians to fight by sending one party of soldiers directly west as usual along the wood road to relieve the train, while the other marched north along the east side of Lodge Trail Ridge and came down into the valley of Peno Creek in the rear of the retreating Indians, who would be caught between the two forces. A good understanding of the terrain and this strategy is necessary to understand the military actions which follow; see Maps 2 and 3 below.

On the morning of December 6, 1866, the wood train, following the usual practice, went to the mountains to cut pine timber for the buildings. At one o'clock that afternoon a messenger reported that the train, on its way back to the fort, was being attacked about four miles to the west. At the same time, Indians appeared upon Lodge Trail Ridge, their pickets riding to the north of the Big Piney, evidently to watch the movements of the garrison. Colonel Carrington ordered every horse mounted, and he placed part of Lieutenant Bingham's cavalry under the command of Colonel Fetterman, who was ordered to take the wood road, relieve the wood party, and crowd the Indians across the Big Piney. Pursuant to the new policy of offensive operations, it was understood that Carrington would lead a party of mounted infantry northward for the purpose of cutting off the Indians and destroying them as they came eastward down the valley of Peno Creek four miles north of the fort. There is a discrepancy in the reports regarding the number of men with Fetterman, the report

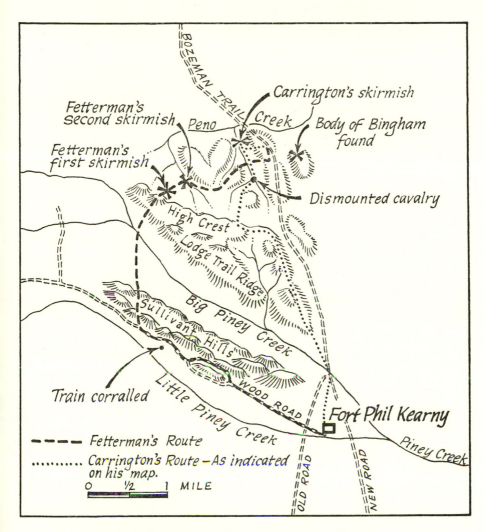

Indian Skirmishes of December 6, 1866

of the Sanborn Commission stating that he had thirty-five cavalry-men of Company C, Second Cavalry, under the immediate com-mand of Lieutenant Bingham, and seventeen mounted infantry-men from his own Company A.[8] Colonel Fetterman, in his official report of the engagement, said that he had about thirty men in all—twenty-five cavalrymen, two officers, and two mounted in-fantrymen who had joined him later at the wood train.[9] Fetter-man's figures are probably correct for Dr. C. M. Hines confirmed that the party consisted of about thirty men,[10] while Colonel Car-rington, who had twenty-five men, later said that the whole force engaged included fewer than sixty men.[11]

Captain Fred H. Brown, who never missed an Indian skir-mish, joined Fetterman's detachment at the train and went along as a volunteer. He and the two infantrymen had ridden to the top of the hill to ascertain the extent of the attack and to see if reinforcements were needed to drive off the Indians. The three men then rode down to the train and were there when Fetterman came up. The little force was further augmented by the arrival of Lieutenant Wands, the regimental quartermaster, who was armed with a Henry rifle. Wands had been ordered to join Car-rington's party but was delayed in changing horses. When he asked the sentinel which way Carrington had gone, he had been misdirected to the wood train. Most of the party were armed with breech-loading carbines, although some of them, probably the mounted infantrymen, had only revolvers.

According to Fetterman's report, the train was corralled four miles from the post, but all other sources, including Colonel Carrington's sketch map, indicate that it was only a mile and a half or two miles away. Upon the approach of the cavalry, the

[8] 40 Cong., 1 sess., *Sen. Exec. Doc. 13*, 63–64.

[9] *Ibid.*, 37–38.

[10] Letter, Dr. C. M. Hines to "Brother John," dated December 15, 1866, *ibid.*, 14–15.

[11] 50 Cong., 1 sess., *Sen. Exec. Doc. 33*, 36.

Indians retreated northwest over Sullivant Hills along their usual escape route.

Colonel Carrington, in the meantime, set out with Lieutenant Grummond and his force of mounted infantrymen. He knew that when the Indians were driven by Fetterman they would follow their customary course of retreat down the valley of Peno Creek. Upon reaching the Bozeman crossing over Big Piney, he found ice had formed, and when his horse broke through, he had to dismount in three feet of cold water and open the way. According to his report, the command then went northward up the eastern slope of Lodge Trail Ridge, bearing a little towards the west to the head of the eastern branch of Peno Creek. Their route was west of the road and near the crest of the ridge, the men probably keeping out of sight as much as possible. From here he could look down and see about one hundred Indians descending to Big Piney from the north slope of Sullivant Hills, followed closely by Fetterman's command which had promptly carried out the order on the left. As Carrington advanced along the ridge, the Indian pickets fell back except for three on the highest point on the ridge. Upon reaching the north edge of the ridge, he saw a party of thirty-two Indians hidden in a ravine, with four pickets on the road to his right. According to his report and map, Carrington galloped westward along the crest of the ridge, a small party of the enemy falling back before his advance. Upon arriving at the north crest of Lodge Trail Ridge, Carrington could look down and see several large parties of the enemy who had now crossed over into the valley of the west fork of Peno Creek, closely pursued by Fetterman's detachment.

After having been pushed northward over one of the saddles on Lodge Trail Ridge, these Indians were reinforced and made a stand in the valley of the west fork of Peno Creek. Seeing Carrington's party marching towards their rear from the southeast, they broke off the engagement and retreated eastward, Fetterman's party following. When Carrington failed to carry out the plan and attack their rear, most of the Indians returned to attack Fetterman, who meanwhile had moved eastward across the west fork. The resurgent Indians again made a stand in front of the low hill between the east and west branches of Peno Creek and offered strong resistance. Fetterman estimated that there were nearly one hundred Indians surrounding his little party on three sides, probably on the north, west, and south.

During this skirmish the soldiers were compelled to retreat, but when the command was given to halt, Lieutenant Bingham beckoned to his men, calling out "Come on," and the cavalry fled southeast with the great precipitancy towards Carrington. It is clear from Colonel Fetterman's official report that the defection of the cavalry was led by Lieutenant Bingham:

> In the most unaccountable manner the cavalry turned and commenced a retreat, which resisted by Captain Brown and Lieutenant Wands, used every exertion to stop them. The Indians corraling and closing around us, it was plain the retreat, if continued, would be a route and massacre. . . . Lieutenant Bingham, while retiring with the major part of the cavalry, encountered the mounted infantry as they were descending the road, and joined them, leaving my party of about fourteen men to oppose a hundred Indians.[12]

Lieutenant Alfred H. Wands described this little skirmish in his testimony before the Sanborn Commission on March 4, 1867, at Fort McPherson, Nebraska:

> After pursuing the Indians about five miles, they were reinforced by a large number and suddenly turned upon us, surrounding us in the shape of a horseshoe. As soon as they turned to attack us, Colonel Fetterman called to our party to halt, but instead of halting, about three fourths of the cavalry

[12] 40 Cong., 1 sess., *Sen. Exec. Doc. 13*, 37–38.

dashed off at full speed in the direction of the post, through the opening left in the Indian lines. About nine or ten of the cavalry remained, and most of these were compelled to dismount by the officers threatening to shoot them if they did not halt and dismount. We were then surrounded by about one hundred and fifty Indians [who] fought us for about three quarters of an hour. The cavalry was not rallied and did not return to the fight. Lieutenant Bingham with the detachment of cavalry met Colonel Carrington on the road, coming to our assistance with a detachment of mounted infantry, accompanied by Lieutenant Grummond.

Colonel Carrington's party was seen by us approaching rapidly at about to [*sic*] miles distant.

The Indians, seeing this party, left us, but the approaching party meeting Lieutenant Bingham's command, and supposing it to be the whole command of Colonel Fetterman, joined and dashed down Peno Creek, leaving us to the left about a mile.

At the place where the junction was made with Lieutenant Bingham's detachment, we could not be seen. The Indians, seeing the party pass on to their right, returned and fought us for about fifteen minutes longer, wounding one man and three horses. They then retired.

As the cavalry broke, the Indians created a great display and made every effort to panic the remaining force. Fetterman dismounted his fourteen infantrymen and with the aid of Captain Brown and Lieutenant Wands succeeded in keeping this small body of men in hand, and by reserving their fire until the enemy were within proper range, they rescued it from annihilation. While thus engaged, Fetterman stated that he saw Carrington passing on the road one-half mile to the east, apparently to get in rear of the Indians who had the low ridge at their backs. After about twenty minutes, the enemy again retreated down the valley, but since Fetterman was unable to overtake them, he decided to join Carrington, striking the road a short distance to the south.[13]

Seeing Fetterman's party engaged, Carrington scrambled down the rough slope of Lodge Trail Ridge in order to play his part in the drama, intending to go around the hill in behind the Indians from the east and crush them between the two forces. According to Carrington's map, he followed down a spur between the upper branches of the east tributary of Peno Creek, about one-half mile west of the road, and after crossing two branch ravines, found the fifteen cavalrymen dismounted and huddled together without an officer. He passed through them, ordering them to mount and follow him at the gallop. This group apparently was so thoroughly demoralized that it remained here until the fighting was over. Carrington's command was strung out during the march so that when he reached the north end of the hill jutting northward into the valley near the creek, and just south of the present ranch house of Eddie Smith on the Brewer Ranch, he suddenly encountered a large force of Indians who, retiring around the hill before Fetterman's advance, charged Carrington and attempted to cut him off. The latter stated that only six men turned the point with him. One of these, a young bugler of the Second Cavalry, told him that Lieutenant Bingham had gone down the road and then around the hill to the right (east). This was hard to understand because Bingham was attached to Fetterman's command, engaged on the other side of the hill to the west. Carrington had the recall sounded, but no one appeared.

The Indians, meeting Carrington head on, charged, and Private McGuire fell with his horse on top of him. The principal chief attempted to secure his scalp, but Carrington dismounted his little force, leaving one man to hold the horses, and drove off the Indians, saving the fallen trooper. The enemy circled around, yelling, nearly one hundred in number, but did not venture to

[13] *Ibid.*

close in after Carrington emptied one saddle with a single shot. At this moment, the fifteen cavalrymen and stragglers from Carrington's command chose to appear, and the Indians retreated eastward down the valley. Because the force with him was small Carrington was unable to crush the Indians between the forces of Fetterman and his own, so he withdrew eastward up onto the road near the point where it descended to Peno Creek. According to his map, this was several hundred yards north of the rocks where Wheatley and Fisher later made their stand. Here he awaited Fetterman, who because of the defection of the cavalry, had been barely able to hold his own.

When Fetterman came up with his force about twenty minutes later, the joint commands started to look for Lieutenant Bingham and Lieutenant Grummond. Although he did not report to Colonel Carrington, Lieutenant Bingham had beckoned to Lieutenant Grummond to join him in the pursuit of the enemy. Dr. C. M. Hines described the incident:

> Lieutenant Grummond left the Colonel's party, and meeting Lieutenant Bingham, they and three or four men started in the pursuit of about thirty Indians, who were apparently retreating; an Indian's horse had almost given out, and Lieutenant Bingham wounded the horse by a pistol-shot, (Lieutenants Grummond and Bingham had nothing but pistols). The Indian then took to his heels, they following him, cutting at him with their swords. Bingham lost one pistol, and after firing the other, so excited did he become that he threw it away. At this time they saw two large bodies of Indians flanking them, when they concluded to run through them; drawing their swords, they laid about them right and left. Lieutenant Bingham did not follow the rest and was killed, stripped and scalped; two sergeants and one more were wounded. Lieutenant Grummond ran against the Indians, and cutting right and left with his sword, got through with the balance. After a while they

were surrounded again by a large number of Indians, drawn in a circle around them with spears, at a charge, and firing upon them; they halted, and Lieutenant Grummond then told the rest to follow him; they did, he using his sword as before. All got through, but Sergeant Bowers no doubt turned around and fired upon his pursuers; they overtook and put an arrow in him and split his skull open above the eyes. They did not scalp him. Our people found him a short time afterwards; he was living and in great agony, but died in a short time.[14]

As the combined forces of Carrington and Fetterman rode eastward to find the missing men, Lieutenant Grummond with three men, hotly pursued by Indians, came riding down a ravine. Grummond was infuriated at Carrington for not coming to the rescue of the surrounded men and angrily asked whether the Colonel was a fool or a coward to allow his men to be cut to pieces without offering help. Grummond then explained that he had met Bingham after descending the ridge and had accompanied him, with the idea that the cavalry were close behind; but that, while chasing a dismounted Indian and cutting at him with their sabers, they were surrounded and Lieutenant Bingham cut off.[15]

The soldiers then went to where Sergeant Bowers was lying and sent to the post for an ambulance and reinforcements. The men with Bowers said that during the headlong retreat he had stopped to make a stand but was cut down after killing three Indians with his revolver. Private John Donovan, armed with a Colt's revolver, saved himself at the last moment by killing two Indians who were trying to pull him off his horse.[16]

After an hour's search, the body of Lieutenant Bingham was found about one mile east of the Bozeman Trail on the north end

[14] Letter, Hines to "Brother John," dated December 15, 1866.

[15] William H. Bisbee, *Through Four American Wars*, 171–72.

[16] William Murphy, "The Forgotten Battalion," Part I, *Winners of the West* (May 30, 1928), 7.

of the next ridge, "in the brush . . . shot with over fifty arrows, lying over an old stump."[17]

When the ambulance came, the two bodies were taken to the fort, and since it was dark the soldiers also returned, arriving about seven o'clock, after a six hours' absence. The casualties were Lieutenant Bingham, Second Cavalry, and Sergeant Bowers, Company E, Eighteenth Infantry, killed; Sergeant Aldridge, Second Cavalry, wounded; and four privates wounded. Three horses had been killed and five wounded. Carrington estimated that ten Indians had been killed, many more being wounded.

The offensive operation had been a failure, although Carrington stated that Fetterman had carried out his instructions properly. It would have been a good fight had Fetterman retained Bingham's command, which was composed mostly of green recruits. The question on everyone's mind was why Bingham led his men away from Fetterman and then dashed off without orders into the ambush. His sergeant said that Bingham's horse had run away with him and that the Lieutenant told him he could not hold the animal.

In his official report of the skirmish, Colonel Fetterman showed more charity towards the dead Bingham than he was to receive himself later on:

> I cannot account for this movement on the part of an officer of such unquestionable gallantry as Lieutenant Bingham; but it is presumed that being unable to prevent retreat of his men, he deemed it most prudent to hold his men in hand as much as possible, and fall back on the mounted infantry who were expected on the road.[18]

Lieutenant Grummond and Private William Murphy blamed Carrington for failing to go to the aid of Bingham's party, on the

[17] John Guthrie, "The Fetterman Massacre," *Winners of the West* (September, 1939), 8.
[18] 40 Cong., 1 sess., *Sen. Exec. Doc. 13*, 37–38.

41

theory that it was on the right flank of the skirmish line and that when Carrington sounded recall and fell back to the higher point on the ridge, he abandoned Bingham's party to its fate. Murphy was the bunkmate of Private John Donovan and presumably got his information from him. Lieutenant Wands indignantly told the Sanborn Commission, "I consider the conduct of the cavalry on that day, disgraceful and of such a character as to induce the belief on the part of the Indians that they could overcome the garrison, or any party from the garrison, in an open fight."

There was no imputation of cowardice on the part of Lieutenant Bingham, it being generally assumed that since he was unused to Indian warfare, he understandably lost his head under the trying conditions. It is surprising, however, that Fetterman, with all his combat experience, was unable to hold his men together. Colonel Carrington, who had no prior combat experience, was at fault in not keeping his men closed up. Lieutenant Grummond lost his head and joined Bingham without authority. However, the two detachments were able to overcome the effects of their blunders by hard fighting.

As a result of the narrow escape of December 6, the rift between Carrington and his officers widened. Fetterman blamed him for remaining on the ridge instead of closing in on the Indians. In his official report, Fetterman claimed that Carrington had come down the north slope of Lodge Trail Ridge on the Bozeman Trail, which would have placed him one-half mile farther east of the action. Lieutenant Wands confirmed this in his testimony. Carrington was also denounced by Lieutenant Grummond for not coming to the aid of the men isolated on the right flank. Although Carrington gave credit to Fetterman for following orders, the cavalry was censured for not staying with their leader.

After the fighting Colonel Fetterman appeared rather subdued, but Captain Brown was as cocky as ever. With Brown as spokesman, several officers proposed to Colonel Carrington that they take sixty civilian employees and forty mounted soldiers on an expedition to the Tongue River to clear out the Indians. Carrington, however, had learned the danger of allowing soldiers to go beyond Lodge Trail Ridge, and he refused the request. The garrison was placed in readiness for the next encounter with the enemy. All available horses were kept saddled from dawn to dusk, with loosened girth and bits taken from their mouths, so that there would be no delay when required for immediate service.[19] The soldiers, who had demonstrated a remarkable lack of discipline, were drilled in preparation for future engagements.

On December 19, the wood train was again attacked, and Carrington sent Major Powell to its relief with the explicit orders, "Heed the lessons of the 6th. Do not pursue Indians across Lodge Trail Ridge." Powell followed orders and drove off the Indians without pursuing them beyond the ridge.

On December 20, Carrington supervised the building of a bridge across Big Piney near the mountains without seeing any Indians. That night Captain Brown called on Colonel and Mrs. Carrington. "Only the night before the massacre he [Brown] made a call, with spurs fastened in the button-holes of his coat, leggings wrapped, and two revolvers accessible, declaring, by way of explanation, that he was ready by day and night, and must have one scalp before leaving for [Fort] Laramie, to which place he had been ordered."[20]

The next day, Friday, the twenty-first of December, it was uncertain whether the wood train would go out in the morning on account of the snow, which was deep in the woods. Although snow had not fallen for several weeks, the whole area around the post was still blanketed. Brevet Major Samuel M. Horton, assistant surgeon at the fort, testified before the Sanborn Commis-

---

[19] Carrington, *My Army Life*, 145.
[20] Carrington, *Ab-Sa-Ra-Ka*, 208.

sion that "there was snow on the ground but the day was pleas-
ant. . . ." Captain Ten Eyck testified that there was "not as much
snow on the road the ascent being more gradual, and the ridge
being intersected by several deep ravines that were partially filled
with snow." The snow was deep on Lodge Trail Ridge,[21] while
Massacre Ridge was covered with ice and snow.[22]

Just before guard mounting, or nearly ten o'clock, Carrington
decided to send the train out with a strong guard. Anticipating
that the Indians might have seen his work of the day before, he
sent with the civilian employees a military escort under the command of Corporal Legrow of Company E, Eighteenth Infantry.
Civilians and escort together totaled about ninety men. It was
nearly eleven o'clock when the picket on Pilot Hill signaled that
the wagons were corralled about a mile and a half from the fort,
under attack by many Indians. Firing was distinctly heard at
the post.

The bugle sounded, and as the troops formed ranks, two Indians appeared on the slope of Lodge Trail Ridge and, dismount-
ing beyond rifle range, wrapped themselves in their red blankets
and sat down near a tree to watch the action inside the fort. Four
more Indians appeared on the north side of Big Piney and shouted
to the garrison, "You sons of bitches, come out and fight us."[23]
In reply to this challenge Colonel Carrington fired three shots
from a twelve-pound howitzer, and one of the shots flushed out
about twenty Indians who scampered out of a ravine near the
road crossing where the shot exploded. The Indians fled northward, taking positions on Lodge Trail Ridge.

Colonel Carrington then ordered Major Powell to command

[21] Testimony of Captain Tenodor Ten Eyck before the Sanborn Commission;
and Timothy O'Brien, Letter to the editor, *Winners of the West* (March 30,
1933), 1.

[22] George Bird Grinnell, *The Fighting Cheyennes*, 242.

[23] Testimony of Lieutenant W. F. Arnold and Private George C. Mackey
before the Sanborn Commission.

a relief party of fifty men to go to the aid of the wagon train, but when Colonel Fetterman claimed the right by reason of his seniority, he was given the command.[24] Having the choice of his own Company A and such additional details as he might select, he picked out, after a hasty inspection, twenty-one men of Company A, nine of Company C, six of Company E, and thirteen of Company H, all of the Eighteenth Infantry. The detachment was formed in front of Fetterman's quarters just as the guard was being mounted and turned over to Lieutenant Wands as officer of the day. Major Powell saw Colonel Carrington talking to Colonel Fetterman, but neither Powell nor any of the others present heard what the orders were. According to Carrington, his instructions to Fetterman were "Support the wood train. Relieve it and report to me. Do not engage or pursue Indians at its expense. Under no circumstances pursue over the ridge, viz., Lodge Trail Ridge, as per map in your possession."

Within fifteen minutes, or about 11:15 A.M., Colonel Fetterman moved out the mill gate at the southwest corner of the post with his infantry, who were armed with the obsolete Springfield muzzle-loading rifles. It was understood that a detachment of cavalry would be sent to join him as soon as it was ready to move. Instead of heading westward along the wood road, Fetterman went northward from the fort and crossed the Big Piney.

While Fetterman was taking command of his infantrymen, Company C of the Second Cavalry was mounted and armed with the Spencer carbines which had been taken from the Regimental Band a few days before. Captain Fred Brown joined the mounted troopers, riding the mottled pony, Calico, which he had borrowed from Carrington's son, Jimmy, and was eager for one more chance to get Red Cloud's scalp. Two civilian employees of the Quartermaster's Department, James S. Wheatley and Isaac Fisher, armed

[24] However, Major Powell claimed in his testimony before the Sanborn Commission that the order was given directly to Fetterman.

45

with repeating Henry rifles, also volunteered to accompany the troopers.

Lieutenant Alfred H. Wands, in his testimony before the Sanborn Commission, described the departure of the cavalry:

> The cavalry company, numbering about twenty-seven men, were all mounted and awaiting orders. At the request of Lieutenant Grummond, who had taken command of Lieutenant Bingham's company, I went to Colonel Carrington, and told him Lieutenant Grummond desired to know who was going to take out the cavalry.
>
> Colonel Carrington then directed me to order Lieutenant Grummond to take command of the detachment of cavalry, and overtake and join Lieutenant Colonel Fetterman's command who were then about one quarter of a mile from the Fort.
>
> Colonel Carrington directed me to inform Lieutenant Grummond that his orders were to join Colonel Fetterman's command, report to and receive all his orders from Colonel Fetterman, and also to tell Colonel Fetterman, and to remember himself that this command was to go out and succor or relieve the wood train, bring it back if necessary, or if Colonel Fetterman thought best, take the train to the woods (it being on its way out) and bring it back, and under no circumstances were they to cross the Bluff in pursuit of Indians. I gave those instructions to Lieutenant Grummond, and while the Corporal of the Guard was unlocking the gate, I returned to Lieutenant Grummond and repeated them, and asked him if he thoroughly understood them. He replied he did, and would obey them to the letter.
>
> Lieutenant Grummond left the Post with his detachment of cavalry and had proceeded about two hundred yards when he was called back by Colonel Carrington, who was on the sentinel's platform at the time, and who called out in a loud voice, repeating the same instructions given to Lieutenant Grummond by me, and asking him if he understood them.

46

He replied I do. Lieutenant Grummond's command was seen to join Colonel Fetterman about a mile from the Post.

There are two accounts which seem to indicate that the cavalry went first to the corralled train and then to join the infantry. Captain William H. Bisbee stated that:

> It was evident that the usual attack was being made on the train and relief was speeding on its way from the Fort: eighty odd soldiers under the command of Brevet Lt. Col. Fetterman, accompanied by Captain Fred H. Brown, Lieutenant Grummond and two experienced frontiersmen. The matter of driving the Indians from the attack was speedily accomplished.[25]

Although Bisbee was not stationed at Fort Phil Kearny during this time and his understanding of the movements rested entirely upon hearsay accounts, this theory is confirmed by Sergeant F. M. Fessenden, of the Regimental Band, who was present at the fort:

> The cavalry had gone to the assistance of the wagon train, as mentioned. Captain Fetterman offered his services, and with Lieutenant Grummond and some soldiers, started out. Instead of going to protect the wood train, they started after the two Indians across the stream. The direction they had to go led them over a hill some little distance away. At the foot of this hill, but on the opposite side, were two ravines which came to a point, over this point was a very large rock. The company of cavalry, not finding the Indians attacking the wood train, as expected, followed them over this point.[26]

Colonel Carrington's statements that the cavalry went north following Fetterman's party are confirmed by a number of eyewitness accounts. Private Timothy O'Brien of Company E, Eighteenth Infantry, was with the wood train:

> Seventeen wagons went out with a citizen driver for each

[25] Bisbee, *Through Four American Wars*, 173.
[26] Hebard and Brininstool, *Bozeman Trail*, II, 100.

wagon and one soldier for each wagon, well armed with rifles and ammunition. I was in Wagon No. 2. We were about one mile out from the fort on our way to the mountains to get our load of logs, when we were attacked by the Indians, about fifty or sixty of them. Corporal La Groe [Legrow] of Philadelphia was in command of our wood train; and after repulsing the Indians, we held a consultation and decided to go on to the mountains for our load of logs. Hearing the fire of our rifles back at the fort, Col. Carrington decided to send a relief to assist us, and this was the occasion of Fetterman being sent out with about eighty men to our rescue. (We of course, knew nothing at that time of Fetterman being dispatched to the rescue of our wood train.) Bringing our wood train to the mountains, we hurriedly pulled logs down the mountain sides through the deep snow and after loading our wagons, we started for the fort. Upon arriving at the fort, I met Col. Carrington at the entrance to the stockade. He asked me, "Were any of your men killed?"

I replied, "No, Col. none of our men have been killed."

Col. Carrington then related that he had sent out Capt. Fetterman with eighty odd men to relieve our wood train, and that evidently Fetterman and his men had all been killed by the Indians.[27]

After the infantry and cavalry detachments had left, Carrington "sent Dr. C. M. Hines with two orderlies to the wood trains, instructing him, if not needed there, to join Fetterman and return with him." In this statement Carrington recognizes that Fetterman was not at the wood train. That none of the relief party was at the wood train is borne out by Dr. C. M. Hines in his testimony before the Sanborn Commission on March 11, 1867, at Omaha, Nebraska:

I was ordered, perhaps an hour after they had left the Fort, by Colonel Carrington, to go to the wood train. His orderly

[27] O'Brien, Letter to the editor, *Winners of the West* (March 30, 1933), 1.

was to accompany me, and a Mr. Phillips, a citizen, was also to accompany me.

I was afterwards joined by Lieutenant Matson, and a mounted infantryman, we joining with some employees of the Quarter Master's Department in one or two wagons. We followed the road toward the wood train, and were satisfied the wood train was safe.

My orders were after being satisfied of the safety of the wood train, to cross to the command of Brevet Lieutenant Col. Fetterman.

Following this road for two miles or more, we then determined to join the command under Colonel Fetterman. Passing down the side of the defile between the Big and Little Piney, we reached the Big Piney. We tried to find a crossing but could not, and were obliged to go lower down the stream to where the road crosses. The firing at this time being very rapid, and the Indians appearing on Lodge Trail, between us and the command, we came to the conclusion that the command was surrounded, and rode into the post for re-inforcements. This was done as expeditiously as possible.

Private John Guthrie, of Company C, Second Cavalry, reported that "Fetterman had taken the old Holiday Coach Road,"[28] referring to the old route which circled northward around the base of Pilot Hill and ran a short distance west of the post, joining the new cutoff road at the regular crossing over Big Piney.

According to Private William Murphy, of Company A, Eighteenth Infantry, "I was standing right there and saw the men start on a double quick and go up over Sullivant's Hill."[29]

It seems that Carrington was correct in saying both detachments went north, and his version is amply supported by reliable witnesses who were present at the post or at the wood train. After Fetterman left the fort, he soon passed out of sight over the east

[28] Guthrie, "The Fetterman Massacre," *Winners of the West* (September, 1939), 8.

[29] Murphy, "The Forgotten Battalion," Part II, *Winners of the West* (June 30, 1929), 7.

shoulder of the Sullivant Hills down into the valley of Big Piney Creek. Carrington reported that:

> Just as the command left, 5 Indians reappeared at the cross-ing. The glass revealed others in the thicket, having the ap-parent object of determining the watchfulness of the garrison or cutting off any small party that should move out. A case-shot dismounted one and developed nearly 30 more, who broke for the hills and ravines to the north. . . .
>
> In half an hour the picket reported that the wood train had broken corral and moved on to the pinery. . . .

It is well established that the cavalry detachment joined Fet-terman's infantry at some point north of Piney Creek, but there is a discrepancy in the accounts concerning Fetterman's route from the post to the creek. Colonel Carrington claimed the com-mand went northwest and crossed the creek west of the road crossing, while on his map he shows Fetterman crossing at an island west of the road. Other accounts claim he crossed at the regular road crossing and marched up the road until he disap-peared over Lodge Trail Ridge. His route over this area probably depends upon whether he continued up the Bozeman Trail or up onto the top of Lodge Trail Ridge.

When Fetterman arrived at Big Piney, there were three courses open to him. He could have turned northwest on the south side of the creek and followed the valley, intending to come in behind, or north of, the Indians. The second course was to cross Big Piney and follow the south slope of Lodge Trail Ridge, parallel with the creek, the route Carrington claimed he had taken on December 6, in an effort to cut off retreat. His third choice was to follow northward up the Bozeman Trail and come down into Peno Creek valley in rear of the retreating hostiles. It is clear that he did not follow the first route, but the eyewitness accounts are sharply divided on whether he followed the second

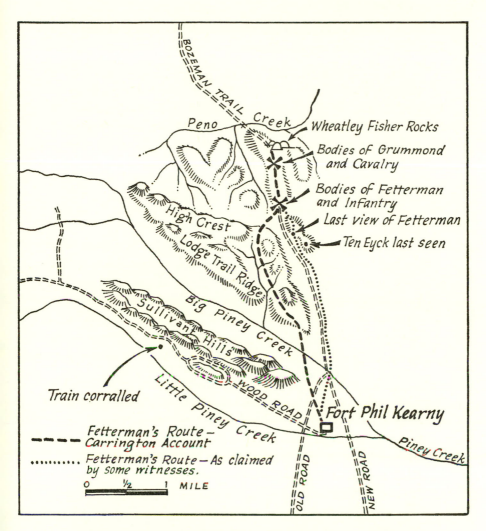

The Fetterman Massacre of December 21, 1866

or third. Colonel Carrington and Lieutenant Wands claimed that Fetterman's party marched northwest along the south slope of Lodge Trail Ridge in an effort to cut off the retreat of the Indians, and this is the route indicated on Carrington's map. All other accounts allege that Fetterman went up the road, after crossing at the regular road crossing, until his skirmish line disappeared over Lodge Trail Ridge.

Colonel Carrington's official report continued:

> Fetterman's command had been joined by Grummond's just west of the ordinary ferry crossing. It moved in good order.
>
> I remarked the fact that he had deployed his men as skirmishers, and was evidently moving wisely up the creek and along the southern slope of Lodge Trail Ridge, with good promise of cutting off the Indians as they should withdraw, repulsed at the train, and his position giving him perfect vantage ground to save the train if the Indians pressed the attack. It is true that the usual course was to follow the road directly to the train, but the course adopted was not an error, unless there was then a purpose to disobey orders. . . .
>
> Dr. Hines came back quickly, reporting the train to have passed safely on; that Brevet Lieutenant-Colonel Fetterman had crossed Lodge Trail Ridge towards Peno Creek, and that Indians were on the western slope, and between him and Fetterman, so that he could not join him. Brevet Lieutenant-Colonel Fetterman evidently disregarded those that were on that slope (if he saw them) and was led off into Peno Valley, perhaps after the party who had been at the ferry crossing, and had attempted precisely the same decoy practiced December 6, 1866. When Brevet Lieutenant-Colonel Fetterman was lost in sight from the post his command was moving westward along the slope of Lodge Trail Ridge, and apparently in good order, with no indication that it would pass over it.[30]

[30] 50 Cong., 1 sess., *Sen. Exec. Doc. 33*, 44–45.

Carrington's wife also reported later that "We had all watched Captain Fetterman until the curve of Sullivant Hills shut him off, and then he was on the southern slope of the ridge, apparently intending to cut off the retreat of the Indians from the train."[31] According to the Sanborn Report, "As he [Fetterman] advanced across the Piney, a few Indians appeared in his front and on his flanks, and continued flitting about him beyond rifle range, till he disappeared beyond Lodge Trail Ridge."[32]

The testimony of Lieutenant Alfred H. Wands before the Sanborn Commision appears to support Carrington's claim about Fetterman's route:

> Instead of proceeding to the wood train as ordered, the command crossed Piney Creek to the other bank, and proceeded up a long ridge on the opposite side of the creek from the wood train, and about three miles from the crossing, to a point about two miles from where the wood train was corralled. They were then seen to halt on the crest of the ridge, about four miles from the Post. There were about forty or fifty Indians riding around the command, firing at them during the march from the crossing at the creek, up the ridge and the command was returning the fire.
>
> About the time the troops were seen resting on the ridge, pickets reported that the wood train had broken corral and had moved on towards the woods. Colonel Fetterman's command suddenly moved over the ridge and the firing increased.
>
> In about ten or fifteen minutes, and about eleven o'clock in the day, the firing increased until it was a rapid and continuous fire of musketry.

Wand's description of the point where Fetterman halted on the crest of the ridge is rather vague, but as near as can be determined on the aerial photograph of this area, two miles from

[31] Carrington, *Ab-Sa-Ra-Ka*, 203–205.
[32] 40 Cong., 1 sess., *Sen. Exec. Doc. 13*, 63–64.

the wagon corral would place Fetterman very close to the point on Lodge Trail Ridge where the road goes over, or possibly a short distance to the west. The corral was actually northwest of the post at the base of Sullivant Hills. But if Wands had meant the point on the ridge where the road crosses, he would have said so. He probably intended to support Carrington's version of the route.

It will be noted that there is a wide discrepancy in the accounts regarding the time schedule of events, probably caused by differences in the various timepieces. Because it is the time intervals which are important, and since Colonel Carrington gives definite times for the more important occurrences, his schedule will be used here. The Colonel's clock was in the adjutant's office and was the official post time.

In sharp contrast with the statement of Colonel Carrington were those of other soldiers who watched Fetterman after he crossed the Creek. Lieutenant W. F. Arnold, testifying before the Sanborn Commission, said:

> When next I saw Colonel Fetterman's command the infantry were deployed as skirmishers along Piney Fork in an entirely different direction from that which the wood train had taken. He then crossed Piney Fork, still diverging from the wood train, and took road towards Peno Valley, and passed over into Peno Valley, which is out of sight of the Post, and about four miles from it. Firing was heard from the direction his command had taken, between, I think, eleven and half past eleven o'clock A.M. but it did not alarm anybody as it was the largest force that had ever been sent out from the garrison.

Private George B. Mackey, of Company E, Eighteenth Infantry, told the Commission on March 9, 1867, at Omaha, that "Between eleven and twelve o'clock heavy firing was heard from the direction of the Big Horn road, in a different direction from the wood train, and from the direction we supposed the troops were in. What I call the Big Horn road is the road to Fort C. F. Smith."

Captain Tenodor Ten Eyck, Eighteenth Infantry, testified on July 5, 1867, before the Sanborn Commission at Fort Phil Kearny:

> Col. Fetterman's command did not take the road [to the pinery] but went down into the bottomlands near the Creek, and was joined by Capt. F. W. Brown who started from the Fort alone. By following up the bottomland the command could have reached the road where it crosses the Big Piney, in about the same distance as if it had taken the road. The usual ford across Big Piney on the Virginia City road, is about a half mile north of the Fort. The command marched a short distance above this ford [west], then countermarched and crossed the Creek at the ford, on the ice. At this time, a few Indians, apparently lookouts or pickets, were visible on the hills on the opposite side of the stream from the Fort, and about three miles distant. The infantry marched up the Virginia City road which follows up a ravine for some miles, being flanked by the cavalry on the ridges. Soon after this the command disappeared from the sight of those in the Fort at a point about three and one half or four miles distant and where the road descends into the valley of Peno Creek.

The testimony of Brevet Major James Powell, Twenty-seventh Infantry, relating to the route that Fetterman followed, is as follows:

> Before moving his command from the Post, I saw Col. Carrington in conversation with Col. Fetterman, what orders or instructions Col. Carrington gave him I do not know, but I observed that Col. Fetterman's command in place of going to the relief of the wood train, filed to the right and went on

the Big Horn road. While they were moving along the Big Horn Road, I endeavored to drive the Indians from their flanks and front by shelling them, which I succeeded in doing. Col. Fetterman's command passed out of sight of the garrison in about two miles, nothing was seen in his front or on his flanks at that time. In the course of an hour from when he disappeared, which was about eleven o'clock, heavy firing was heard in the direction which he took, which continued for fully an hour.

After the elapse of this hour, about twelve o'clock, I requested Col. Carrington to arm all the civilian employees, at the Post, and at once send some person to the relief of Col. Fetterman with ammunition and wagons; Col. Carrington gave his consent to my request and asked my opinion upon the matter. I armed those men, had the wagons prepared, organized the detachment, consisting of employees and soldiers; Col. Carrington ordering Captain Ten Eyck to take command.

It is impossible to give full credence to Major Powell's statements because his claim that he drove the Indians from the flanks of Fetterman's command by shelling them is not substantiated by any other source. The shelling seems unlikely since it would have been as dangerous to the soldiers as to the Indians. His statements that Colonel Carrington turned the command of the post over to him and that he assumed command are not confirmed by any other accounts. However, it should be remembered that it was Major Powell who successfully carried out the orders of December 19 in driving the Indians away from the wood train without loss and without crossing Lodge Trail Ridge. Several days after giving his testimony at Fort Phil Kearny before the Sanborn Commission, Powell conducted the valiant defense of some woodcutters and their military escort at the famous Wagon Box Fight five miles northwest of the fort. His statements of fact are entitled to consideration even though it is difficult to assess their accuracy.[33]

The writer, over a period of years, has tried to locate definitely the route Fetterman took from Peno Creek to the crest of Lodge Trail Ridge and has covered the course claimed by Carrington and all of the crest of the ridge with a metal detector. A cavalry spur of the type used during the period was the only thing found, and it was discovered on the long plateau extending northward to the crest and about one-half mile west of the present highway. While this is directly in the route indicated in Carrington's map, nothing else was found, and the one item alone has but little significance. The spur had been spread apart at an obtuse angle, probably, in the opinion of Lieutenant Colonel E. L. Nye, U.S. Army, Retired, a recognized authority on cavalry equipment, from being caught in the stirrup when the rider was thrown and then dragged by a bolting horse. It is not surprising that nothing else was found in the area because shots fired by the old muzzle-loading Springfields of the infantry would leave no trace except

[33] Major Powell's statements have been strongly criticized by Michael Straight in his article, "The Strange Testimony of Major Powell in the Fetterman Massacre Inquiry," New York *Westerners Brand Book*, Vol. VII, No. 1 (1960). However, the criticism is based largely upon material covering a period of forty years placed in the custody of the public library in Sheridan, Wyoming, by Colonel Carrington himself. There are written statements by Carrington and letters received in response to inquiries during efforts to clear his name. Most of the statements were made years after the battle when many of the persons involved had disappeared or were dead. Under such circumstances, this material does not seem to have much weight when compared with the direct testimony of the witnesses before the Sanborn Commission taken down only a few months after the event. Major Powell's brilliant military record and the fact that the President and the higher army officers believed him lend support to his statements. In those days it was a common practice for army officers to emphasize their own importance at the expense of their fellow officers. Powell boasted about his part in the affair, downgrading Carrington, while the latter carried on a continuous assault upon the character and actions of Fetterman for forty years in his frantic efforts to clear himself of responsibility for the disaster. It should also be pointed out that most of Powell's testimony was substantiated by other sources.

the small flattened-out primers, while the Spencer cartridges of the cavalry were very small, about one inch long. Unless trodden into the earth, such small items would have been washed away years ago. Northward from the Piney crossing, the old Bozeman Trail lies over farm ground before extending on to join the present highway. The writer has worked down along the road site but found nothing significant.

There is another test by which it might be determined where Fetterman's skirmish line was strung out along the ridge just before it disappeared from sight of the post. As noted before, the only place on the crest of the ridge west of the old Bozeman Trail in sight of the post is the peak of the hill which is the highest point on the whole ridge. An area about one hundred feet wide is visible from the fort, the rest of the ridge being obscured from the view by the southern edge of the Lodge Trail Ridge. It seems extremely unlikely that either cavalrymen or infantrymen climbed this peak covered with ice and snow, and it is more probable that the skirmish line was located along the ridge immediately east of the Bozeman Trail since it is in plain sight of the post. The present highway cuts through the ridge where the old road went over, and this area was in sight of the fort before the deep cut was made. Therefore, it is probable that Fetterman's infantry went up the road with the cavalry along the slopes on each side as flankers, the skirmish line extending from about the middle of the present highway eastward along the ridge.

This conclusion is supported by a critical examination of Carrington's statement that Fetterman was cutting westward along the ridge to head off the Indians who were expected to arrive in the valley at the west end of Lodge Trail Ridge. In his map Carrington shows the Indians retreating from the wagon train northwesterly over Sullivant towards the valley leading to Peno Creek. It would have been impractical to intercept the enemy by this route because the soldiers would have had to march at least two miles farther westward along the broken ridge through the snow and over deep gullies, while the Indians on their fleet little ponies would only have had to travel a similar distance from the wagon corral to arrive at the interception point at the west end of Lodge Trail Ridge. The impossibility of arriving by this route ahead of the Indians, even with mounted troopers, was demonstrated on December 6, when Carrington arrived on the crest of the ridge only in time to see the Indians already engaged with their pursuers far down in the valley of Peno Creek. Some students of the battle believe that the Indians' escape route from the wagon corral was straight northeastward over Sullivant Hills and through a break in Lodge Trail Ridge situated about one mile west of the road. I do not think this route was used, especially with snow on the ground, because the country is extremely rough, being covered with gullies, ravines, and broken slopes and ridges. The easier route for them, although a little longer, was around the west end of Sullivant and Lodge Trail Ridge as shown in Carrington's map. This drawing is fairly accurate but is faulty in that it does not show Lodge Trail Ridge extending far enough west. On the aerial photograph of the area the ridge extends exactly two miles from the road on the east to the most westerly spur, although the distance is actually farther along the ridge as it bows towards the south. Carrington may have shortened the ridge on his map so as to make it appear that the distance was short enough that Fetterman could have gotten to the west end of it in time to cut off the retreat of the Indians, thus sustaining his contention that Fetterman took that route. Possibly, Carrington intended for Fetterman to maneuver to get in rear of the Indians without engaging them so that the latter would leave the wood corral. But if Carrington intended only this, why did he not send a messenger ordering Fetterman back to the post when he saw that the party was taking the road towards the crest of the ridge? In taking that route, Fetterman could hope to inter-

59

cept the Indians only in the valley of Peno Creek, which would mean that the movement was intended to be strictly offensive.

It was generally agreed that during this time back at the post there was no anxiety or activity until about twelve noon. It was shortly after twelve that Fetterman's skirmish line disappeared from the view of the fort, then scattered shots were heard, followed by four volleys, and then a continuous and rapid fire, indicating that a pitched battle was in progress. According to Carrington, twelve o'clock sounded just after the sound of firing began, and his office orderly immediately told him that the sentry at the door reported firing. Carrington said he then went to the top of his house, where a lookout was posted, and heard a few shots apparently from the direction of Peno Creek, but could see neither Indians nor soldiers through the glass. At this point there are the usual discrepancies. Major Powell said that Carrington continued sitting on top of his house listening to the firing until the relief party was sent out, but both agreed that the relief party was not ordered out for some time after Dr. Hines returned. However, Dr. Hines and Captain Ten Eyck both said the party was sent out immediately after the doctor returned with his report of heavy firing on the other side of the ridge.

The relief party was sent out under the command of Captain Eyck with orders to take the most direct route and join Fetterman at all hazards. It left within seventeen minutes at the double quick after an inspection of the men, arms, and ammunition. Ten Eyck gave this account of the march in his testimony before the Sanborn Commission:

> At this time [when Dr. Hines returned] I received an order from Col. Carrington, to take command of a party of about forty infantry and dismounted cavalry, and proceed as rapidly as possible to the scene of the action, and join Col. Fetterman if possible. As soon as the detail was formed, which occupied but a very few minutes, I started, and following the course

which Col. Fetterman had taken, crossing the creek at the same place, and marching up the road. Lieut. Matson at my request was allowed to accompany me, and Dr. Hines was likewise sent out by Col. Carrington. Several citizens joined my party as volunteers.

My reason for taking the road was that I could accomplish the distance sooner, and with less fatigue to my men, there being not as much snow on the road, the ascent being more gradual, and the ridge being intersected by several deep ravines that were partially filled with snow.

After proceeding about four miles I came upon the crest of the hill where the road descends into Peno Creek Valley, and here I first came in sight of the Indians. This march occupied but little, if any, over an hour. Up to the time we crossed the creek, we heard heavy firing, apparently in volleys, after which very little firing was heard by me.

From the point on the hill where I first came in sight of the Indians I could see a distance of several miles along the valley of Peno Creek. From this point the road descends for near half a mile abruptly, then a gradual ascent for about a quarter of a mile, to the summit of a small hill from which the road follows a narrow ridge, for about a mile and then descends abruptly to the valley of Peno Creek. Upon both ends of this ridge are a number of large rocks lying above the surface and beside of the road.

When I first came in sight of the Indians they were occupying the ridge just described and extending a distance of a mile or more beyond the further point of the ridge. About one hundred mounted appeared congregated about the pile of rocks nearest to my position. Many were passing backwards and forwards on the road, but no indications of a fight going on.

I could discover none of Col. Fetterman's party. I thought that they might be surrounded near the further point at which I could see Indians, or that they might have retreated to the west and joined the wood party at the Pinery. I dispatched a mounted courier to the Fort asking the commanding officer for reinforcements and artillery. I then marched my men along the crest of the ridge in a westerly direction by which I could gradually approach the nearest point of rocks without losing my commanding position on the higher hills. As I advanced I observed that the group of Indians nearest the rocks named, became much less as I approached so that when I arrived within about six hundred yards of the rocks, there were but four Indians remaining at that point. I was then able to discover a large number of naked bodies lying there. I then fired a few shots at the Indians remaining who retired precipitately and joined the main body, who were slowly retiring along the road.

About this time I was joined by about forty employees of the Quartermaster's Department with three wagons and an ambulance, who I afterwards ascertained, were sent from the Garrison before my courier arrived. The Indians at this time to all appearances were forming in line of battle on the high hills across the valley about two miles distant.

Q: From your experience in estimating the numbers of men during the late war how many Indians do you think you saw at that time?

A: I am sure that there were not less than 1500 and I think over 2000.

Q: How long was it after you came in sight of the Indians before you were joined by the Citizen Employees which you have mentioned?

A: About three quarters of an hour.

Q: Did the Indians retire from sight while you were on the hill?

A: They did not, on the contrary I was expecting an attack every moment until I left for the Post.

Q: After the wagons arrived did you advance to the point of rocks where you discovered the naked bodies?

A: I did.

Q: How far, from the nearest point, where the first bodies were found was it to the most remote bodies?

A: About one mile, and at the further point of rocks spoken of in my testimony.

Q: How many were found at that point of rocks?

A: I think five or six, and among them Jas. S. Wheatley and William Fisher, two citizens.

Q: Where were the remaining bodies found?

A: Scattered along the ridge road between the two points of rocks, most of them nearest the point of rocks towards the post.

Q: Where was the body of Lt. Grummond found?

A: About forty rods beyond the point of rocks where the first bodies were found. And the body of Col. Fetterman near that of Captain Brown's at the first point of rocks.

When the two couriers sent by Ten Eyck arrived at the post, Colonel Carrington sent one of them, Orderly Sample, directly back with the following written instructions, "Captain—Forty well-armed men with 3000 rounds, ambulances, etc. left before your courier came in. You must unite with Fetterman; fire slowly and keep men in hand; you would have saved two miles towards scene of action if you had taken Lodge Trail Ridge. I order the wood train in, which will give fifty more men to spare."

The statement in the order that Ten Eyck went two miles out of his way was unfortunate in that it implied cowardice on the part of Ten Eyck and also suggested that if he had marched directly to the scene of action he might have been able to save Fetterman's command, or at least part of it. Captain Ten Eyck failed to mention in his testimony that in marching to the relief of Fetterman, he diverged eastward from the Bozeman Trail and went on top of the ridge, which was at that point variously estimated at from eight hundred to one thousand yards from the nearest bodies. His route was correctly indicated in Carrington's battle sketch, which shows that Ten Eyck marched three or four hundred yards east of the road to a small peak which commanded the view of the surrounding country. It seems obvious that the captain did this in order to avoid the dangerous defile at the point where the road went over the ridge. The damage was done, however, and this ordinary prudence resulted in Ten Eyck's disgrace and in his being the victim of rumors and whispers behind his back that he detoured because of cowardice. Ten Eyck began drinking heavily and was permitted to retire from the army with the rank of captain, another casualty of the Fetterman massacre.

Over one-half of the material in a small pamphlet which Carrington later wrote is entitled "Vindication of Capt. Ten Eyck" and is a labored attempt to undo the damage caused by his hasty note. He reaches the belated conclusion that Ten Eyck was to be commended for avoiding the dangerous defile and that in any route he might have taken he would have been too late to aid Fetterman. At this time Ten Eyck was dead, but the vindication was for his long-suffering widow and daughter. Carrington also protested against the injustice done Ten Eyck when the latter's reinstatement and retirement were before Congress. In the pamphlet it appears that Ten Eyck crossed the creek with much difficulty, which may have been caused by the two ambulances and the extra ammunition. The next day he showed his courage in accompanying Carrington to bring in the rest of the bodies.

Dr. C. M. Hines, who accompanied Captain Ten Eyck's relief party, described his experience in his testimony before the Sanborn Commission:

> Captain Ten Eyck was then sent out, with which command Lieutenant Matson, myself, and the others who had been out, joined. We crossed the Big Piney at the regular crossing, on the ice, marched up the road nearly opposite the Indian picket left on Lodge Trail Ridge, and he descended, joining other

Indians then there. We then took a position on Lodge Trail Ridge, where we received re-inforcements and ammunition.

We remained about one hour. The Indians were gradually moving off on horseback. A few remained near the bodies. Captain Ten Eyck, and some of the men fired to drive them off. They were from six to nine hundred yards distant. The Indians were apparently waiting to gather some things. Captain Ten Eyck then advanced his line to those bodies, which were by the road side.

Q: How far were you when you heard the last shot fired?

A: When we arrived at the point where we had a view of the position, where the bodies lay, they were surrounded by Indians, and there was some firing then.

Q: About this time how many shots were fired?

A: Not many. The shots appeared to be from the arms captured by the Indians.

J. B. Weston, a lawyer who was at the fort at the time, was one of the group of civilians who joined Captain Ten Eyck's party at the Big Piney. He gave the following account:

About 12 M. of that day [December 21] myself in company with several citizens viz: J. Fitch Kinney, Mr. Welch, Mr. Blodgett, and others hearing heavy firing over the hills started with the intention of joining Col. Fetterman's party if possible, and at the Piney Creek we fell in with Capt. Ten Eyck's party. We marched on the double quick most of the way until we came to the hill which overlooks the valley of Peno Creek, about four miles from the Post, where I had a good view of the Indians; whom I then estimated and still think were 150 in the immediate vicinity of the greatest number of dead bodies; a quarter of a mile in their rear apparently drawn up in line of battle on horseback, about 500, and thence down the valley of Peno Creek upon the ridge and in the ravines on both sides and upon the bluffs to the left, appeared a compact body of Indians, as also as far as we could see down the Peno valley.

I have never estimated the number, but believe it to be much greater than is generally supposed.

Q: How long was it after heavy firing was heard, in the direction that Col. Fetterman took, until you left the Post?

A: Upwards of thirty minutes.

Q: How long did the firing continue after you left the Post?

A: We heard the heaviest volleys as we were crossing Big Piney Creek within three quarters of a mile from the Post; and we heard a few faint volleys after crossing the Creek and occasional shots as we were going up the road. Just as we got on the crest of the hill, I thought I heard groans and screams; and after we got on the crest we saw and heard several shots fired around where the greatest number of dead bodies were found.

Q: Did you suppose that these last shots were fired by Col. Fetterman's party or the Indians?

A: I am certain now that they were fired by the Indians; but it was the supposition of Capt. Ten Eyck at the time that it was Col. Fetterman's party who fired these shots.

Q: How far were you at the time of this last firing from the Indians who were then around the mass of the dead bodies?

A: We were above them and from 800 to 1000 yards distant.

Q: How long after you occupied that position, did the Indians who were about the dead bodies, leave?

A: They did not leave until Capt. Ten Eyck advanced, probably twenty minutes after we came in full view. They did not fall back very much until the QMR wagons appeared which were sent out from the Post; and they probably took the wagons to be artillery.

Q: Did you encounter any Indians on your way from the Post?

A: Not exactly encountered any, but passed near some of their pickets, which we supposed at the time to be white men. We saw two loose Indian ponies which we captured. I think

66

these horses were left for a decoy with the intention of destroying our party at that place, as it was well chosen for the purpose; which in my opinion was only prevented by the timely
appearance of the QMR's wagons and men appearing in our
rear, and which as I stated were believed to contain artillery
by the Indians.

After Captain Ten Eyck's group departed to join Fetterman,
Lieutenant W. F. Arnold was helping to organize the Quartermaster's party:

> The Quarter Master's employees, some fifty in number, were
> then called up and armed, and sent to Captain Ten Eyck, with
> three wagons and ammunition. This was about half an hour
> after Captain Ten Eyck's party had left. About dusk all the
> reinforcements returned with some forty nine bodies of Colo-
> nel Fetterman's party, all of whom had been massacred and
> multilated. . . . At about one o'clock after all the troops had
> left, there were 119 armed soldiers at the post while 80 were
> with the wagon train. . . . The troops had between 20 and 40
> rounds of ammunition at guard mount and there was no in-
> spection before the troops left.

Lieutenant Alfred H. Wands told the Commission about the
relief sent out to Captain Ten Eyck:

> Before Captain Ten Eyck's party reached the crest of the
> ridge overlooking Peno Creek the firing had entirely ceased
> except an occasional shot.
>
> As soon as Capt. Ten Eyck's party reached the top of the
> ridge, he sent back a mounted man with information that he
> could see nothing of Colonel Fetterman's party and that he
> could see thousands of Indians, and requested a howitzer to
> be sent to him. More employees of the Government were
> mounted and sent to reinforce him. Captain Ten Eyck and
> party returned about sunset, with the wagons loaded with the
> dead bodies of the officers and soldiers of Colonel Fetterman's

command, numbering thirty nine [*sic*], all the wagons would hold, and stated that other bodies could be seen stretched along the road for a mile ahead. The wood train came in loaded with timber about the same time that Capt. Ten Eyck's party arrived.

The Indians did not molest Capt. Ten Eyck's party but retired as he advanced to pick up the bodies.

Q: Were any empty shells of Spencer ammunition on the ground near where the large number of bodies lay?

A: Very few, if any. But from that point to a mile beyond, where the fight evidently commenced, a large number were strewn along the road, and a great many near where the dead bodies most remote from the fort lay, and where the heavy fighting commenced.

Dr. C. M. Hines went down from the ridge with Captain Ten Eyck's party to the first group of dead bodies and described the area to the Sanborn Commission:

Behind and in the neighborhood of these rocks, I should judge in an area of ten or fifteen yards in diameter, there were some fifty or sixty dead men. Stripped of everything, their heads apparently radiating from a comman centre, with the appearance of having died there. Then passing on the road I found five or six, some of them not more than twenty feet from the other bodies. The heads of the horses and men were lying in the direction of the main body of the dead. No body was found between the large body and the Fort.

Captain Brown, to the best of my knowledge, and Colonel Fetterman, were with the large body of men. Lieutenant Grummond was on the road, some distance off. Some three or four were from a quarter to a half mile from the large body.

Q: Were there any cavalry soldiers with the main body?

A: There were. There was a dead horse between this body of men and the fort, and another to the right, in some bushes, not quite dead. There were no dead men near the horse.

Q: Would you judge from the appearance of the ground, that one party advanced and the other halted on the ground where they were lying?

A: My impression is, from viewing the ground, that the cavalry were in advance of the infantry; that the Indians decoyed them on, and that the Indians rose up from the defiles in the rear of the entire command, that the cavalry dismounted and fought on foot, that they retreated or fell back to join the infantry. I think they fought in a circle, being attacked on all sides. . . .

Q: Was this circle standing in order or was it a crowded circle?

A: It appeared to me to be an ordered circle, and in ranks. I do not recollect of seeing the smoke of pieces discharged. On reaching the point, we heard a tremendous yell or cry, then the guns were discharged. The rapid firing had ceased half an hour before.

Q: How many Indians did you see on the field that day?

A: From this point where we saw the bodies, to a point beyond Peno, the Indians were scattered over a distance of two or three miles. There was a large body around the dead bodies, and at the end of the three miles, there was another large body drawn up as it were across the road. I estimated the number from 1500 to 3000. I make my judgment from what I have seen of troops, while serving with the army in the south.

Brevet Major Samuel L. Horton, assistant surgeon at the post, told the Sanborn Commission on July 25, 1867, at Fort Phil Kearny, that the men had been shot with pistol balls and arrows and had been mutilated and attacked with clubs after being wounded. He then described the bodies and wounds with clinical detail, stating that not more than six of the men were killed by balls.

The next morning Carrington led a party of eighty men to the scenes of action and retrieved a few bodies from the north end of the ridge, the rest being found near that of Lieutenant Grummond, between the two extremes. At the farthest point, between two rocks and apparently where the command first fell back from the valley, realizing their danger, were found the remains of civilians James S. Wheatley and Isaac Fisher, both of Blue Springs, Nebraska, who, with their Henry rifles, had tried to stem the red tide. Nearby lay the bugler, Adolph Metzger, whose death was an epic of raw courage.

> The bravery of our bugler is much spoken of, he having killed several Indians by beating them over the head with his bugle. . . . The Indians mutilated every body in Fetterman's command with the exception of the bugler who fought so courageously that his remains were left untouched but covered with a buffalo robe.[34]

With this group were the bodies of several veteran troopers who knew better than to turn their backs on the enemy. Some of these may have been infantrymen since a common practice of that day was for rugged foot soldiers to march along with cavalry for short distances hanging on to the stirrups in order to reach an engagement at the same time as the cavalry.

There were no survivors of the fight and no witnesses (other than the Indians) from the time the party disappeared from the view of the fort until seen by Ten Eyck's party. What happened during the one-hour period is one of the great mysteries in American military history. Since Fetterman was in command of the party presumably sent out to relieve the wagon train, it has been assumed that he foolishly, and in disobedience of express orders, led his men into the trap. There is no question but that the Indians planned to entice the soldiers far enough away from the fort to surround and destroy them. The Cheyenne Indians were in ambush along Peno Creek west of the road, while the Sioux

[34] Elmo Scott Watson, "The Bravery of Our Bugler Is Much Spoken Of," *Old Travois Trails*, Vol. I, No. 6 (1941), 21–24.

were in hiding east of the road and behind the next ridges to the east. Decoy Indians had led at least some of the troops down the ridge close to Peno Creek where the trap was sprung, all the Indians charging the soldiers at once.[35]

It has been suggested by one authority that Fetterman's party was driven northward over the ridge by the Indians returning from the wood train together with the thirty who had been flushed out of the brush at the crossing.[36] This is highly improbable because the firing was light while the soldiers were in sight of the post, and no Indians were visible except for the few who hovered about the flanks. Had there been an attack in force, the Indians, in driving the soldiers northward, would have been visible from the post. The fifty or sixty Indians from the wood train and the thirty who fled from the brush would not have been enough to drive eighty-one soldiers and civilians. Such an attack would have interfered with the decoy plans; in fact, those attacking the wood train were but decoys playing their part in the strategy.[37]

In trying to figure out what happened during that one-hour period that Fetterman's party was out of sight, the late L. C. Bishop and the writer made a complete coverage of Massacre Ridge with metal detectors. The place where Fetterman, Brown, and forty-seven other soldiers were found is well known, and a large rock monument with an access road has been built on the site. Colonel Carrington and other soldiers returned in later years to identify the spot and dedicate the monument. In confirmation, the writer has found at this site two steel lance points, uniform buttons, fired percussion caps of the type used with the

[35] Grinnell, *Fighting Cheyennes*, 233–41; O'Brien, Letter to the editor, *Winners of the West* (March 30, 1933), 1; David, *Finn Burnett*, 125; and Carrington, *Ab-Sa-Ra-Ka*, 200.

[36] Charles Edmund DeLand, "The Sioux Wars," *South Dakota Historical Collections*, Vol. XV (1930), 89–94.

[37] Grinnell, *Fighting Cheyennes*, 236.

muzzle-loading Springfields, pistol bullets, round musket balls, several bullets fired from the Springfields, and one expended Spencer cartridge case, all deep in the ground. This place is about one-quarter of a mile down the hogback from Lodge Trail Ridge, right on the old Bozeman Trail.

North of the battle position is a hill on the ridge, and the ruts of the road lead directly from the monument along the crest of the hill, sloping down the north side to a level area which extends for about one-half mile. North from the monument, on this level area, were found battle relics indicating that this is the place where Lieutenant Grummond and his cavalry detachment were overwhelmed. The ruts in the road are several feet deep at this point and plainly discernible, the crest of the ridge being about fifty feet wide. The level space terminates in a little point where the present fence crosses, the road descending for three hundred yards to the rocks where Wheatley and Fisher made their stand. From here, the road descends by a series of terraces, finally angling towards the northwest down to Peno Creek, about one-quarter of a mile away from the rocks.

The present highway runs north and a little west along the western base of Massacre Ridge, and all three sites can be seen from several positions along the road. The three sites correspond closely with the positions shown on Carrington's map, and there can be no question but that these are the actual battle locations. Since forty-nine bodies were found at the monument site, it is probable that most of the twenty-seven cavalrymen fell with Lieutenant Grummond at the middle site, while Wheatley, Fisher, Metzger, and several others died at the rocks. At the last place, we found one soldier's uniform button and three flattened-out bullets which had struck the rocks on the northwest. We checked the surrounding area but found nothing except relics farther up the slope to the south. We looked for some of the .44-caliber Henry cartridges, but finding none, we assumed that they had been picked up years ago when General Crook's army passed here on two campaigns in 1876. The rocks are close beside the road on the east, while the ridge is very narrow here.

Commencing two hundred yards southward up the slope from the rocks were found lead bullets and .52-caliber Spencer carbine cartridges on the west side of the ridge, becoming more numerous towards the little hill where they were thickest. Extending for 125 yards south of the hill, the shells were found as far as 50 feet down the slope and as far east as the road. Several were found east of the road. The greatest concentration was immediately south of the little hill, becoming less numerous towards the south. Thus the battlefield extended 225 yards north and south along the top of the ridge and for 50 feet down the west slope. The present fence, running east and west over the ridge, cuts through the middle of this area. Farther down the ridge are rock formations, but nothing was found around these, the soldiers having been higher up on the ridge. Since Grummond's cavalry carried Spencer carbines, many expended Spencer cartridges were found together with round, lead balls, probably pistol balls, obviously fired by the Indians. The following is a list of the relics found here:

2 .52-caliber Spencer cartridges which had misfired
2 .52-caliber Spencer cartridges unfired
36 .52-caliber Spencer cartridges fired
1 soldier uniform button
1 hand-hammered $\frac{3}{8}$–inch iron wagon nut
1 oblong steel $\frac{1}{16}$–inch ring, $3\frac{1}{2}''$ x $1\frac{3}{8}''$, probably part of equipment
5 round musket balls about .50 caliber which had been fired
1 round musket ball about .40 caliber which had been fired
1 lead bullet flattened out and then doubled up, which had obviously found its mark
3 lead Spencer bullets unfired of about .52 caliber

2 lead Spencer bullets which had mushroomed, of about .52 caliber

The cavalry was armed with the .56–.56 Spencer carbines which had the bore measurement of .52 inches. The .56–.56 refers to the chamber diameter, which was straight. There was also in use at that time the .56–.50 Spencer carbine which used a tapered cartridge and had a bore measurement of .50 inches. The .56–.52 Spencer was not made until 1867 and was never used by the army. It also had a bore measurement of .50 inches.

Having located the three battle sites on the ridge, we ascertained the distances of the various points from the fort using aerial photographs of the area. The distance from the fort to Fetterman's crossing, as indicated on Carrington's map, is thirteen hundred yards, while to the regular road crossing it is a little less. To the north crest of Lodge Trail Ridge at the point where the road crosses it is two and one-half miles. From the post to the monument where the infantry were killed is three miles; to the cavalry site is three and one-half miles; to the Wheatley-Fisher rocks it is three and three-fourths miles; while it is four miles to Peno Creek. The hill from which Captain Ten Eyck first saw the battle site is two miles from the post, as Lodge Trail Ridge turns towards the southeast at the point where the road crosses.

Since the country was very rough and Fetterman did not go in a straight line, he actually went farther than the distances indicated. According to Carrington's map, he first went north across the Big Piney, then angled northwest on the lower slope of Lodge Trail Ridge, then northward over the plateau to the area of the top of the hill at the north crest, then down the north slope to the infantry site, a total distance of three and one-half miles. The route by the Bozeman Trail was nearly three miles, with a gradual ascent from the Creek to the crest of the ridge.

The heavy firing was heard when Fetterman's men, spread

out as skirmishers, disappeared over the ridge at twelve noon, or forty-five minutes after he had left the post. Since it is not definitely known just where on the ridge the troops were, it is interesting to speculate about the distance he and his infantry could have marched during this period, under the circumstances. According to Brigadier General Charles D. Roberts, U.S. Army, Retired, who was an infantry officer for many years, "small bodies of infantry could easily make three miles per hour on open level ground. In snow this would be reduced to one or two miles per hour for short distances." And in Roberts' opinion, ". . . Fetterman and his foot troops could hardly have gotten over two miles when the firing was heard from the fort about noon."[38]

It seems clear that in hurrying to cut off the retreating Indians, Fetterman made very good time in marching the two and one-half miles up the road to the crest where he disappeared in the forty-five minute period, considering that he was going uphill most of the way with snow on the ground. It is equally clear that the party could not have gone any farther during this period because of the time and space limitations. It seems doubtful that he could have marched the three and one-fourth miles over the Carrington route, where the terrain was rougher and the snow deeper, in this amount of time. Nor does it seem reasonable that the Indians and pursuing troopers would go over the high point on the ridge, which was the only place visible from the post west of the road, when they could have gone on either side of it. But if they did not go over the high peak, they would not have been visible from the post, so it seems highly improbable that Fetterman's men took the course Carrington indicated.

Cavalry, on the other hand, usually marched from four to six miles an hour but of course could go much faster for short distances. During this forty-five-minute period, the cavalry could easily have ridden either route to Peno Creek. None of the ac-

[38] Letters, Charles D. Roberts to the author, dated June 10 and July 28, 1963.

counts indicate that the cavalry was seen with Fetterman on Lodge Trail Ridge, so it is possible that the cavalry went on ahead down the road, leaving the infantry in a skirmish line along the ridge. That both were together up to the crest is borne out by the Indians, who claimed that the cavalry moved slowly so as not to get too far ahead of the infantry.[39] According to the Cheyenne Indian accounts, there were scattered shots and two volleys fired before the soldiers came in sight over the ridge, with several more volleys fired at the decoy Indians retreating down the valley west of Massacre Ridge.[40] This conforms fairly well to the reconstruction of events by those at the fort.

It has been assumed in most of the modern accounts that Fetterman's infantry and Grummond's cavalry advanced together to Peno Creek, and that the infantry then retreated southward for one mile along the road to the place where they were destroyed. This reconstruction seems to be substantiated by the fact that bodies of infantrymen were found with Wheatley and Fisher, while cavalrymen were found back with the infantry. But the positions indicated by this reconstruction could not have been possible under our time-versus-distance formula. The infantry could not have marched the four miles to Peno Creek over Lodge Trail Ridge in the snow and then retreated back up Massacre Ridge in the ice and snow for one mile while under attack, and then all be killed within the small area at the battle site. They could not have gotten that far before all would have been killed by the surrounding Indians, most of whom were on horseback. It seems clear that it was the cavalry which moved ahead to Peno Creek, while the infantry only marched as far north as its battle site when it was attacked, probably retreating a short distance to the rocks. At some point, the cavalry broke ahead of the infantry in hot pursuit of the decoy Indians, probably leaving the infantry

[39] Grinnell, *Fighting Cheyennes*, 239.
[40] *Ibid.*, 242.

deployed as skirmishers on Lodge Trail Ridge until the trap was sprung at Peno Creek. During this time, Fetterman, powerless to prevent the advance, may have watched from the crest of the ridge. The heavy firing which commenced just after the skirmish line disappeared was probably the firing between the cavalry and the attacking Indians. When the enemy swarmed to the attack, it was the duty of Fetterman, in the emergency, to go to the aid of the mounted force. It might be speculated that he just had time to march down to his battle site, one-quarter of a mile along the road, before he was under attack himself. Thus he may have deliberately marched into the trap in going to the aid of his comrades.

The Cheyenne accounts state that when the Indians attacked, the infantry was also within the trap, implying that it was far enough down the ridge so that it could not escape. If this were the case, Fetterman may have felt obliged to follow along in support of the cavalry even if it had advanced contrary to orders. The other alternative is that all the soldiers were committed to an offensive operation in trying to intercept and destroy the Indians in Peno Valley, and that the cavalry was at its usual place at the head of the column.

Whatever the explanation, it is certain that the three bodies of troops were isolated and destroyed in detail, each out of sight of the other. Fetterman's infantry did not have much chance because they had the obsolete muzzle-loading Springfield muskets which could not be fired very fast, while their position was on an exposed narrow ridge with no cover except a few rocks. The Indians could fire their arrows very rapidly from concealed positions in the rough terrain along the sides of the ridge. The bodies of the infantrymen were found in a very small area facing outward in a small circle, where they had huddled together and were easily overcome by the large numbers of the enemy attacking from all sides. That several horses were found dead headed for the post makes it probable that several of the cavalrymen broke away from Grummond and rode back to the infantry. Captain Brown may have been one of these because his body was found with those of the infantrymen. Private Guthrie indicated that there were some cavalrymen at the scene,[41] while the Cheyenne Indians said "the last of the cavalry were killed where the monument now stands."[42] In confirmation of this, Colonel Carrington said some unexpended Spencer cartridges were found with the bodies of the infantrymen, while the writer found one expended Spencer cartridge here, buried deep in the ground.

The cavalry was far down the ridge, nearly to Peno Creek, when the enemy attacked, and they retreated southward up the ridge. The civilians and some veterans, knowing it was fatal to retreat from Indians, stopped at the rocks and made their stand until cut down by enemy attacks from the northwest and northeast. The rest of the mounted men retreated up the ridge to take cover behind the little hill, firing as they retreated. Here they turned their horses loose, pouring in a heavy fire from their Spencers on the enemy towards the north and west down the slope. It is probable that they were finally cut down by the Indians from the east coming up in their rear. Their carbines did not have the Stabler cutoff attachment which prevented the firing of the weapon as a repeater because the only weapon the army had acquired with these appliances designed to prevent the soldiers from firing too rapidly was the .50-caliber Spencer carbine.[43] Although the cavalrymen could fire the seven shots in the magazine rapidly, they were particularly vulnerable when compelled to reload or insert another magazine. Their position was also exposed with no cover on the east, south, or west. Several expended

[41] *Ibid.*, 244; Guthrie, "The Fetterman Massacre," *Winners of the West* (September, 1839), 8.

[42] Grinnell, *Fighting Cheyennes*, 244.

[43] Colonel Arcadi Gluckman, *United States Muskets, Rifles, and Carbines,* 439.

78

Spencer cartridges have been found along the road several hundred yards south of the cavalry site, and it is possible that they were fired by Captain Brown or some of the cavalrymen escaping towards the infantry detachment. Captain Brown started out riding the pony Calico, but Brown's body was found with Fetterman, while the dead horse was found near the rocks where the civilians died. It seems unlikely that Brown would turn his pony over to someone else during the chase, so one might guess that when Calico was killed, Brown jumped on another horse and raced back to Fetterman.

As to the sequence of events, the Cheyennes claimed that the infantry was destroyed first, then the civilian party, and last of all the cavalry.[44] On the basis of various sketches which show the Indians in hiding along Peno Creek, it seems more likely that the civilian party and the cavalry were wiped out first, being nearest the enemy, and last of all the infantry, which was farther back. The reconstruction is supported by the fact that the escaping cavalrymen rode directly to the infantry. If the infantry were heavily engaged or had been wiped out at that time, these men would not have ridden back there. Each of the battle sites is out of view of the others. The cavalry and civilian sites cannot be seen from the monument because the hill to the north of the civilian site blocks the view. The rocks where Wheatley and Fisher made their death stand are visible only from that portion of the cavalry site on the north side of the little hill which shuts off the view from the south.

That the infantry was some distance behind the cavalry is supported by the statement of the Cheyenne Chief Two Moon, to George Bent, when the chief was visiting in Colony, Oklahoma:

> When Fetterman came out few Indians with best horses went and met him and they had instructions to lead him on

[44] Grinnell, *Fighting Cheyennes*, 242–43.

hills where Indians hid behind the hills. He [Two Moon] says some of troops were coming up about ½ mile behind Fetterman. He says there were so many Indians when they came out on hills. Fetterman started to turn back but seen the Indians were all around his men dismounted and turned their horses loose.[45]

While Two Moon mistakenly assumed that Fetterman was with the mounted advance party, it was actually Lieutenant Grummond who was in command of it. The importance of Two Moon's statement lies in his assertion that there was another body of troops coming up one-half mile behind, which would place Fetterman near his battle site.

This view was, in effect, accepted by the Sanborn Commission, which reported: "Our conclusion, therefore, is . . . that Colonel Fetterman formed his advanced lines on the summit of the hill overlooking the creek and valley, with a reserve near where the large number of dead bodies lay. . . ."[46]

Although it is hearsay evidence, the testimony of Michael Boyer, post guide and interpreter at Fort Kearny, on July 27, 1867, before the Sanborn Commission, also supports this assumption. Boyer had known since childhood one of the Sioux Indians who was in the fight and had great confidence in his veracity. The warrior's description of the fight had been corroborated by other Indians and was believed by Boyer to be true:

> He also stated that the Indians who came to the Post and attacked the wood train, drew the soldiers out on the ridge road, and a large number of Indians lay concealed in the ravines on either side of the road, and when the soldiers got where they wanted them, the concealed Indians surrounded

[45] Letter, George Bent to George E. Hyde, dated December 5, 1904, now in Coe Collection, Yale University Library, New Haven, Connecticut. This is probably the same letter referred to by Colonel Carrington which appears in Hebard and Brininstool, *Bozeman Trail*, I, 338–39.

[46] 40 Cong., 1 sess., *Sen. Exec. Doc. 13*, 65.

The grave of Lieutenant John R. Brown. The road beginning in upper right is the old Bozeman Trail.

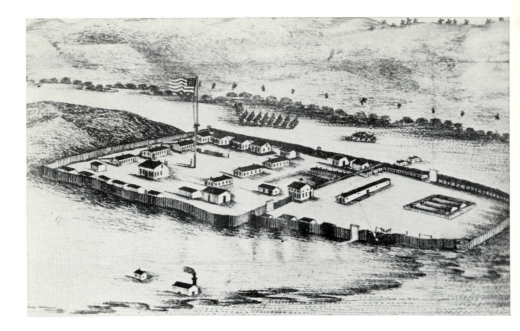

Fort Phil Kearny, as sketched in 1867 by Bugler Antonio Nicoli.

View from Fort Phil Kearny looking north over shoulder of
Sullivant Hills to Lodge Trail Ridge in distance.

Photograph by the author

Site where Lieutenant Grummond and cavalry were killed. Looking northeast, Wheatley-Fisher Rocks are at left beyond the picture.

Roahen Photos
Billings, Montana

The rocks where James S. Wheatley and Isaac Fisher were killed.

The site of the Hayfield Fight. Warrior Creek lies in middle ground, and the bluffs are in background.

Photograph by the author

General George "Three Stars" Crook, 1875.

One guard on duty could see for more than a mile in all directions, giving ample warning of attack.

Issuing arms and supplies to the friendly Indians in Crook's army, June 15, 1876.

them and killed them all. He also said that the soldiers fought bravely but by huddling together gave the Indians a better opportunity to kill them, than if they had scattered about. He said that the soldier's [*sic*] ammunition did not give out, but they fired to the last. He said the Indians took all the ammunition the soldiers had left, but some soldiers had no ammunition left.

Q: Who did you understand were the principal chiefs in the fight?

A: "Red Cloud" "Iron Goggle" and "Lone Bear" of the Ogallah band, "Pretty Bull" of the Minneconjou band, and "Red Horn" of the Unk Papas or Missouri Sioux. There were some Breulah [Brulé] Sioux, young warriors who were fighting under the leadership of "Bull Head" who was killed. There were about 60 Arapahoes without any chief of their nation, but were fighting under the Sioux. . . .

That the fight did not last very long, about an hour. That some of the soldiers were a mile in advance of the others, and when the Indians rose up from the ravines, the advance soldiers were killed in retreating to the main body, and that the main body huddling together were killed as before stated.

Regardless of who was to blame for the disaster, there are several facts which are well established by the time-versus-distance formula. First, Fetterman with his infantry was never farther north along Massacre Ridge than his battle site. This being true, the cavalry, for some reason, outran their support so that neither party was within supporting distance of the other, permitting each to be destroyed in detail. If the soldiers had stayed together or within supporting distance of each other, the result of the encounter might have been different.

In reconstructing the action occurring on the twenty-first, there are so many unknown factors that it is impossible to assess the blame for the disaster, if indeed anyone was at fault. In the first place we do not know definitely what Carrington's orders were to Fetterman because no one overheard them. If Carrington merely wanted the Indians driven away from the wood corral, the relief party only needed to march westward towards the corral, as on previous occasions, and the Indians would have dispersed. There was no point to Fetterman's getting in rear of the Indians unless some punitive or offensive action was intended.

If we accept Carrington's assertion that he told Colonel Fetterman to relieve the wood train but not to move across Lodge Trail Ridge, the question immediately arises why he then permitted Fetterman, and later Grummond, to move northward toward the ridge and at right angles to the direction of the wood corral which he was to have relieved. There is no question but that Carrington ordered Grummond and the cavalry to report to Fetterman and to follow his orders, and that Grummond was in turn to relay to Fetterman the order not to cross Lodge Trail Ridge. Here, again, we do not know if Grummond gave these orders to Fetterman, and even if he did, they may have been in conflict with verbal orders already given Fetterman before he left the post. The order given Grummond may have been an afterthought by Carrington, who knew the order would be disregarded. In examining the various possibilities, it should be borne in mind that the Indians could not have been surprised at the wood corral or elsewhere since their pickets were stationed all over the hills.

When Carrington saw that Fetterman and Grummond had crossed the creek and were heading away from the wagon corral towards Peno Creek valley, he must have known that they were intending to intercept the Indians. He could easily have sent a mounted messenger to overtake the troops, whichever route they actually took. It seems clear, then, that when Fetterman's men were in a skirmish line along the crest of Lodge Trail Ridge, Fetterman had thus far complied with Carrington's orders, whatever they were, because he had not been recalled. By this time, the picket had signaled from Pilot Hill that the Indians had left the wood train, but Carrington still made no effort to have the troops return even though firing was heard while the troops were still in sight.

If Fetterman directed or collaborated in the advance of any of his command over onto the north slope of Lodge Trail Ridge, contrary to orders given him by Carrington personally or through Grummond, he would be solely responsible for the disaster. However, there is no evidence (except Carrington's testimony) that Fetterman received such orders or that he authorized the advance. When the cavalry at some point separated from the main body, the excited men and horses could have dashed after the decoy Indians without Fetterman's consent. It would have been impossible for a dismounted infantry officer to prevent mounted troops at the head of his column from bolting in hot pursuit of the enemy. If Fetterman did not authorize the advance past the ridge by the cavalry, but marched to its aid when it became heavily engaged, he would have been without actual fault, although technically responsible for violation of orders by troops under his command. If he saw the cavalry riding down Massacre Ridge on the heels of the decoy Indians, in violation of orders, he would have been justified in following to support them in anticipation of an attack. In either case it was Fetterman's duty to go to their support because such an unforeseen emergency would nullify Carrington's order (if it were actually given Fetterman) not to go over the ridge. While taking the blame from one man only places it on the shoulders of another, it does seem that putting the entire responsibility on Fetterman is unjust, especially as he may have been entirely without fault and a victim of the disobedience of others.

It should be pointed out in Fetterman's behalf that no official condemnation or reproach was cast upon him, but Colonel Carrington was immediately relieved of his post by General Cooke, who was, in turn, removed as department commander by General Sherman, a friend of Carrington's. Whether he was actually to blame or not, Carrington's career was ruined, and he later resigned his commission. It took him twenty years to absolve himself from blame, which he accomplished by convincing Congress and the public that the disaster was caused by Fetterman's disobedience of orders.

General Grant and the army high command blamed Carrington for the disaster. His alleged ordering of Fetterman not to engage the Indians "at its [the wood train's] expense," while at the same time permitting him, and shortly thereafter, Grummond, to march northward must have appeared inconsistent to them. Also possible is that the army thought Carrington deliberately permitted the three combat officers to take the dangerous course in the hope that they would learn a lesson or, possibly, just to get rid of them after their repeated insults and slurs upon him because of his lack of combat experience. A study of Carrington's character both during and after his army career indicates that he was not the kind of person who would have allowed personal considerations to influence him in this manner. However, in the light of recent research, Carrington was at best a controversial figure while in the army.[47]

Colonel Carrington was invited to Sheridan, Wyoming, to dedicate the new monument on the nearby Fetterman field on July 3 and 4, 1908. The dedication was accomplished with much ceremony, and during his visit he presented to the Sheridan Public Library a pamphlet compiled by him and entitled "Fetterman Massacre. Based on Colonel Carrington's Testimony as regarded by Lieutenant General W. G. Sherman." What Sherman had to do with the pamphlet is not clear since the narrative is by Car-

[47] See Straight, *Carrington*; R. E. Banta, "General Carrington's Hoosier Debacle," New York *Westerners Brand Book*, Vol. IV, No. 3 (1957); and Frank L. Klement, "Carrington and the Golden Circle Legend in Indiana During the Civil War," *Indiana Magazine of History*, Vol. LXI (March, 1965), 31–52.

rington, but it may be assumed that Sherman agreed with its conclusions. The proceedings of the military Court of Inquiry are
described, and then, as we have mentioned earlier, Captain Ten
Eyck's route to the scene of action is justified. In addition to the
pamphlet, Carrington presented a bound manuscript, compiled
and signed by him under date of July 3, 1908, entitled "Wyoming
Reopened, 1866." Of significance in this volume is the chapter
consisting of pages 33–42, entitled "Explanation of Congressional
Delay for Twenty Years," wherein he tells about his experiences
and frustrations after the disaster. This chapter is set forth in full
in Appendix A herein and states Carrington's side of the controversy.

Another chapter, contained on pages 63–77 of the manuscript,
is a reply to the testimony of Major Powell before the Sanborn
Commission, and Carrington refers to this testimony as an "Ex
Parte Affidavit," on the theory that Kinney had no right to represent the Commission. This chapter is itself in the form of an affidavit but is neither dated nor signed by a notary public, though
it is signed by the Colonel at the end. This is one of the most remarkable documents relating to the Fetterman disaster, for it
contains a highly detailed account of actions at the fort before,
during and after the events of December 21 and 22. One is impressed with the straightforwardness of most of it, and some of
the testimony of Major Powell and the other officers is also probably true. This document, which is set forth in full in Appendix B
herein, reiterates that Carrington's report of January 3, 1867,
"is the true version of the Phil Kearny Massacre." This report,
therefore, is included herein as Appendix C. A blueprint showing the various burial sites in the post cemetery was also filed with
the Library. In his July the Fourth oration in 1908, Carrington
gave a new version of the disaster which is published herein as
Appendix D.

It has been noted that there are serious discrepancies in the official reports of Fetterman, Wands, and Carrington concerning the affair of December 6, and since there are other questionable and inconsistent statements and actions by him, it is possible that Carrington may have colored his accounts of the disaster of December 21 in his efforts to clear himself. The testimony and reports of the persons who were at the fort during the disaster were given against the background of the mutual distrust, animosities, and jealousies of the small community. Colonel Carrington's statements in Appendix B point up the extent of the open hostility and bickering between the officers. When Fetterman was permitted, by seniority, to take out the relief on December 21, Major Powell became so angry that he objected to any of his company's going along. In a general way, it seems that Carrington, Wands, Grummond, and their friends were aligned against Fetterman, Powell, Brown, Kinney, Dr. Hines, and their followers.

Nearly all looked down on Carrington because of his lack of combat experience and aggressiveness, while the Colonel considered his fellow officers ignorant of Indian warfare and beneath him socially. After the disaster it soon appeared that he had been openly feuding with Major Powell and Mr. Kinney, the post sutler. The testimony of Major Powell which was taken on July 24, 1867, by Mr. Kinney as the representative of the Sanborn Commission was immediately forwarded to the Interior Department, which in turn submitted it to General Grant. Since Grant knew Major Powell personally and believed his statements, he prohibited the publication of Colonel Carrington's official report of the battle. General Sherman, a friend of Carrington's, dissuaded Grant from bringing court-martial proceedings, and the military Court of Inquiry which was decided upon subsequently cleared Carrington and Ten Eyck after hearing only Carrington's testimony.

Secretary of the Interior Browning had known Carrington during the Civil War and sent him a copy of the testimony. Carrington then went to see Generals Sherman and Grant to secure the publication of his report, but the report remained buried in the dusty files of the Interior Department for twenty years. Carrington, after writing to his friends to obtain evidence to offset Powell's testimony, received a letter from Wands dated November 27, 1867, which refuted most of Powell's charges. A copy of Wand's letter was sent to Captain Ten Eyck, who was then retired, and the reply dated November 23, 1903, affirmed in general terms the contents of Wand's letter. Carrington finally persuaded the Senate in April, 1887, to call upon the Secretary of the Interior for the evidence given by Carrington at Fort McPherson, which was produced and appeared as *Senate Document No. 33, 50 Cong., 1 sess.* This material did not include the minutes of the proceedings of the Sanborn Commission nor the testimony taken before it, and Carrington has never at any time referred to the testimony of any other person before the Commission other than his own and Major Powell's. Much testimony was given by other soldiers at Fort McPherson and at Omaha, and he surely must have known of it because he was the commandant at the former post, and the meetings of the Commission were held in his own house. One wonders why he neither acknowledged nor referred to this additional testimony. Of the testimony of the other officers and men at Fort Phil Kearny he has nothing to say except to reply to the "Affidavit" of Major Powell. He may not have known of the other testimony taken at Fort Kearny, but he surely knew of that at the other two posts. Carrington seems to have regarded Powell and Kinney as enemies who had conspired to effect his disgrace. Carrington's ignoring the sworn testimony of all the other witnesses, much of which was adverse to him, places him in an unfavorable light.

Carrington had a copy of Major Powell's testimony shortly after it was given, so why did he not confront Powell with it at that time instead of waiting so many years? The actual date of their meeting is not known, but apparently both were old men at the time. When the subject was revived just twenty years after the disaster, nearly all the principals were dead or unavailable, and by 1908 very few would still be living.

It appears from Carrington's statements in Appendix B, and the fact that Major Powell's statements are mostly unsupported, that much of Powell's testimony is untrue. The unreliability of Powell's testimony may be explained by the mental illness with which he was afflicted after his years of exposure and hardship in the army. His "blowing" and other expressions of delusions of grandeur are manifestations of the illness. In view of the old gentleman's mental condition, it seems best to disregard the disputed and unsupported parts of his testimony, although his military ability and accomplishments must be recognized. One cannot doubt but that he performed his full duty at the post on December 21, but his statements that he superceded the Colonel and took personal command of the post are surely untrue, especially since he was outranked by Captain Ten Eyck.

Mr. Kinney had been a justice of the Utah Supreme Court, and although he had a grievance against Carrington because of the latter's denial of his claim against the government for some goods allegedly stolen by soldiers, sufficient grounds do not exist to accuse him of the serious crime of procuring witnesses to perjure themselves. The minutes of the Sanborn Commission indicate that he was authorized to represent the whole commission at Fort Phil Kearny, and the government furnished a large cavalry contingent to escort him there so he could take the testimony.

While the discrepancies between Carrington's official report and his account of the disaster in the Fourth of July speech in Appendix D are probably explained by the failure of memory over a lapse of forty-two years, it is interesting to note the Colonel's various attitudes towards Captain Ten Eyck. In the note Carrington had sent Ten Eyck by Orderly Sample, he told him that he had lost two miles in going to Fetterman's aid. In the battle sketch drawn by Carrington later, Ten Eyck's route is shown as going to a hill a short distance east of the Bozeman Trail, only a slight variation from the direct course. In the "Vindication of Ten Eyck" in the pamphlet, Carrington actually praises Ten Eyck for his foresight in not going up the road into the defile where he could have been ambushed. While in this instance he was charitable to Ten Eyck, he never showed any mercy to Fetterman. A study of Carrington's shifting statements and actions makes the student wonder just what his instructions to Fetterman were on that frosty morning a century ago.

There is another rather startling possibility in view of all the evidence. If Fetterman's party was the largest one sent out from the fort up to that time, as one witness testified, an offensive movement may have been agreed upon by Carrington and Fetterman during their conversation, with the former repenting the decision after the party had left. General Cooke had been harping on an offensive to punish the Indians for their depredations, and this little expedition may have been launched for the purpose of fighting the fifty or sixty Indians who had attacked the wood train as they retreated down the Peno valley. Perhaps Carrington felt the mistakes of December 6 could be corrected by sending forth the compact body of eighty-one men, surely enough to cope with the small body of Indians attacking the wood train and hovering about the flanks of the command. But instead of encountering a small body of the enemy, Fetterman's party rode into the ambush of warriors variously estimated from fifteen hundred to three thousand. If this expedition was intended to be an offensive movement in response to General Cooke's orders (and Colonel Fetterman's urging), then the disaster was one of the misfortunes of war, and none of the officers involved was to blame. In such an event, Fetterman, Brown, Grummond, and all their men were heroes who fell fighting overwhelming numbers

of the enemy. None of them can be blamed for not knowing of
the large concentration of warriors awaiting them. On the other
hand, if it was an offensive movement, why did not Carrington
admit it? Perhaps the answer would be that the admission would
shift responsibility to him.

The new evidence and testimony that have been brought to
light offer new grounds for speculation concerning what actually
occurred on those snowy slopes long ago. The weight of the testimony seems to indicate that the Fetterman party went straight
north across the creek and up the Bozeman Trail over Lodge
Trail Ridge and into the valley of Peno Creek. Since Colonel
Carrington made no effort to prevent the movement, the movement was probably an offensive one intended to punish the Indians who were attacking the wood train. If anyone should be
blamed for the disaster, it is the high command which allowed
twelve companies of well-equipped soldiers to remain back in
Fort Laramie while five companies of poorly armed infantrymen
and one company of newly recruited cavalrymen were trying to
fight off the Indians while building a new army post in the heart
of their territory.

3
The Hayfield Fight
⊓⊔⊓⊔⊓⊔⊓⊔⊓⊔⊓⊔⊓⊔⊓⊔⊓⊔⊓⊔⊓⊔⊓⊔

I N 1867, FORT C. F. SMITH was the most northerly of the forts built by the army to protect emigrants and miners traveling the Bozeman Trail to the gold fields of Montana. It was an isolated post for Fort Phil Kearny lay ninety-five miles to the southeast, while the little mining settlements were far to the north. Since the Bozeman Trail ran through the heart of the Indian country, these far-flung army posts were subject to constant attacks by the hostile Sioux and Cheyenne Indians. In the summer of 1867, after their annual sun dance, a large encampment of these tribes on Powder River decided to wipe out the two posts but could not agree upon which one to attack first. It was finally decided that a band of Sioux led by Red Cloud would attack Fort Phil Kearny, while the other group, composed of Cheyennes and some allied Oglala and Minneconjous Sioux, would mount their assault against Fort Smith.[1]

On August 1, 1867, the Cheyenne contingent, while on its way to Fort Smith, encountered a small force of soldiers and civilian hay cutters in a little corral and immediately attacked. After a battle lasting all day, the Indians were repulsed with heavy losses and returned to their home lodges. The next day the band under Red Cloud, heading toward Fort Phil Kearny, encountered a wagon box corral of soldiers and woodcutters and in the fierce battle which followed suffered such severe losses that they also abandoned the campaign. While the famous

[1] George E. Hyde, *Red Cloud's Folk*, 158–59.

91

Wagon Box Fight has been adequately described by many survivors, the equally important fight at the hayfield has been neglected by historians. With official documents now available from the National Archives, it is possible to reconstruct this engagement with the aid of army reports.

Fort Smith was situated on a high plateau three hundred yards south of the Big Horn River, which broke out of the Big Horn Mountains about two miles west of the post. The river ran eastward past the fort but soon jogged towards the northeast. The plateau extended eastward parallel with the river for about one mile where a spur extended a quarter of a mile northward. Here the valley widened out as the bluffs ran southward for about one mile, where they resumed their former course a few degrees north of east.

On July 23, 1867, the permanent garrison at the post had been augmented by the arrival of Lieutenant Colonel and Brevet Brigadier General Luther P. Bradley,[2] the new commandant of the fort, and Companies H and I of the Twenty-seventh Infantry. Accompanying the troops was the wagon train of the post sutler, A. C. Leighton, which, in addition to the usual supplies, brought haymowing machines and some of the new Allin-modified .50–70 breech-loading Springfield rifles.[3] The long-awaited weapons were eagerly received by the troops.

[2] Luther Prentice Bradley was born in Connecticut and appointed lieutenant colonel in the Fifty-first Illinois Infantry on November 6, 1861. Appointed colonel on October 15, 1862, he was commissioned brigadier general of volunteers on July 30, 1864, serving until June 30, 1865, when he resigned. After one year of civilian life he returned to the army with the commission of lieutenant colonel in the Twenty-seventh Infantry, holding this rank at the time of the Hayfield Fight. He served in the Ninth Infantry from March 15, 1869, to March 20, 1879, when he became colonel of the Third Infantry Regiment. He was retired on December 8, 1886, as colonel of the Thirteenth Infantry. During the Civil War, Bradley had been a combat officer, receiving the rank of brevet colonel on March 2, 1867, for gallant service at the Battle of Chickamauga and brevet brigadier general on the same date for gallant service at the Battle of Resaca, Georgia.

[3] James D. Lockwood, *Life and Adventures of a Drummer Boy; or, Seven Years a Soldier*, 182–83; and Hebard and Brininstool, *Bozeman Trail*, II, 162.

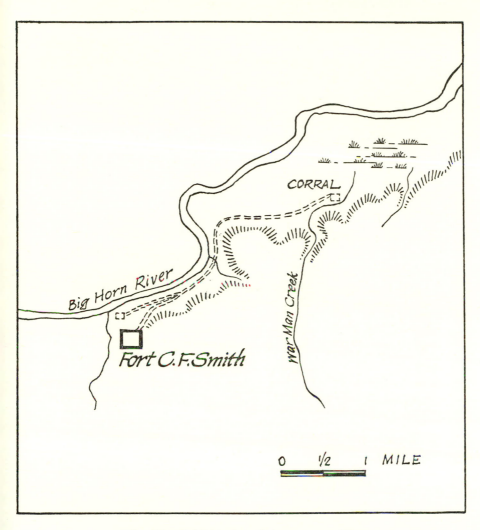

The Hayfield Fight of August 1, 1867

The garrison now consisted of Companies D, E, G, H, and I, of the Twenty-seventh Infantry. Company D was under the command of Second Lieutenant Paul Harwood because Captain E. D. Harding, normally the commanding officer, was on detached service, while First Lieutenant George M. Templeton had left to serve as post adjutant at Fort Phil Kearny. Company E, whose commanding officer, Captain I. D. Isay, was also on detached service, was commanded by First Lieutenant Winfield S. Watson and Second Lieutenant George H. Palmer. Company G was commanded by the sturdy Civil War veteran, Captain and Brevet Major Thomas B. Burrowes, and a young Prussian, Second Lieutenant Sigismund Sternberg.[4] Company H was under First Lieutenant R. H. Fenton[5] and Second Lieutenant E. R. P. Shurly,[6] as

[4] Sigismund Sternberg, born in Prussia, was appointed first lieutenant in the 175th New York Infantry on September 26, 1862. After his resignation from the army on February 13, 1864, he was commissioned captain in the Seventh New York Infantry on October 22, 1864, serving until the end of the Civil War. Appointed second lieutenant in the Regular Army only a few months before his death on August 1, 1867, he had been sent immediately to the frontier.

[5] Born in New York, Reuben H. Fenton began his military career in October, 1861, as a private in Company C of the Ninth New York Cavalry. Reaching the enlisted grade of sergeant, he received his commission as second lieutenant on January 16, 1863, resigning March 31, 1863. After the war he secured an appointment as second lieutenant in the Eighteenth Infantry on February 23, 1866, and was promoted to first lieutenant on July 28, 1866. When the Eighteenth Infantry was divided, he was commissioned captain in the Twenty-seventh Infantry, serving until January 1, 1871. He was serving in the Sixth Cavalry when he left the army on May 22, 1872.

[6] Edmund Richard Pitman Shurly was an Englishman living in Illinois at the time of his appointment as first lieutenant in the 126th New York Infantry on May 21, 1861. Commissioned captain on August 7, 1861, he was honorably mustered out on April 25, 1863, becoming a captain in the Veteran's Reserve Corps on August 28, 1863. From his record it appears that his being wounded at Fredericksburg was the reason for his joining the Reserve Corps, which was composed mostly of men who had been discharged because of wounds. He was brevetted major of volunteers on March 13, 1865, for gallant and meritorious services in the Battle of Fredericksburg, December 13, 1862. He was further honored by an appointment as lieutenant colonel of volunteers on March 13, 1865, for gallant services during the war.

Apparently recovering from his disability, Shurly entered the Regular Army as a second lieutenant in the Eighteenth Infantry on May 11, 1866. Transferred

Captain Andrew S. Burt was on detached service. Company I was commanded by Captain Edward S. Hartz and Second Lieutenant E. S. McCaullay. According to the post return for August, 1867, the post strength was 293 officers and men, not including 58 men of Company E who were absent at the end of the month. Since the men of Company E were at the post on August 1, the total was 351, of which about seventeen were in the guardhouse and fourteen in the hospital, assuming that the number in each remained fairly constant from month to month. According to the muster roll of Company D, forty men left the post at 2:00 A.M., on August 1 to escort the supply train on its return to Fort Phil Kearny. If our calculations are accurate, there were approximately 280 men present and on duty on August 1 when the attack on the hay corral occurred. Twenty-one men were actually at the corral, leaving about 260 at the fort. The soldiers were occupied with garrison duty, in escorting the wood and hay parties, and in building new quarters.

The post had a number of oxen, mules, and horses, and it was necessary to gather up grass growing near the fort to provide hay for them during the winter. A. C. Leighton had the contract to supply hay for the post and had brought with his wagon train a crew of civilians to work in the hayfields. These men were immediately put to work cutting hay with the new mowers and hauling it to the post in wagons which were provided with hay racks instead of the usual wagon boxes. The hay was being cut from meadows east of the fort, between the plateau on the south and the Big Horn River on the north. Since the meadows were too far away from the fort for wagons to travel to them and back

to the Twenty-seventh Infantry on September 21, 1866, he participated in the Hayfield Fight. Possibly in recognition of his services in this engagement, he was commissioned first lieutenant on September 29, 1868, but retired the following December. On March 15, 1867, he had received the brevet ranks of first lieutenant and captain in the Regular Army for gallant services at Fredericksburg and during other actions during the Civil War. He was evidently quite a competent officer to have received commissions in the Regular Army despite the handicaps of his war injuries.

in one day, a strong corral was built on the north bank of Warrior Creek, about three hundred yards north of the plateau and slightly more than two and one-half miles northeast of the fort. This little stream flowed from the bluffs and ran north for three hundred yards then turned northeast for another four hundred yards. Here it angled towards the east for another one hundred yards where it again swung northeast for fifty yards, coming out of the bench onto the bottomland. The south side of the hay corral was located about forty feet north of the creek at a point where the stream ran eastward just before making the last turn. The fort could not be seen from here because the eastern edge of the plateau cut off the view. A road was built from the Quartermaster's corral down near the riverbank under the post eastward along the bottomland for one mile where it circled to the north and then south around the spur, and then took the direct route easterly to the corral. Portions of this old road can still be seen although in places it runs across what are now plowed fields. Another road went from the fort along the bluffs for about one mile and then dipped down to the river bottom, joining the other road. The distance by road to the corral was three miles by modern speedometer measurement.[7]

The corral was about one hundred feet square and well constructed with heavy double-upright posts every six feet. Pole stringers were fastened to the posts halfway to the top, and another row was fastened at the top. Heavy logs were laid on the ground between the posts. On this framework, willow branches and other foliage were interlaced so as to hide the occupants from view. A row of four wagon boxes with their bows and canvas tilts were placed end to end just inside the west side of the corral, while north of these were three soldiers' tents. At night the stock were tied to a picket line which ran north and south over

[7] Data on the terrain is obtained from aerial photographs and personal reconnaissance.

toward the east side. The only opening, on the south, was closed at night by chaining a wagon's running gear by its wheels to the entrance posts. The kitchen tent stood just outside the corral at the southwest corner near the stream. A dense growth of willows grew all along the creek, while to the north was a little grove of trees. Trenches thirty feet long were dug at the northwest, northeast, and southeast corners of the enclosure for defensive purposes, while a picket was stationed on the point of the bluffs seven hundred yards down the valley to the east.[8]

The crew of civilian employees, guarded by a detachment of infantry from the fort, worked harvesting hay during daylight hours, but the soldiers and hay cutters all stayed at the corral during the night. Loading of the wagons was accomplished during the afternoon, and the hay was hauled to the fort the next morning so that the hay cutters were always busy. During these operations, the hostile Indians frequently attacked the corral four or five times a day. When the hay was dry and ready to load on the wagons, the Indians would attack, driving the workers into the corral and burning the hay.[9] The friendly Crow Indians, enjoying a temporary truce with the Sioux and Cheyennes, were around the area constantly. The Crows, who visited in the hostile camps, often brought tales to the soldiers of the plans of the enemy. On July 29 a band of Crows stopped at the hayfield and told the men that the Sioux and Cheyennes were planning to attack the next day in great strength, but the men had been warned so often that they paid no attention to the story. The Crows then went to the fort, where their story was again ignored.[10]

On the morning of August 1, 1867, the loaded hay wagons and a mounted escort, following the usual practice, were sent to

[8] David, *Finn Burnett*, 162–63, 168.
[9] *Ibid.*, 163, 166; see also the official report of Lieutenant Colonel Luther P. Bradley, dated August 5, 1867.
[10] David, *Finn Burnett*, 166.

the fort, leaving a force of nine civilians and twenty soldiers under the command of Lieutenant Sigismund Sternberg, thirty men in all. While the post return for August, 1867, and the annual regimental return for 1867 give the number of soldiers as nineteen in addition to the Lieutenant, it is probable that the official report of Colonel Bradley, dated August 5, 1867, giving the number of soldiers as twenty in addition to the Lieutenant, is more accurate. Bradley's report is supported by Private Lockwood's assertion that there were twenty-one soldiers present.[11] According to Finn Burnett, a young member of the hay crew, the nine civilians were D. A. Colvin, Zeke Colvin, Al Stevenson, Robert Wheeling, Robert Little, George Duncan, William Haynes, John G. Hollister, and Burnett.[12] From the company muster rolls and official reports the names of some of the soldiers have been found: Second Lieutenant Sigismund Sternberg and Private Henry C. Vinson of Company G; Private James D. Lockwood of Company D; Sergeant James Horton and Privates Richard Colclough, George Brambier, James L. Leavey, Thomas Riley, Rudolph Raithel, and Edward Holloran, all of Company I; Private Navin of Company H; and Privates Francis M. Law and Charles Bradley of Company E. The names of the other eight men have not been located since most of the muster rolls did not mention the soldiers at the corral unless they were wounded.

The soldiers were armed with revolvers and the newly issued .50–70 Springfield rifles and were well supplied with ammunition. The civilians had Spencer, Henry, and Model 1866 Winchester repeating carbines, although Zeke Colvin used his favorite Enfield muzzle-loading musket which he had picked up on the battlefield of Wilson's Creek in Missouri during the Civil War. Another man had a shotgun.[13]

There are two eyewitness accounts of the battle, one by Finn

---

[11] Lockwood, *Drummer Boy*, 182.   [12] David, *Finn Burnett*, 167.
[13] Hebard and Brininstool, *Bozeman Trail*, II, 162; and *ibid.*, 174.

Burnett and the other by Private James D. Lockwood, who was "learning music." Although both were written years afterwards, they are believed to be fairly accurate despite differences in minor details. The official reports of Colonel Bradley and Captain Burrowes are important in giving the point of view of the soldiers at the fort and details of the later stages of the engagement. The soldier's accounts are biased in their own favor, and little mention is made of the heroic part played by the civilians. On the other hand, Burnett emphasizes the part played by his comrades, while accusing the soldiers at the post of cowardice for not coming immediately to the rescue of the hay party. The antagonism which existed was not unusual during the Indian Wars, with each writer seeking to magnify his own achievements at the expense of others, and as a consequence the truth must be sought somewhere between a mass of conflicting claims and charges.

When the hay wagons departed for Fort Smith, the mowing machines were driven into the fields while the soldiers and some of the civilians lounged about the corral. This peaceful setting and the attack by the Indians are graphically described by Private Lockwood:

> The mowers rattled on for some time without interruption, and there had been a quantity of hay cut, and the boxes had been taken off from the wagons and placed upon the ground in a circle around the camp, they being replaced upon the wagons by racks, for the drawing of the hay.
>
> While these arrangements had been progressing, the soldiers had been lounging around the encampment, playing cards, wrestling, pitching horseshoes in lieu of quoits, and striving to pass time pleasantly, as soldiers usually do at remote stations where there is no society aside from their own.
>
> Upon the day of which we write, the following conversation was held at the camp among them in reference to their estimation of the value of their new breech-loading arms:

First private—"Sergeant, how many Indians do you think our squad here, could lick with these ere new guns of ours?"

Sergeant—"We can wallop the devil out of all the Indians that could stand between here and that hill" (which was about three hundred yards distant).

Second private—"By jinks, I should like to try them a crack," sighting over his rifle and then resuming, "I have an idea that I could make some of them scratch where they didn't itch."

Third private—"So cud I, aisy enough, be jabers; fur it wud be on the ground that they's be afther scratchin."

Sergeant—"Well, boys, we shall have no such good luck, I fear, for, damn them, they won't fight fair, and they never come when you are ready for them. But now I think of it, some of you loosen the screws in the lids of those ammunition boxes, so that if we do need them, we can get at them quick. I am of the opinion that if they come and stay long enough to have those five thousand rounds pumped into them, there will be a number of them in need of the doctor."

Fourth private—"An by the same token, there will be a pile of them that divil a docther wud be only good to."

The sergeant wound up, musingly, with the remark, "I wish that 'boss' haymaker had taken this grass up from around the camp here, as I requested him to do—a fire here would play the devil with us."

The boys, as soldiers are always called, had not finished this conversation above a half hour, when shots were heard down the valley, where the mowers were at work, and the machines began coming into the camp helter skelter, their mule teams on a gallop; they were followed by a band of Indians, who occasionally fired a shot at them, with the only effect to make them more expeditious in getting to the soldiers at the encampment.

The soldiers, as we have seen, were eager for a fight and were not long in getting in shape for it. A few shots were fired by them at the Indians at long range, but seemingly without effect. Some of the hot headed ones wished to follow them, and give them battle. This, it subsequently appeared, was precisely what the Indians wished them to do.

But the sergeant, who was the right man in the right place, had profitted by the lesson which the Indians taught in the recent massacre at Fort Philip Kearney, and refused point blank to stir from the encampment, but, wisely, set the citizens to work with picks and shovels to fortify it, by digging a trench around on the inside of the circle of wagon boxes, and throwing the dirt from the trench into them, rendering them a substantial protection from bullets, and that was the salvation of the little band.

When the savages saw that it was useless to try to draw the soldiers out after them, they began congregating in great numbers in sight of the devoted little party, and it was clear that they intended to make an attack. The chief harangued them at considerable length; and their squaws and children were brought in sight upon the bluffs, beyond rifle range, to see their warriors kill the white men.

Suddenly a band of five or six hundred of them assembled and rode, yelling and whooping, down upon the little fortified camp. They received a close, regular, sweeping volley, and circled away; their ranks were then joined by nearly twice as many more and, thinking to reach the little band before they could reload their guns, they rode furiously upon them. Then, indeed, the battle was properly on. The little camp was one steady, continuous circle of fire from the breech loaders; the rattle and roar of them in the hands of those few regulars was as steady and continuous as the rumbling of a mill, or the hum of machinery. The soldiers were delighted. The Indians, surprised and dumbfounded, scattered in all directions. Seeing that nothing could be done by direct assault, they got around to the windward and set fire to the hay. The flames started, leaping and racing at a frightful speed, for the apparently doomed encampment of soldiers. They never once slackened their fire, as they knew it was death to surrender, and they determined to fight as long as there was a man to pull a trigger.

Our hero [Private James D. Lockwood], who was on the right of the circle near the river, frequently dipped his gun into the water to cool its heated breech block.

The fire came on in rolling billows, like the waves of the ocean, the Indians whooping behind it. When it arrived within twenty feet of the barricade it stopped, as though arrested by supernatural power. The flames arose to a perpendicular height of at least forty feet, made one or two undulating movements, and were extinguished with a spanking slap, like the flapping sound of a heavy canvas in a hard gale; the wind, the succeeding instant, carried the smoke of the smoldering grass away from the providentially saved encampment, into the faces of the attacking Indians, who improved the opportunity, under cover of it, to carry away their dead and wounded.

There was one body which they could not get, as it was too close to the camp for them to venture; this was the body of an Indian, who had actually crawled up to the wagon-box containing the provisions of the party, and had abstracted therefrom a mess-pan full of molasses, during the battle. He was seen by a teamster, who, still having one of the old Springfield muzzle-loaders, and being short of ammunition for it, had loaded into it a handful of thirty-two calibre pistol cartridges, copper shells and all. It is hardly necessary to state that this dose did the business for the brave who possessed such an inordinate fondness for sweets. After the battle, he was still lying "taking his rest," with his pan and molasses around him.[14]

According to Burnett, the action started about 9:30 A.M. when the picket on the bluff seven hundred yards to the east fired his gun and came galloping in, followed by a solid mass of warriors advancing up the valley. The Indians charged so quickly upon

[14] Lockwood, *Drummer Boy*, 183–89.

the enclosure that there was not time to man the rifle pits. The soldiers threw themselves upon the ground behind the large logs and opened fire. The first charge was repulsed, but Lieutenant Sternberg was killed at the south entrance by a musket ball through the head while he was ordering his men to stand up and fight like soldiers. The young lieutenant had joined his company only a few days before the engagement. Unaccustomed to Indian warfare, he was spoken of by the men who fought under him at the corral as having acted with great coolness and gallantry.[15] The command then devolved upon Sergeant James Horton, who was shortly thereafter shot in the shoulder. He was out of action as a result of his wound except that when the enemy made their charges, he took his place at the line with his revolver. One of the civilians, D. A. Colvin, who had been a captain in the Union Army, then assumed command.

When Sternberg fell, the Indians rallied and charged again from the bluffs on the east and south. As they were again repulsed, they commenced long-distance sniping from the bluffs and benches overlooking the position on the west, south, and east. Some fired from the willows along the creek and the grove of trees to the north and northwest.

Shortly after noon, the Indians disappeared, and the men were able to eat and fill the water barrel from the creek. During this brief respite, they prepared for the next attack, digging holes behind the ground logs in which to take refuge.

The next assault, led by a Cheyenne medicine man, was from the bench to the west, and as the red tide swept down, the soldiers rushed to the west side of the stockade and poured in such a heavy fire that the Indians again withdrew and resumed their tactics of firing from behind the bluffs, benches, and trees surrounding the corral. All during the battle, the Indians along the creek and on the bench to the west kept firing arrows at the

[15] Annual Record of the Twenty-seventh Infantry, 1867.

animals on the picket line. The wounded mules frantically kicked and plunged, sending clouds of dust over the corral and adding to the general confusion.

After an interval, the enemy was rallied by a Minneconjou chief who led a charge on foot from the bluffs to the south, but after splashing through the creek, which was about three feet deep, they were driven back by the fire of the men who had rushed to the south side of the stockade to meet the attack. In retreating on foot over the benchland rising to the bluffs, the Indians were fully exposed and suffered heavy casualties. Most of them abandoned the attack and started back down the valley, leaving some of their number to continue the long-distance sniping.[16]

> As soon as the firing ceased, a brave soldier named Bradley [Private Charles Bradley] volunteered to ride to the garrison for aid, which he did, narrowly escaping with his life, for the Indians had secreted themselves in a ravine, the mouth of which opened upon the river valley within a few hundred yards of the fort, and as he was passing they strove to intercept him, but being an excellent horseman, and better mounted than the Indians, he escaped them.
>
> The commandant of the fort instantly ran out one of his little howitzers and cracked a shell down into the ravine, making the "poor Los skedaddle" all sorts.[17]

Earlier that morning the wood train had departed as usual from Fort Smith for the mountain slopes west of the post, and the hay wagons from the corral arrived at the fort and were unloaded. Captain Hartz, who was in command of the wood train, saw the battle at the hay corral and galloped back to the fort and

[16] David, *Finn Burnett*, 168–89; and Hebard and Brininstool, *Bozeman Trail*, II, 162–69.

[17] Lockwood, *Drummer Boy*, 189.

reported the engagement to Colonel Bradley. Just as Hartz arrived a few Indians approached the fort, attempting to molest the wood train which was returning from the mountains, so Bradley ordered the gates of the post closed.[18] This was probably a short time after noon, the time when the Indians disappeared from the corral. Apparently deciding not to attack the fort and wood train, the hostiles returned to the stockade where they resumed the siege by charging from the west.

Colonel Bradley has been condemned for cowardice in failing to send troops immediately to the relief of the stockade. He states in his official report of the action five days later that:

> I did not know of the fight until it had been going on some hours, very little firing was heard, and not a large body of Indians were seen, though a few rode near the post, and threatened the timber train, which was out in an opposite direction. Wishing to send out the train of hay wagons in the afternoon I directed 20 mounted men under Mr. Shurley [*sic*] to go in advance and reconnoiter. They developed a large number of Indians and were obliged to fall back. I then sent Maj Burroughs with Companies "G" and "H" and a howitzer when the Indians were driven back and the party at the stockade relieved.

The statements that very little firing was heard and that Bradley did not know of the fight until it had been going on some hours are questionable. The firing must have been heard by the pickets stationed at the post, though possibly they did not report it. According to Burnett, the Indians had been in the habit of attacking the corral four or five times a day, so the attack on August 1 was not unusual, and since relief had not been sent to the corral on previous occasions, the pickets and Bradley, if he did in fact know of it, did not think the action too serious. Both

---

[18] Hebard and Brininstool, *Bozeman Trail*, II, 167; and David, *Finn Burnett*, 183.

Lockwood and Burnett mention only two direct attacks upon the corral during the morning.

Bradley may have thought the force of thirty men, protected by the corral and armed with the latest type of rifles and repeating carbines, sufficient to defend themselves. His decision to send a reconnoitering party of only twenty men to see if the hay wagons could return to the corral makes it appear that he did not fear for the men back at the corral. He probably thought it best not to send out a large party until the wood train returned to the post. There are so many factors which may have dictated his actions that he cannot be categorically charged with fault or neglect. The charge that he cowered behind the walls of the post, afraid to send relief to the corral, is belied by the fact that when advised of the seriousness of the attack by the messenger from the corral, he immediately sent one-third of his total force to its relief. Colonel Bradley was not censured by the army and had a long and distinguished record in the service, later commanding the District of the Black Hills.

Captain Burrowes,[19] who has also been accused of timidity and cowardice in the presence of the enemy, gave a detailed account of his part in the engagement in his official report dated only three days after the action. Since the entire report pertains to the Hayfield Fight, it is set forth in full:

FORT C. F. SMITH, M.T.
August 3rd 1867

SIR:

I have the honor to report that at 4 o'clock P.M. August 1st

---

[19] Thomas Breden Burrowes, born in Pennsylvania, was commissioned first lieutenant in the Eighteenth Infantry on May 14, 1861. For some reason he was dismissed on June 17, 1863, but was reinstated February 27, 1864. Since he was commissioned captain on November 13, 1863, before his reinstatement, it is possible that his dismissal was because of some wound or other disability. When the war ended he remained in the Regular establishment, being transferred on September 21, 1866, to the Twenty-seventh Infantry. On September 1, 1864,

1867 I was ordered with "G" Co 27 U.S. Inf. to go to the relief of Lieut. E. R. Shurley [*sic*] 27 US Inf who was in charge of twenty mounted infantry and citizens (employees) and sharply engaged with Indians whilst reconnoitering the ground between the garrison and the hay field.

I proceeded with my force until I formed a junction with Lieut. Shurley, when the Indians with whom he was engaged retired out of range. When I had secured Lieut. Shurley from danger I was about to return to the post when I received a re-inforcement of a detachment of "H" Co. 27 U.S. Inf. 1st Lt. R. F. Fenton comdg; one mountain howitzer and its gun-squad; with orders from Bvt. Brig. General L. P. Bradley Lieut. Col. 27 U.S. Inf comdg post to move forward with my command to the hay corral, relieve them, bring back the killed and wounded and do whatever I might deem best after I ar-rived there and discovered the exact status of affairs.

In obedience to these instructions I moved forward throw-ing out Lt. Shurley and his mounted party to protect my flanks and guard against surprise. The mounted men were supported by an infantry skirmish line Lieut Fenton in charge.

I arrived at the hay corral at sun-down having had desultory skirmish firing with the Indians for a mile and a half before reaching it.

When I arrived at the hay ground I found the following cas-ualties to have occurred—viz:

Lieut Sigismund Sternberg "G" Co 27 Inf Killed

Pvt-Nevins "H" Co 27 Inf Killed

Serg Norton "I" Co 27 Inf wounded—left shoulder.

Pvt. Henry C. Vinson "G" Co 27 Inf wounded—both legs—right leg fracture.

Pvt. Francis M. Law "E" Co 27 Inf wounded—Knee

Citizen J. G. Hollister wounded—chest—since died.

he was honored by being commissioned brevet major for gallant service during the Battle of Jonesboro, Georgia, and he retired from the Ninth Infantry on March 20, 1879. He died on October 12, 1885.

Upon surveying the position I found it untenable from its nearness to a thickly brushed creek from which the enemy could come very close and deliver their fire unseen, without great sacrifice of life.

I immediately threw out a line of skirmishers, Lieut Fenton in charge and ordered the dead and wounded to be loaded at once and all the available mules to be harnessed. I then discovered that out of twenty two mules two had been killed and seventeen wounded many of them severely having from three to nine arrow wounds each. With this limited and inefficient motive power I found I could not transport all the property. I therefore ordered all heavy articles to be left such as wagons, wagon beds and the mowing machines and the wagons loaded to the utmost capacity of the mules with more valuable property, judging that the enemy would not disturb the property thus left. The result has proven its correctness for today these articles were recovered uninjured. I was obliged for want of transportation to abandon some wagon sheets and articles of like description as the owners preferred to save lighter articles of more value. The articles so abandoned I burned to prevent them falling into the hands of the enemy.

I made these dispositions as rapidly as possible for the wounded men were sadly in want of medical attendance. During this time quite a lively skirmish was kept up with the Indians.

They appeared on the bluffs all around me in numbers which I estimate at from 450 to 500 whilst on the bluffs in rear a party of about 300 more were within supporting distance of the main force. Upon conversing with the contractors and men on the hay detail I found my estimate considerably lower than theirs.

When ready to return I opened on the Indians with the artillery and cleared the bluffs under cover of the fire I ordered Lt. Shurley to take possession of the bluffs and Lieut Fenton to support him with his skirmishers whilst I with my company and the train moved toward the garrison by the river road. I moved forward after these dispositions were made in the manner heretofore described only being obliged to halt once and clear some Indians off a bluff round the base of which I was obliged to pass with the train. Here the howitzer was again called into use. I arrived at Ft. C. F. Smith at 8:30 o'clock P.M. Aug 1st 1867. The distance marched was about 7 miles. I lost neither men or animal. Lieut. Shurley was slightly scratched on the hand in the action. My command in going to relieve the hay party was eighty men in returning it aggregated about one hundred.

Credit is due both Lieut Fenton and Lieut Shurley for the zeal displayed and the fidelity with which they carried out all my instructions.

I deem it proper to add that from personal inspection of the corral (which was but a brush screen, rifle pits having been constructed after the first dash of the Indians was made) that the fight was a success to us. The Indians were certainly very determined and the number of arrows in and around the work shows that they came very close.

When I arrived I found one Indian lying dead within fifteen paces of the work. I am fully convinced that the number of Indians killed must be from eighteen to twenty-two or three, with a goodly number wounded.

All agree in this that the men behaved exceedingly well that they were calm and deliberate seldom wasting a shot although their comdg officer Lt. Sternburg was killed at the first onset and Sergt. Norton the second in command placed "hors de combat" shortly after.

The new breech loading musket gave the men an opportunity to fire much more rapidly when the occasion demanded and with less exposure of the person than the Springfield rifle. Whilst the superiority of the sights gives more accuracy to the aim. The confidence which it gives the men from the rapidity with which it can be fired and the telling effects of the shots tends to keep them calm, composed and confident under fire.

The Indians engaged were Sioux, Cheyennes and Arapahoes.

I am Sir Very Respectfully Your Obt Servt
T. B. Burrowes, *Capt 27 US Inf*
Bvt Maj. U.S.A.

To
1st Lieut Geo. M. Templeton
27 U.S. Inf
Post Adjutant
Ft C. F. Smith M Terry

When Company H and the howitzer were sent to Burrowes with orders to relieve the corral, they must have been sent in response to the message brought by Private Charles Bradley because Burrowes was specifically instructed to bring back the killed and wounded. Colonel Bradley could not have known of the killed and wounded without having had word from the corral.

From all accounts the action lasted from nine-thirty in the morning to eight-thirty that night. Private Lockwood reported that:

> Before leaving the ground they scalped the dead Indian in the latest and most artistic western style, then beheaded him, placing his head upon a high pole, leaving the carcass to his friends or the wolves. The general verdict was, "that he came to his death on account of his extreme fondness for government molasses," the soldiers, of course, making due allowance for the ignorant savage's perverted tastes.[20]

Sergeant Horton and Privates Vinson and Law must have been severely wounded, for their company bimonthly muster

[20] Lockwood, *Drummer Boy*, 189–90.

rolls indicate they were still on the sick list at the end of August. The personal effects of Lieutenant Sternberg were gathered together and held subject to the order of his father in Berlin.[21]

The Indians suffered such severe casualties that they did not return to molest the hay party. "Big Bat" Pourière, who arrived at the post the day after the fight, said the Indians admitted that seven or eight were killed and "quite a number wounded."[22] Captain Burrowes' estimate that there were eighteen to twenty-three Indians killed seems more realistic. The repeated statements by Burnett that dead Indians were "piled up" outside the corral are not substantiated by any other source. Finn Burnett claimed that the bodies of fifty dead Sioux were found in a sandstone ledge two miles east of the corral several days later by newly arrived cavalrymen.[23] These could have been bodies of Indians killed in both the Wagon Box Fight and the Hayfield Fight, including those who died of wounds some time after the engagements. On the other hand, the number of bodies found may have been exaggerated over the years, as this claim is not substantiated by any other source.

The attack showed that the corral's position under the bluffs was untenable, and a new corral was built one-half mile to the north and was guarded with one company of soldiers and a howitzer.[24] Remnants and relics of the new corral have been found on the north side of the farm of Archie Wilson. According to "Big Bat" Pourière, John Richaud, Jr., took over the hay contract and completed it within several weeks, because Leighton had lost part of his stock and had sustained other damages to his

[21] Muster roll of Company G, Twenty-seventh Infantry, dated August 31, 1867.

[22] Ricker "Interviews," tablet 15, pp. 75ff. These remarkable manuscripts are in the custody of the Nebraska State Historical Society.

[23] Hebard and Brininstool, *Bozeman Trail*, II, 169; and David, *Finn Burnett*, 193.

[24] David, *ibid.*, 195; see the official report of Lieutenant Colonel Luther P. Bradley, dated August 5, 1867.

outfit.[25] Burnett, however, states that Leighton completed the hay contract.[26]

Some historians have wondered why cavalry at the fort did not sweep out and disperse the Indians with a dashing cavalry charge. The best answer is that there were no cavalry troops at Fort C. F. Smith at this time,[27] and there were only enough horses to mount an infantry detachment. The terrain at Fort Smith, as at the sites of most of the other engagements in Wyoming and Montana, was too rough and broken to permit cavalry charges. Soldiers could fight Indians better dismounted in rough country, and infantry armed with long-range rifles were especially effective. From descriptions of the corral after the fight, it appears that everything above the level of the ground logs was riddled with bullets and arrows, and the men were wise in preparing their defenses so they could lie prone behind the ground logs and wagon boxes filled with dirt.[28] Captain Burrowes and Private Lockwood paid tribute to the new .50–70 Springfields with which the soldiers were armed, and a statement in the annual record of the Twenty-seventh Infantry, 1867, says that "the new arms, handled with great coolness, saved the party from massacre." These weapons were single-shot rifles taking metal cartridges which were inserted at the breech. When the breech was opened after firing, the empty cartridge was ejected, leaving the chamber ready for the insertion of the next cartridge. Thus, after the gun had been thrust through the wall of the stockade and fired, it did not have to be withdrawn since all the reloading action took place at the breech. It could fire much more rapidly than the old Civil War type Springfield muskets which were loaded from the muzzle. Had the old Springfields been used at the corral, the defenders might not have been able to fire fast

[25] Ricker, "Interviews," tablet 15, pp. 75ff.
[26] David, *Finn Burnett*, 199.
[27] Post Return of Fort C. F. Smith, M.T., for August, 1867.
[28] David, *Finn Burnett*, 191; and Lockwood, *Drummer Boy*, 186.

enough to hold back the enemy. Reloading was quite an involved process with this type of weapon. After firing, the gun would have had to be withdrawn from the wall of the corral and swabbed out with a ramrod. The paper cartridge would then be bitten off at the end so that the powder would be exposed and then inserted into the muzzle of the gun and rammed home with the ramrod. A patch or wadding would then be tamped down to hold the cartridge firmly in place. After a percussion cap was placed on the nipple, the gun would have to be thrust back through the wall for firing. The men in the corral would have found it very difficult to reload these muskets while lying behind the ground logs.

It was a favorite tactic of the Indians in fighting soldiers armed with muzzle-loading weapons to provoke a volley from them and then rush upon the soldiers before they could reload. This was tried at the Hayfield and Wagon Box Fights in the belief that the men were still armed with the old style muskets. When they charged after the volley, they were close to the enclosure and perfect targets for the second volley from the new weapons. Captain Burrowes also mentioned in his official report that the sights were better and gave the men more confidence. While the new guns were much more powerful than the Winchesters, Spencer carbines, and the .44-caliber Henrys of the civilians, they could not be fired as rapidly.

The exact site of the old corral became lost, and for many years the late Dr. W. A. Russell, of Hardin, Montana, searched for it. As each new shred of evidence appeared, he weighed and compared it with the terrain, making repeated trips over the area. With a view to establishing the true location, he planned a celebration and dedication to be held on August 1, 1923, the anniversary of the battle. Many of the old-timers, Indians, and historians were invited to attend.[29]

[29] Letter of Miss Marion J. Russell, daughter of the late Dr. Russell, to the author, dated June 28, 1962.

One of the letters received, dated July 18, 1923, was from W. L. Simpson, of Thermopolis, Wyoming, who handled Burnett's correspondence. Apparently written for Burnett, the letter stated that Burnett would arrive two or three days before the celebration so that he could go over the field with Russell. The location of the old corral was said to be situated on Warrior Creek about one-half or three-fourths of a mile below the mouth of the little canyon where the creek flows through the bench out into the valley. Its exact position could be determined with reference to the point on the bluffs where the picket was kept, about seven hundred yards away.

A letter was also received from W. M. Camp, who regretted that he would be unable to come but gave the location as about ninety-five rods down the creek from the point where it was intercepted by the big irrigation ditch. Camp claimed that he had visited the place in the company of soldiers and Indians who had been in the battle. They had pointed out a dense thicket with tree stumps lying between the corral and the river from which some of the Indians had poured in their fire on the stockade.

The night before the celebration it began to rain, and a steady downpour continued all the next day. Since the road to the scene of the fight was not graveled, it was impassable, so the program was held in a hall in Hardin.[30]

Burnett and Russell went over the field and decided upon the corral site where a marker would later be placed. The location agreed upon was the point where the two roads now intersect. In 1923 these roads were mere trails, while in 1910 an irrigation ditch fifty feet wide had been built south of the road from Fort C. F. Smith but north of Warrior Creek. Finn Burnett was sure of the location, although C. H. Asbury, then superintendent of the Indian Field Service at Crow Agency, who was present, said that

[30] *Ibid.*

114

"they placed a stone on, or very near, the site of this fight."[31] Apparently nothing was found in the area to confirm the location, and the wife of Dr. Russell wrote the writer that nothing was found at the time. The marker was erected that fall at the northwest corner of the intersection of the two roads, which are now graded up and heavily graveled. Relics of the battle have not been found around the marker nor along the creek south of it, although a number of people have gone over the area with metal detectors.

The true site of the corral has not been definitely located, although the writer and many others have searched extensively for it. It is probably south of the marker and north of Warrior Creek, being covered by the large irrigation ditch, its embankments, and the graded-up road north of it. Besides being the location made by Finn Burnett, this site is the approximate place shown on the map of Captain Hartz in the National Archives and on the sketch made by Professor Grace Hebard under the direction of Finn Burnett.[32] A series of benches lead up to the bluffs three hundred yards to the south, while the new corral is one-half mile to the north. Spencer and .50–70 Springfield cartridge cases have been found around the trees northwest of the marker, but it is likely that many metal cartridges and other relics have been either covered over or scraped up in the process of constructing and grading the roads.

That the marker is situated on the exact site of the corral is claimed by an old Crow Indian, Carl Crooked Arm, of St. Xavier,

---

[31] Letter, C. H. Asbury to Professor Grace Raymond Hebard, dated September 18, 1923, the original of which is in the archives of the University of Wyoming.

[32] This sketch appears in David, *Finn Burnett*, 171; and Hebard and Brininstool, *Bozeman Trail*, II, 163. It is believed to be fairly accurate and was made from the high bluff south of the stockade. The bluffs at the extreme left appear closer than they are, being a mile and a half to the west.

Montana, who is well versed in local history. He says that each year during the spring, Warrior Creek, being very narrow where it comes out of the bluffs, floods the whole plain northward to the Big Horn River because of the high water caused by snow thaws and heavy rains. The whole hay meadow is thus irrigated, making it very productive.[33] The absence of relics on the site may be easily explained by the flooding waters, which have probably washed away everything not fastened to the ground and may have even covered up the ground with silt and debris washed down from the bluffs.

It is to be regretted that the original site of this heroic stand has not been preserved intact as part of our national heritage.

[33] Letter, dated November 20, 1965, to author from Ed Kopac, of Hardin, Montana, who went over the marker site with Carl Crooked Arm.

4
The Rosebud Campaign
ɼᴜ̄ᴜ̄ᴜ̄ᴜ̄ᴜ̄ᴜ̄ᴜ̄ᴜ̄ᴜ̄ᴜ̄ᴜ̄ᴜ̄ᴜ̄ᴜ̄

TENSION BETWEEN THE GOVERNMENT and the Sioux and Cheyenne Indians had been building up for many years, but when the Indians refused to sell the Black Hills in 1875, popular clamor compelled the government to adopt a "get tough" policy with the tribes who were opposing the surging tide of white civilization. Abandoning its policy of appeasement, the Indian Bureau turned the problem of Indian management over to the army, which had long favored General William T. Sherman's aggressive policies towards the hostile tribes.

When the Indians refused to go to the reservations set aside for them, General George Crook led an expedition northward from Fort Fetterman on March 1, 1876, for the purpose of destroying the small, scattered Indian bands whose ponies were still weak from lack of forage during the winter season.[1] One portion of Crook's force, led by Colonel Joseph J. Reynolds, destroyed a Cheyenne village on Powder River on March 17. Reynolds and his men were driven back without decisive results, however, and the column, which had suffered severely from the cold and a shortage of provisions, returned to Fort Fetterman to recuperate. It was believed at the time that the failure of the expedition was caused by mismanagement and cowardice on the part of some of the officers, so court-martial proceedings were commenced against three of them, including Colonel Reynolds.

[1] See Vaughn, *The Reynolds Campaign.*

117

General Crook immediately began organizing another party to hunt down the village of the Oglala war chief, Crazy Horse, whom he believed responsible for the successful defense against Reynolds' attack at Powder River. This column was larger than the one led by Reynolds, and the Crows and Shoshones, who were bitter enemies of the Sioux, had promised to send some of their warriors to act as scouts. The army's overall strategy called for Crook to move northward, acting in concert with another force under General John Gibbon coming down the Yellowstone from the northwest and a third column from the east under the command of General Alfred Howe Terry. The tactical plan envisioned the Indians routed by one column being caught by another of the forces; this force would compel the Indians to move onto their reservations. Gibbon had commenced his advance in February and was already somewhere along the Yellowstone, while General Terry's expedition, which included General George A. Custer and his ill-fated Seventh Cavalry, was expected to leave Fort Abraham Lincoln early in the spring.

In May, 1876, Fort Fetterman began bustling with the concentration of troops and supplies being sent there in preparation for the new advance into hostile territory. Lieutenant Colonel William B. Royall, Third Cavalry, led a detachment of cavalry and infantry northward from Fort D. A. Russell, and after being joined by units from Fort Laramie, crossed the new iron bridge over the North Platte and marched westward over the Morman Road along the north side of the river to Fort Fetterman, where camp was made in a river bend across from the fort. Major Andrew W. Evans, Third Cavalry, led another detachment which traveled via Union Pacific to Medicine Bow, and from here it marched northward to Fort Fetterman, camping on the south side of the river. A large pack train accompanied by a number of army wagons was brought up from Camp Carlin loaded with huge quantities of supplies and ammunition. The troops camped south of the river at the fort were moved across on a small ferry-boat whose cable was broken several times by the swift current of the flood-swollen river. Despite some delay, all the troops and supplies were moved across, and soon everything was in readiness for the long march ahead.

General Crook's column, whose movements were later known as the Big Horn and Yellowstone Expedition, consisted of ten companies of the Third Cavalry and five companies of the Second Cavalry under the command of Lieutenant Colonel Royall and two companies of the Fourth Infantry and three companies of the Ninth Infantry all commanded by Major Alex Chambers. Crook's staff included his aides-de-camp, Captain Azor H. Nickerson and Lieutenant John G. Bourke; the chief of scouts, Captain George M. Randall; the chief engineer officer, Captain W. S. Stanton; the chief quartermaster, Captain J. V. Furey; the chief commissary officer, Lieutenant J. W. Bubb; and the medical director, Assistant Surgeon Albert Hartsuff.

The units and officers serving with the expedition were:

Company A, Third Cavalry. Lieutenant Joseph Lawson and Lieutenant Charles Morton.

Company B, Third Cavalry. Captain Charles Meinhold and Lieutenant James F. Simpson.

Company C, Third Cavalry. Captain Frederick Van Vliet and Lieutenant Adolphus H. Von Luettwitz.

Company D, Third Cavalry. Captain Guy V. Henry and Lieutenant William W. Robinson, Jr.

Company E, Third Cavalry. Captain Alexander Sutorius and Lieutenant Henry R. Lemly.

Company F, Third Cavalry. Lieutenant Bainbridge Reynolds.

Company G, Third Cavalry. Lieutenant Emmitt Crawford.

Company I, Third Cavalry. Captain William H. Andrews, Lieutenant James E. H. Foster, and Lieutenant Albert King.

Company L. Third Cavalry. Captain Peter D. Vroom and Lieutenant George F. Chase.

Company M. Third Cavalry. Captain Anson Mills, Lieutenant
Augustus C. Paul, and Lieutenant Frederick Schwatka.

Company A, Second Cavalry. Captain Thomas B. Dewees and
Lieutenant Daniel C. Pearson.

Company B, Second Cavalry. Lieutenant William C. Rawolle.

Company E, Second Cavalry. Captain Elijah R. Wells and
Lieutenant Frederick W. Sibley.

Company F, Second Cavalry. Captain Henry E. Noyes and
Lieutenant Fred W. Kingsbury.

Company G, Second Cavalry. Captain Samuel M. Swigert and
Lieutenant Henry D. Huntington.

Company C, Ninth Infantry. Captain Sam Munson and Lieutenant Thaddeus H. Capron.

Company G, Ninth Infantry. Captain Thomas B. Burrowes
and Lieutenant William L. Carpenter.

Company H, Ninth Infantry. Captain Andrew S. Burt and
Lieutenant Edgar B. Robertson.

Company D, Fourth Infantry. Captain Avery B. Cain and
Lieutenant Henry Seton.

Company F, Fourth Infantry. Captain Gerhard L. Luhn.

The press was well represented by John F. Finerty of the
Chicago Times, Robert E. Strahorn of the Denver *Rocky Mountain News,* W. C. McMillan of the Chicago *InterOcean,* Joseph
Wasson of the *New York Tribune,* and R. B. Davenport of the
New York Herald. The dispatches sent back by these reporters
from time to time are a valuable source of material on the campaign. The guides and interpreters were Frank Grouard, Louis
Richaud, and Baptiste ("Big Bat") Pourière. The large wagon
train was under the charge of Charles Russell, while the mule
pack train was under the boss packer, Tom Moore. Just before the
departure of Crook's column, friendly Indians brought into the
post a warning from Crazy Horse that the soldiers were not to
cross the Tongue River. Crook had already learned that Terry
and Custer had left Fort Abraham Lincoln on May 17.

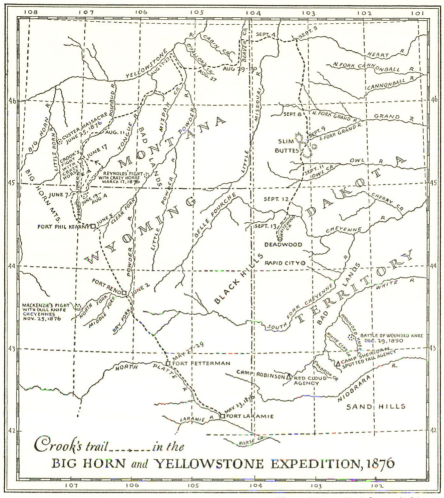

Crook's trail ---->--- *in the*

BIG HORN *and* YELLOWSTONE EXPEDITION, 1876

From Martin F. Schmitt (ed.),
General George Crook: His Autobiography

Moving out about noon on May 29, Crook's force of cavalry and infantry headed north and a little west along the old Montana Road; fairly easy marching was expected, and wood and water were believed to be sufficient at the various campsites along the route. As the exodus began, dancehall girls with waving handkerchiefs and bartenders in their white aprons bade the troopers and infantrymen a fond farewell as they filed past the hog ranch one-half mile north of the river.

The line of march was four miles long with the cavalry leading the way, followed by the infantry and the wagon train and beef herd. The packers and their mules rode in single file on the right of the soldiers, receiving the full benefit of dust kicked up by the horses and men. Having left in the middle of the day, they made only a short march before camping on Sage Creek. The next day the column marched twenty miles and camped on the South Cheyenne River. The march could not be rapid for the pace was set by the infantry which averaged two and one-half miles an hour. On May 31 the North Fork of Wind River was reached, while the next day's camp was made near the head of the Dry Fork of Powder River. Smoke signals were seen every day after this camp, showing that the Indians were warning each other of the approach of the troops. After a short march on June 2, down the Dry Fork, the column forded Powder River and camped east of the ruins of old Fort Reno. When Crook did not find his Crow and Snake allies here as expected, he sent his three scouts— Grouard, Richaud, and Big Bat—west to locate and bring in the promised warriors. The burned ruins of the old fort and the mutilated post cemetery inspired the whole command with a burning desire to seek out the village of Crazy Horse and avenge these atrocities.

At Fort Reno one of the teamsters was found to be the fabled Calamity Jane dressed in men's clothing. Just how she was discovered is not clear, but one statement has it that she attracted attention because she did not lash her mules and swear at them as artistically as the professional teamsters. She was kept with the supply train and was later returned to Fort Fetterman.

Crook did not linger at Fort Reno but pushed on to Clear Creek, where sixty-five miners going to Montana joined the command for protection. The day after leaving Clear Creek the column reached the site of old Fort Phil Kearny and camped for a mile and a half along the Big Piney east of the fort. The men visited the old post cemetery, where they paid tribute to Lieutenant Colonel Fetterman and his men who had been killed by the relentless foe in 1866. The next morning the Montana Road was followed along the ridge of the long hogback north of Fort Phil Kearny where Fetterman and his men had been wiped out. Crook intended to go to Goose Creek, but since his guides were absent he mistakenly turned to his right at the north end of Fetterman Ridge, traveling down Prairie Dog Creek. On the evening of June 6, he discovered his mistake upon unexpectedly arriving at Tongue River. Because the men and animals were exhausted from the march over the rugged and steep road which crossed and recrossed the stream, Crook decided to wait here for the arrival of the Indian allies. On the following day a soldier of Captain Meinhold's company, who had accidentally shot himself while chopping wood, was buried on a small bluff overlooking the camp. In later years the body was transferred to a national cemetery, but the partially filled hole was still visible a few years ago. That night, an Indian was heard shouting from the bluffs north of the river, and Crook sent Ben Arnold, a scout and courier with the command, to try to talk to him. Arnold, befuddled with sleep, answered the Indian in the Sioux language, and the unknown voice was heard no more. The Indian, it was learned later, was a Crow messenger looking for the command, but upon hearing the

Sioux dialect he was frightened away in the belief that it was a hostile camp.

While the men were at supper on June 9, several hundred Indians appeared on the bluffs north of the river and rained down bullets on the camp. Captain Anson Mills was ordered to take four companies of the Third Cavalry and drive away the intruders. Riding across the river, the troopers left their horses in a little grove, climbed the bluffs, and pursued the retreating Indians from one ridge to another until they disappeared. The Second Cavalry had a minor skirmish over on the left when some of the Indians forded the river. An attack by a small band from the south was repulsed. Several infantry companies occupied the bluffs during the night and, being without shelter, were drenched in a cold rain.

It was fortunate that the soldiers were at supper when the attack began, because their tents were riddled with bullets. One man was slightly wounded in the arm and another in the leg, by spent balls. Three horses and one mule were so badly wounded that they had to be destroyed. One of the horses belonged to Lieutenant Robertson and another, a fleet little animal, was the personal property of Captain Burt, who prized him very highly. That afternoon Burt's horse had won two short-distance scrub races over a course hastily improvised with a can of corn or tomatoes as the stake.

At the height of the attack the packers, who were always ready for a joke, amused the camp by their antics. An Indian wearing a tin hat rode back and forth on the bluffs in front of the soldiers in such a rhythmic manner that the packers, acting as if they were trying to catch him, ran in the same direction he did, yelling and tumbling, and then would turn and run the other way as if following the warrior when he turned and rode back.

One amusing sequel to the attack was the reporting of a bullet which passed through the pipe of Captain Mills's stove; the eastern newspapers reported that the bullet had gone through his "stovepipe," and an editorial condemned him for wearing a stovepipe hat on such a campaign.

The troops enjoyed the excitement of the attack and believed that Crazy Horse was renewing his warning against crossing the Tongue River. It is generally believed now, however, that the Indians were Cheyennes because these bluffs were one of their favorite camping places. This belief is sustained by the Cheyenne warrior, Woodenleg, who said in later years that he was with some Indians when he saw the troops at this point.[2]

From maps and sketches made at the time, it appears that the wagon train was corralled north of the Perkins ranch house, while the main camp was on the west side of Prairie Dog Creek in the angle formed by its confluence with the Tongue River. The infantry and pack trains were directly beneath the bluffs where the attack occurred. The Third Cavalry camp was south along Prairie Dog Creek, and the Second Cavalry camp was on the extreme left on the Tongue River.

While in camp here, Crook got word that the Fifth Cavalry had been ordered up from Kansas to reinforce him, and that 120 Shoshone warriors were riding to join him from their reservation in the Wind River Range. Encouraged by this news, Crook moved the command westward to the confluence of the forks of Goose Creek, where there was more wood and better pasturage, to await the arrival of his allies. The new camp was on the site where the present business district in Sheridan, Wyoming, is now situated; and from a sketch made by one of the packers, Crook's headquarters were located approximately where the Crescent Hotel stands. The cavalry camp was sprawled along Little Goose Creek towards the southeast, while the infantry camp was strung out along Big Goose Creek towards the southwest. That the camp-

2 Thomas B. Marquis, *A Warrior Who Fought Against Custer*, 194.

site shown in the sketch is the site of present Sheridan has been
verified by Herbert Zullig of that city, who came there in 1884.

Private William Nelson of Company L, Third Cavalry, died
in the hospital and was buried on the banks of Big Goose Creek.
The body has been removed, but the grave site behind the J. C.
Penney store could still be seen several years ago.

On the afternoon of June 14, General Crook was delighted
by the appearance over the bluffs to the north of the contingent of
176 Crow warriors under their chiefs, Old Crow, Medicine Crow,
and Good Heart. Shortly thereafter, eighty-six Shoshones under
Chief Washakie came in from the opposite direction, and in honor
of the occasion General Crook formed his command in a regimental front to impress his new allies. Mrs. Tom LaForge, a
Crow woman who was raised by Old Crow, pointed out to F. H.
Sinclair the place in north Sheridan where the ceremony was
held. The regimental front, nearly one mile in length, was truly
an impressive sight. Quickly making themselves at home, the
warriors set up their tipis near Crook's headquarters. In a council
of war held that night Crook outlined his plans for the campaign,
Frank Grouard and Louis Richaud acting as interpreters. The
wagons and most of the pack train were to be left behind under a
guard of one hundred soldiers together with the teamsters and
packers. A stockade of wagons was formed on a little island in
Goose Creek where the Sheridan Bottling Works now stands. The
cavalry and mounted infantry would strike out towards the north
with four days' rations, moving as rapidly as possible in order to
surprise the wily Crazy Horse. Twenty "horny-handed" packers
were to accompany the column with the medical supplies packed
on one sumpter mule and pioneer tools loaded on another.

In order to find mounts for the infantry, mules and saddles
were taken from the wagon and pack train, and June 15 was devoted to teaching the infantrymen how to ride the mules. Since

few of the men had ever ridden before, and since the mules had never had saddles on their backs, the lesson in equestrianship was something of an ordeal for both, but it was vastly amusing to the spectators. The "Walk-a-Heaps" finally learned to ride, and Lieutenant Bourke estimated that there were 175 who were mounted so that they could keep up with the fast moving cavalry. Crook's army now totaled at least 1,325 men, including the Indian allies, packers, and Montana miners. The soldiers were impressed with their warlike allies, while the latter were eager to meet their hereditary foes. The council of war and all-night war dances had worked the Indians into a frenzy. Morale was high; and as the Crow warrior, Plenty Coups, put it, "My heart was on fire."

Early on June 16, the command forded Big Goose Creek and rode northward, crossing the Tongue River and, in order to avoid rough ground, turned northeast on the bluffs, parallel with Tongue River. During the march, Captain Stanton, the engineer officer, had an odometer drawn by a mule to measure the distance traveled. The odometer was a two-wheeled gig which he had loaded with creature comforts. The contraption had the appearance of a peddler's wagon, and the envious soldiers, who were continually passing and re-passing, embarrassed the Captain by crying out, "Mother's Pies. Mother's Cakes." Because of the extremely rough terrain the odometer finally broke down and was abandoned.[3] However, Stanton kept a record of the distances traveled until the instrument gave out, and also a record of the compass bearings of the directions of the march. This data he included in his official report.[4]

Reaching Spring Creek, about five miles north and one mile west of Decker, Montana, the column turned northwest up the divide between the two forks and rode to the foot of the divide

[3] Anson Mills, *My Story*, 402.

[4] The official report of Captain William S. Stanton covering the expedition appears in Lloyd McFarling, *Exploring the Northern Plains*, chap. 32 and 33.

separating the Tongue River basin from the big bend of the Rosebud. Here the men stopped to rest while the scouts were sent ahead to see if any of the enemy were in the area. Huge herds of buffalo were sighted during the march "through country green as emerald," and the Indian allies slaughtered over one hundred of them in reckless disregard of Crook's orders against unnecessary noise during the march. No hostile Indians were seen north of the ridge, except for a small hunting party, so the command crossed the divide, coming down to one of the south tributaries of the south fork of Rosebud Creek, and made camp. The cavalry arrived first and formed three sides of a square, leaving the other side open for the slower moving mounted infantry. Major Chambers, eager to make a good impression, brought his men up smartly for the benefit of the onlooking cavalry officers, but when the mules were halted, they began to bray as loud as they could. The cavalrymen were convulsed with laughter, and Major Chambers was so provoked that he threw his sword to the ground and stalked away. Pickets were posted on the bluffs surrounding the camp, and the men ate a cold supper, not being allowed to build fires. General Crook called upon the Crows and Snakes to furnish men to scout ahead early in the morning in search of the enemy.

While the soldiers were sleeping on their arms at the headwaters of the Rosebud, the hostiles were already aware of their presence, and after a council of war, bands rode from the large encampment at the forks of Reno Creek to intercept the soldiers. Some went eastward with Two Moon, Young Two Moon, and Spotted Wolf, striking the Rosebud at Trail Creek, eleven miles north of the big bend, where they rested and went through the elaborate ceremonies of preparing for the fight. Other bands went up the south fork of Reno Creek, some going down Corral Creek, others coming through Sioux Pass, all converging upon the big bend where Crook would be at a disadvantage in the rough country with its narrow valleys.

The soldiers were on the march down the Rosebud early the next morning, riding on both sides of the creek. The creek runs eastward along the side of the divide for several miles, turns north for about one mile, and then joins the north fork running east for about three miles through a valley. It forms the big bend in making a right-angled turn again northward, continuing in that direction until it flows into the Yellowstone. The big bend is about forty miles north of present Sheridan, Wyoming.

Scouts had been sent out during the night, and when Crook reached the valley half-way between the two bends, having marched about five miles, he went into bivouac about 8:00 A.M. as word was sent back that the enemy was near. General Crook, back with the infantry, started playing cards beside a little spring. Horses and mules were unsaddled, and the men were glad of the chance to rest after the hard march of the day before. The soldiers boiled coffee and visited about the campfires, while the young warriors raced their ponies to give them their second wind. The camp was strung out for about one mile on both sides of the creek, with the cavalry at the head of the bivouac about where the Kobold house is now situated, followed in order by the infantry, pack train, and warriors.

The lead scouts unexpectedly encountered an advance party of Sioux on the high hill on the William Rowland place, nine miles north of the big bend, and immediately headed back to camp, exchanging shots with their pursuers. At about eight-thirty, after the command had drowsed for about thirty minutes, the scouts' shots were heard from the northeast, but it was assumed that the scouts were killing more buffalo. In a few minutes, however, the small party came tearing down the hillside, led by a wounded Shoshone named "Limpy," who was shouting "Lakota,

Lakota." The camp was immediately in an uproar with officers shouting orders and soldiers catching and saddling their horses and mules. General Crook rode to the plateau above the spring to observe the approach of the enemy. The Indians were approaching rapidly, and Captain Nickerson and Lieutenant Colonel Royall gave orders for the command to deploy to meet the enemy.

The extremely rough terrain combined with the unorthodox tactics of the Sioux made the Battle of the Rosebud very complicated, and it actually consisted of a series of disconnected actions. The valley south of the creek is about one-fourth mile wide with steep bluffs rising beyond. North of the creek is a series of bluffs rising to a high ridge about one mile distant and extending westward from the east bend for five miles, where the bluffs rise to a high promontory now called Andrews Point. Here, forming an acute angle, it is joined by another ridge, or series of ridges, coming in from the southeast commencing at the west bend of the Rosebud. In the valley between the two ridges is a dry creek, known as Kollmar Creek, which rises in the high angle at Andrews Point and runs southeasterly into the Rosebud about one mile east of the west bend. Most of the action occurred on these two ridges, the battlefield being thus five miles long and about two miles wide.

The soldiers were first attacked from the northeast by a small band of Sioux and Cheyennes riding over the bluffs close upon the heels of the scouts. As the party of enemy warriors came near the command they were cut off and killed by the Crows and Snakes. When he first heard firing, Captain Mills rode southward, and from the side of the bluff he saw the Indians swarming on the long ridge one mile north of the creek. Captain Nickerson immediately dispatched two companies of cavalry led by Captain Van Vliet and Lieutenant Emmitt Crawford to occupy the bluffs south of the bivouac. They arrived just in time to drive back a band of Sioux which was trying to gain the rear of the soldiers.

The main attack, from the northwest, was met on the plateau above the rear of the camp by the Crow and Snake warriors. Here a fierce battle raged for about twenty minutes as the allies held off the enemy until the infantry appeared on the plateau. The soldiers found one Crow warrior propped up against a tree watching the fight and yelling like a madman. A shot in his thigh had shattered the bone as he was making a series of "bravery runs" in front of the enemy. The injured warrior was later identified as Bull Snake. Another Crow warrior, Fox-Just-Coming-Over-Hill, renamed Old Coyote, was also wounded in the fight.[5]

The Sioux and Cheyennes withdrew when the infantry arrived, moving farther eastward and attacking down a large ravine from the gap in the ridge north of the Kobold house. By this time, the Second Cavalry had rushed forward as dismounted skirmishers, every fourth man staying to hold the horses. Seeking the cover of a small ridge, the cavalrymen with a withering fire turned back the charge. The attacking Sioux and Cheyennes then divided, retreating northward up the sides of the ravine. When the attacking Indians had withdrawn from the infantry front, the soldiers had moved forward to occupy the long ridge one mile north of the creek, but when they got within five hundred yards they were pinned down by the fire from hostiles occupying the ridge.

While the infantry were advancing north of the west bend, and the Second Cavalry were meeting the enemy just east of the infantry, Captain Mills was deploying his cavalry in a column of mounted companies on the flat a little east of the Kobold house, in response to orders. As soon as his formation was completed, there was a hell-bent-for-leather cavalry charge which cleared two lines of bluffs in his front and reached the summit of the ridge east of the gap, the enemy retreating westward across the front of the approaching soldiers. Mills arrived on the ridge just as the

[5] Mark H. Brown, *Plainsmen of the Yellowstone*, 267–68.

Second Cavalry took the ridge and gap to the west of them. The Sioux and Cheyennes retreated to the west, taking position on a high hill situated on the long ridge north of the infantry, which was later called Crook's Hill, and began pouring a heavy fire on the soldiers around the gap. In order to dislodge them, Captain Mills, together with the three companies of Lieutenant Colonel Royall, which had just joined him, made another cavalry charge and occupied the position, the Indians retreating to another hill about twelve hundred yards to the northwest which the soldiers called Conical Hill.

This enemy retreat enabled the infantry to advance and occupy Crook's Hill and the ridge east of it without opposition. The packers were sent forward to occupy a large rock formation four hundred yards to the west to act as sharpshooters. For some time, small bands from Conical Hill made bravery runs towards the troops, and there was long-distance firing from both sides. The unorthodox tactics of the Indians in retreating westward across the front of the soldiers left the infantry and Second Cavalry occupying the long ridge north of the big bend, facing north, with none of the enemy in their front. None of these two units, except two companies of infantry called to support Royall's retreating forces towards the end of the fight, were seriously engaged for the remainder of the battle. The led horses and the mules were sent for and brought up near the troops. The action above described took place over a front of about two miles, extending from a short distance east of the Kobold house to Crook's Hill, which is one mile north of the west bend of the creek. In this area are now situated the ranches of Elmer Kobold, Burt Young, and Charlie Young, the latter bordering on the Crow Reservation on the west.

The heaviest fighting occurred on the left, west of the west bend of the creek where Royall's men were engaged. When the fight first began, Captain Guy V. Henry was sent with two cavalry companies to occupy a ridge on the south side of the creek facing west to block a band of Indians who were trying to flank the camp by coming down the creek from that direction. Royall took three cavalry companies up the creek to the west, and General Crook later complained that when he returned to camp after first observing the enemy, the last of Royall's men were just disappearing behind a ridge. Royall led his men out of the valley and joined Mills in his second charge, which cleared Crook's Hill. During the charge Royall saw Indians occupying a row of ridges about one mile to the southwest, across the wide valley of Kollmar Creek, so he detached his three companies and drove the Indians northwest along the crest of the ridges. Captain Andrews' company was divided so that the Captain led one platoon in advance far along the ridges to the high promontory later called Andrews Point, about two miles west of Crook's Hill. When more Indians were seen on another parallel ridge to the south, Lieutenant James E. H. Foster was detached with the other platoon, charging westward along this ridge until he was some distance west and south of Andrews. Seeing that Foster had advanced too far and that the Indians were trying to cut him off, Andrews sent a trooper to Foster, ordering him to cut across the wide valley between them and rejoin the company. Since Andrews was also too far advanced, Royall ordered him back to a ridge where his company, and Captain Meinhold's company, and the two companies of Captain Henry (which had been ordered up) took position. This ridge on the south side of Kollmar Creek was Royall's first position and is just west of the fence on the Crow Reservation and one mile southwest of Crook's Hill, being on the land of Bill Rugg. Military cartridge cases have been found for three hundred yards along this ridge well below the crest.

There was a one-mile gap in the soldiers' line, and Crook sent word to Royall to extend his right so as to join the main command around Crook's Hill. Instead of complying, Royall sent Captain Meinhold's company to Crook, his other three companies spread-

ing out to occupy the vacated space on the ridge. The ridge was
held for two hours, and the men were subjected to fire from the
higher ridge to the north across the valley, and from an enfilading
and plunging fire from the Indians who had occupied Andrews
Point and a spur running south from it. Expended military cartridge cases have been found down the side of the slope and behind spurs leading down from the crest, indicating that the men
huddled behind the spurs to avoid the flanking fire from the west.
The firing was too heavy to withstand, and as the men were preparing to withdraw another order came from Crook telling Royall
to rejoin the main command immediately. Crook wanted the
group to join him because he needed the extra men to participate
in his planned attack on Crazy Horse's village, which was believed to lie six miles down the canyon.

Royall tried to comply, but it was now too late. The soldiers,
surrounded by Indians on all sides except the southeast, had to
retreat in that direction. The led horses were taken back first
while the soldiers retreated slowly, covering the horses. In this
manner another ridge was reached about one-half mile to the
southeast, known as Royall's second position, where a stand was
made facing north. When the Indians then tried a flank attack
from the west and rear, Royall sent two companies to occupy
rocky ledges extending about one-half mile to the southwest,
leaving the other company in place. The soldiers fired from behind the protection of the ledges, and the Indians rode away.
Royall then commenced a movement along the ridge towards the
southeast, and there a vigorous battle ensued when the Indians
tried to stampede the led horses. Part of this retreat, which covered about one mile, was over open ground, but the continuation
of the ridge was soon reached, and the troops moved along the
north side as the Indians followed on the south slope.

When the command arrived at the point directly south of
Crook's Hill and about one mile across the valley of Kollmar

Creek, it was necessary for Royall to make the break to join Crook, since further progress would have placed him farther away from the main command. In order to expedite this movement, he had the led horses brought up and placed in a ravine (a side gulley extending northward from Kollmar Creek) at the rear, and sent Captain Vroom's company to line the crest in order to protect the rear while the men mounted their horses. More Indians were on the south side of the ridge than Royall thought, and they immediately swarmed over and around Vroom's company, which formed a circle, holding off the Indians until the rest of Royall's men came to the rescue. The command was pinned down on the bluff, because the Indians occupying the next ridge to the south were so close that the men did not dare make the break for their horses. The troopers answered their constant fire, standing far enough back from the edge of the bluff that only their heads were visible to the enemy. This was Royall's third position and marked the heaviest fighting of the battle. A row of expended military cartridge cases has been found along the ridge for 325 yards, while near the east end of the line cases were found in a rough circle, probably indicating the place where Vroom's men were surrounded. The Indians charged first from the east, and the line swung around to meet them. The next attack was from the west and rear, and again the line bunched up to drive the enemy back.

Finally the big charge came, directly from the south. At this point, Captain Henry was temporarily blinded by a shot across his face, and he fell from his horse.[6] The soldiers became panicky upon seeing their fallen leader and started to give way when the Snakes and Crows arrived just in the nick of time and drove the enemy back. Snake and Crow warriors occupied the ridge to the east of the soldiers, holding the hostiles back until the soldiers

[6] Brevet Brigadier General Guy V. Henry, "Wounded in an Indian Fight," *Collections of Wyoming Historical Society*, 1897, 190. See Monthly Report for June, 1876, Big Horn and Yellowstone Expedition, signed by A. Hartsuff, Assistant Surgeon, U.S.A., Medical Director.

could get down the ravine to their horses. Colonel Crook, upon seeing Royall's men hard pressed, sent two infantry companies under the command of Captain Andrew Burt and Captain Thomas B. Burrowes to occupy several ridges south of Crook's Hill. From here, the infantry with their long-range rifles kept the Indians from pursuing the cavalry too closely. After Royall's men were mounted, they rode eastward down the valley of Kollmar Creek and then turned northward towards Crook's Hill, passing to the east of the infantry positions. While crossing the low ground north of the creek, two cavalrymen who had lost their horses and could not keep up with their retreating comrades were overtaken and killed in plain sight of the whole command. It can safely be said that if the Crow and Snake scouts had not made their charge at the right time, and had not the two infantry companies held the enemy back as they did, Royall's command would have been destroyed.

As Royall's men rode for the safety of Crook's Hill, the Indians made a grand assault from the south and west all along the line and overran a ridge held by the packers and miners, swarming past all the other positions facing west. One band rode down the valley of the Rosebud where the soldiers had bivouacked, where they killed and scalped a little Shoshone boy who had been left to herd the ponies. Some of the Indians, after this final attack, rode down the valley of the canyon north of the field, although some withdrew to the ridges north and west of Crook's Hill to prepare for another attack. Upon reaching Crook's Hill, Royall's men were used with the packers, miners, and infantry to hold that position because most of the cavalry had been detached to ride down the canyon. The battle was finished on this part of the field.

Meanwhile, after Captain Mills occupied Crook's Hill, the Indians made a charge from the Conical Hill southward in the gap between the main command and Royall's first position. The cavalry had to call up some of the infantry to stop the attack, and while this fighting was going on, the Crows and Shoshones made a concerted charge westward along the ridge from Crook's Hill, catching the Indians in the flank. The Sioux and Cheyennes retreated on their fast little ponies but stopped to make a stand in a little valley in the ridge, while the pursuers also dismounted for a moment and poured in a volley. According to Lieutenant Bourke, who accompanied the charge, the two forces came together in the "trough of the valley" and after a short hard fight, the valley was strewn with dead ponies. The hostiles then retreated pell-mell to the high promontory at Andrews Point about one mile to the west of the little valley, where they made a stand and in turn charged the Crows and Shoshones, who were forced to retreat back to the main command. It was at Andrews Point that Sergeant Von Moll, who was afoot, was rescued from under the noses of the enemy by the little hunchbacked Crow named "Limpy," who dashed in long enough for the long-legged sergeant to jump up behind him. Many .44-caliber Winchester and .50-caliber Springfield cartridge cases have been found on Andrews Point where the Sioux and Cheyennes made their stand, and in the summer of 1960, Elmer Kobold and the author found the little valley in the ridge where the two Indian forces had their sharp encounter. About fifty .44-caliber Winchester and .50-caliber Spencer cartridge cases and various sized bullets were found here, although there was no trace of horse bones.

When Burt and Burrowes were ordered to the aid of Royall's hard-pressed forces, the remaining three infantry companies formed a skirmish line across the ridge and drove from Conical Hill the Indians who had been keeping up an annoying fire on the command. A wide variety of cartridge cases, numbering several hundred, have been found on the hill.

When Royall was unable to join Crook when ordered, it was decided that a portion of the cavalry would be sent down the

137

canyon of the Rosebud to destroy Crazy Horse's village, which
was believed to be about six miles north of the east bend. The
two companies of Van Vliet and Crawford were withdrawn from
their position south of the creek to help hold Crook's Hill. Captain Mills took four companies of cavalry and rode southeast into
the valley, thus taking the easiest course down the canyon. Upon
reaching the east bend, where the Penson ranch is now located,
the detachment was fired upon by Indians on a ridge, but the
company of Captain Sutorius cleared the position after a dashing
cavalry charge. Mills rode northward on both sides of the creek
until he reached the point where the valley narrows to only 150
yards, with fallen timber and beaver dams blocking the way.
Frank Grouard advised against trying to go through the canyon
because it would have been a perfect trap if the Indians were
hidden there in ambush. Just as Mills was debating on whether
to advance, Captain Nickerson and his orderly galloped up,
carrying orders from General Crook to return to the field at once
because Royall was in trouble and needed reinforcements. Just
behind Nickerson came the five companies of the Second Cavalry
under Captain Henry E. Noyes, who had been sent to help Mills
destroy the village. Following the quickest route back, Mills,
followed by the Second Cavalry companies, defiled to the west
at the point where the Helvey ranch house is now situated, two
and one-half miles north of the big bend; and after climbing to
the north side of the ravine, he circled around to the west and
south so that he came in behind a contingent of Sioux who were
preparing for an attack on Crook's Hill from the north. The Sioux
were disconcerted upon seeing the enemy in their rear, and they
broke off the fight and rode to the northwest towards their encampment, the cavalry pursuing for several miles. The main part
of the battle was over at 2:30 P.M., having lasted six hours, though
some reports say it lasted until dark.

The exhausted men made camp at that morning's place of

bivouac, and the three infantry companies held Conical Hill until 7:00 P.M. Most of the accounts state that the dead were buried on the banks of the creek, while several claim they were buried on the field where they fell. None of the burial places has been definitely located, though Frank Grouard pointed out to Jim Gatchell a depression near the Kobold house where five men were said to have been buried. The bodies are not there now, although the earth has been found to have been disturbed for a depth of four feet. General Crook reported that nine soldiers and one scout had been killed, while twenty-one soldiers had been wounded. However, Frank Grouard said that twenty-eight soldiers had been killed and fifty-six had been wounded.[7] Ben Arnold claimed that thirteen soldiers were killed in one company, while five Crows and seven or eight Shoshones were killed, probably referring to Captain Vroom's troop which had been cut off on the bluff.[8] Lieutenant Bourke and T. B. MacMillan, a newspaper correspondent, mentioned the "mortally wounded" in addition to the listed dead.[9] The Shoshone boy was buried in the bed of the creek that night with much ceremony. The surgeons were busy building travois on which to carry the wounded.

Crook decided to return to his base; the rations were about exhausted, and he had many wounded who needed care. No trace had been found of the columns of Gibbon and Terry which were to co-operate with him. Crook had been confident of a victory that morning, and the strong attack by the Indians surprised and disconcerted him. His troops had been roughly handled and would have suffered a disastrous defeat except for the support of the Crows and Snakes at critical times.

The Sioux and Cheyennes rode back to the forks of Reno Creek, leaving a few warriors to watch the soldiers. The officers

[7] Joe DeBarthe, *Life and Adventures of Frank Grouard*, 122.

[8] Lewis F. Crawford, *Rekindling Campfires*, 250.

[9] Lieutenant John G. Bourke, "Diary, III, 413; T. B. MacMillan, "On the Warpath," *The Chicago InterOcean* (June 24, 1876), 5.

estimated that fifteen hundred warriors were in the fight. John Stands-In-Timber told the author that there were between ninety and one hundred Cheyennes in the battle under Spotted Wolf, and that the rest of the hostiles were Sioux led by Crazy Horse. Sitting Bull was present giving encouragement to the warriors but was unable to join in the fighting because he was still weak from the tortures of the Sun Dance which he had undergone about ten days before. After watching Crook's men leave, the Indians moved westward to the Little Big Horn, where Custer found them eight days later.

Early on the eighteenth, Crook's column started southwestward, following on the north side of the south fork until the summit of the Wolf Mountains was reached, where it turned south along the ridges. As there were many wounded on travois, Crook decided to avoid the numerous little ravines and gullies running water, which had been crossed during the march to the field, although the new route was rougher. After a march of twenty-two miles, camp was made that night on the west side of the divide. At noon the next day, after marching twenty-five miles, Crook's column located its supply camp on Little Goose Creek two and one-half miles south of the island where it had been left. Crook moved the command two and one-fourth miles farther up Little Goose Creek where there was plenty of fresh grazing. On June 21, the wagon train left for Fort Fetterman bearing the wounded and accompanied by Calamity Jane. Crook decided to wait in this area until the promised reinforcements arrived before making any further moves against the enemy. It was not until August 3 that he set out with a much larger force in search of the hostile Indians in what is known as the "Starvation March" or "Mud March," which finally routed a small band of Indians at Slim Buttes in the present state of South Dakota, on September 9.

The Indians returned to the battlefield and marked with piles of rocks the various points of interest, and most of the markers are still there. John Stands-in-Timber, the historian of the Cheyenne tribe, showed the author where they are and explained their significance as told to him years ago by the warriors who were in the fight. At the beginning of the battle, when the scouts were pushing the Indians northward up the gap, the Cheyenne Chief Comes-in-Sight made a bravery run along the east side of the gap. His pony was shot from under him, and after nonchalantly removing the pony's bridle in the best tradition, he calmly awaited the enemy. As several Crow scouts started for him, a solitary figure on horseback came swiftly from the enemy lines north of the gap and stopped long enough for the Chief to jump on the pony behind the rider and be borne to safety. The rescuer was his sister, Buffalo-Calf-Road-Woman, and in honor of this brave deed, the Cheyennes called this battle "Where the sister saved her brother." The pile of rocks is gone now, having been plowed under, but John showed us the place, and a photograph was taken of him standing on the spot. Across the gap and on a little flat is another pile of rocks marking the place where a soldier was shot and killed by Indians in ambush. On Royall's line of retreat to his last position and south of a rock formation is a large rock which played an important part in the rescue of a Cheyenne Warrior who had one leg shorter than the other and was called "Limpy." He and three other Indians made bravery charges from the west in front of the retreating troops when Limpy's horse was shot from under him. He was between the lines and an easy target for the soldiers. Young Two Moon, nephew of Two Moon, raced his pony to rescue Limpy, but at the first try Limpy could not get on the horse because of his deformity. Young Two Moon then made another try amid a hail of bullets, and this time Limpy got on the big rock and was able to jump on the pony as it paused by the rock, and escape. On Royall's third position the Indians placed three large flat rocks to mark the spot near the south edge of the bluff and a few yards east of the Kobold fence, where Captain

Guy V. Henry was wounded. Three hundred yards to the east on the same ridge is a pile of rocks marking the place where a fifteen-year-old Sioux boy was pulled from his horse and killed. He and a Cheyenne made a bravery charge on the ridge not knowing that the scouts were behind it, so when they got close, the scouts dashed out and killed the Sioux boy while the Cheyenne escaped. These markers confirmed our conclusions concerning the battle terrain.

Four of the soldiers received the Congressional Medal of Honor for bravery in the Rosebud fight. They were Michael A. McGann, Trumpeter Elmer A. Snow, John Robinson, and John Henry Shingle. Trumpeter Snow was shot through both wrists during the charge of the Snakes and barely made it back to his lines, holding the reins between the stumps of his wrists. Robinson was in Captain Henry's company and brought up the led horses at the critical moment. John Henry Shingle was in command of the led horses of Royall's men during the fight on the third position. Upon seeing the line waver after Captain Henry was shot, Shingle left the horses in command of Robinson, mounted his horse, and rushed into the thickest of the fight, rallying the breaking ranks and holding the Indians at bay. At the time of the battle, this man was enlisted under the name of "John Henry." It appeared that he had enlisted under his two given names in order to avoid ridicule from his comrades. As his last name was "Shingle" he had been continually embarrassed during a previous enlistment by his comrades asking him if he had the shingles.

Quite a variety of arms and ammunition were used during the Rosebud fight. The cavalry carried the .45-caliber 1873 Springfield breech-loading, single-shot, carbine, which used a metallic cartridge with fifty-five grains of black powder and a 405-grain lead bullet. The infantry used the same weapon with a longer barrel and ramrod, called the "Long Tom." It took the same cartridge as the carbine except that it had seventy grains of black powder. The effective range of the carbine was six hundred yards, while that of the rifle was one thousand yards. The Indians were afraid to come near the accurate rifles in the steady hands of the infantry, which might explain why the infantry was never in trouble in the fight. The cavalrymen carried the .45-caliber Colt single-action revolver, but none had the saber.

The Indians, consisting of the younger warriors eager to fight, were fairly well armed, having .44-caliber 1866 Winchesters, .44-caliber 16-shot Henry rifles, 7-shot Spencer carbines in .50 and .52 calibers, and .50-caliber Springfield rifles which had been furnished them by the Indian Bureau for hunting purposes. The Winchester and Henry .44-caliber shells are quite small, only about one-half inch long, most of them had the raised H head-stamp and were fired with the forked firing pin, making two dents on opposite sides of the rim. The Spencer cartridges are three-fourths of an inch to one and one-fourth inches long and are rim fire. They look like they might be revolver cartridges. The .45-caliber and .50-caliber Springfield cartridges are about two and one-half inches long and the government variety was of copper, while most of the commercial brands were of brass, with outside primer. The government cartridges were made at Frankfort arsenal and had an inside center fire primer crimped into the head of the case. The Snakes were armed with the .45-caliber Springfield carbines, while the Crows had mostly the .50-caliber Springfield rifles. Twenty different kinds of cartridge cases have been found on the field, most of them of various commercial brands. While there are seven or eight hundred cartridge cases and bullets in the author's collection, but few other items have been found. Larger relics have long since been picked up by Indians and early settlers in the area. Mr. Kobold and the author spent more than five years combing the area with a metal detector; and with the aid of three maps made by soldiers who were in the battle, we were able to identify the various battle positions.

The types of shells found and their location and position on the ridges confirmed the positions as shown on the maps. Wherever possible, the soldiers as well as the hostile Indians fired from behind rocks and ridges far enough down the slope that they could just barely see over the crest, thus being protected by the terrain.

In appraising the results of the Rosebud campaign in later years, General Crook stoutly maintained that he won the battle because the enemy withdrew, leaving him in command of the field. Inconsistently, however, he remained bitter concerning the results of the battle, blaming Captain Nickerson for "scattering" the troops in the beginning, and Royall for failing to join the rest of the command when first ordered to do so. Regardless of blame, it seems clear that the Indians won the battle, for they succeeded in keeping the army away from their camp and prevented Crook from joining Terry and Custer in the concerted action against them. If Crook had won a decisive victory at the Rosebud, or had he brought sufficient rations and ammunition to maintain his position in the area, he might have been able to join with Custer and overwhelm the concentration of Sioux and Cheyenne warriors. This is pure speculation because Custer did not arrive in the vicinity for seven days, and during that time the warriors might have made another attack on Crook's forces; but with Crook out of action, Custer was an easy prey for the Indians.

During the past several years, Joe Dent and Elmer Kobold, under the auspices of the Eastern Montana Historical and Archeological Association, have placed concrete markers at the main points on the battlefield, most of which can be reached by automobile. The battlefield, one of the largest in the Indian Wars, lies in a peaceful little valley west of the graveled road which runs past the east bend northward from Decker, Montana, to Miles City.

5

Major Reno's Skirmish Lines in the Valley

⊓⊔⊓⊔⊓⊔⊓⊔⊓⊔⊓⊔⊓⊔⊓⊔⊓⊔⊓⊔⊓⊔⊓⊔⊓⊔⊓⊔⊓⊔⊓

Today the motorist driving along modern Highway 87 six
miles south of Crow Agency in southern Montana will pass
between a railroad siding on the west and a store building on the
east, which, together with nearby ranches, comprise the little
community of Garryowen. South of the store a deep, crescent-
shaped old riverbed, about one hundred yards wide and covered
with trees and brush, juts almost to the highway, while one-half
mile to the west are low bluffs. On the east a line of trees shows
where the Little Big Horn River follows its tortuous course down
the valley overlooked by high bluffs. Only a few who pass this
way know the importance of this ground to Western frontier
history, for the highway cuts through the middle of the little
battlefield where Major Marcus A. Reno and three companies
of the Seventh U.S. Cavalry were routed by the warriors who
later annihilated General George A. Custer and his five companies
of cavalry on the bluffs across the river.

One of the many controversial questions in the Battle of the
Little Big Horn concerns the actual positions occupied by Major
Reno during his attack on the Indian village north of Garryowen.
Owing to the extensive changes in the terrain, there has been no
positive evidence concerning the location of Reno's men except
statements by participants, which have been vague and inconsistent. Several theories have been advanced by students of the
engagement, while some writers have declined to pinpoint the

145

battle positions. In the fall of 1964, the writer commenced a coverage of the area with a metal detector in the hope of finding tangible evidence of the location of the fighting. After much study and hard work, the writer believes that his findings, supported by other evidence, have definitely located the various positions. Since a wealth of material has been published on the details of this fight in the valley,[1] this chapter will be limited to discussions of the actual sites of the two skirmish lines and Reno's route of retreat out of the river bottom.

By way of background, it is generally agreed that at about two-thirty on the afternoon of June 25, 1876, Major Reno crossed a ford of the Little Big Horn River with Companies A, G, and M, consisting of 134 officers and men and 16 scouts,[2] under orders from General Custer to attack the Indian village several miles northward down the river. After marching about two miles, Reno approached an open space about one-half mile wide between the river, which angled westward in a series of bends, and the low bluffs to the west. Upon seeing a part of the village through the opening, and large numbers of warriors advancing from a ravine in his front, Reno dismounted his troops and formed a skirmish line towards the left, extending from a point of woods near a river bend, out across the prairie towards the bluffs.

After scouting the woods on his right, the led horses were taken to that position and later removed to an old riverbed during the fighting on the prairie. Reno then ordered the skirmish line to advance, and the men went forward seventy-five or one hundred yards where they lay down and commenced firing at the warriors approaching across a wide front. Reno, fearing for the

---

[1] See William A. Graham (ed.), *The Official Record of a Court of Inquiry Convened by the President of the United States at Chicago, Illinois, January 13, 1879, by Request of Marcus A. Reno, to Investigate His Conduct at the Battle of the Little Big Horn, June 25–26, 1876*; and Edgar I. Stewart, *Custer's Luck*, chap. XV.

[2] Stewart, *ibid.*, 343.

safety of his horses, took part of Company G from the right of the line down into the bottomland and deployed the men along the bank of the river, north and south, to protect the horses from the enemy infiltrating from the east and northeast. The remaining men on the skirmish line extended their intervals so as to close at least part of the line so vacated.

After some long-distance fighting the Indians charged, but the heavy firing of the troops caused them to veer towards the bluffs so that they came around the left end of the skirmish line. The soldiers, being outflanked, were ordered to march to their right in single file towards their horses, the last platoon on the left being forced to deploy at right angles to the retreating line in order to face the Indians attacking from the new direction.[3] After this sideways movement, the soldiers turned to the right flank again and formed another line along the bank of the old riverbed, facing the Indians approaching from the bluffs. As the Indians continued their wide sweep, they rode toward the left and rear of the new line, outflanking the soldiers again, so Major Reno gave the order for the men to fall back to their horses in the bottomland to their rear. A few minutes later, when the soldiers were surrounded and subjected to fire from all directions, including their recent position on the riverbank, a hasty retreat was made up out of the bottomland onto the prairie, across the river, and onto Reno Hill, where a successful defense was made until the arrival of General Alfred Howe Terry with the relief column, several days later.

In attempting to locate the first skirmish line, Dr. Charles Kuhlman followed the Maguire map which was used at the Reno Court of Inquiry.[4] The line had been drawn, on the basis of information furnished, by Lieutenant Edward Maguire from the

[3] Testimony of Captain Myles Moylan, Graham, *Official Record of a Court of Inquiry*, 186.
[4] Charles Kuhlman, *Legend into History: The Custer Mystery*, chap. IV.

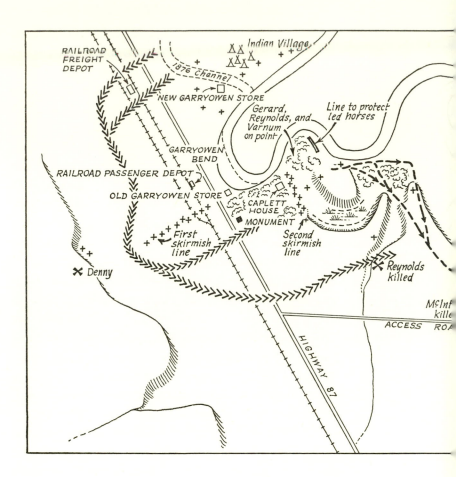

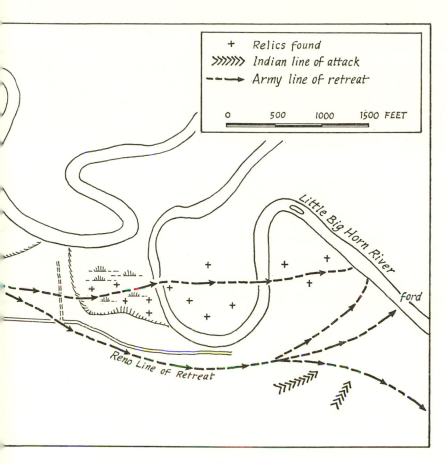

Little Big Horn River

ford

Reno Line of Retreat

Reno's Fight in the Valley, June 25, 1876

south end of the second bend of the river from the east, and extended in a south southwesterly direction towards the bluffs. The Indians came out of a ravine several hundred yards to the west, attacking the troops from the west and south. The line, in retreat, went northward to the bank west of the river bend where it turned east along the bank and faced the Indians approaching from the south. The area described by Dr. Kuhlman, and as indicated on the Maguire map, has for many years been covered by the ranch house, farmyard, and outbuildings of the Pitsch ranch. A lane now runs southward from the buildings about one hundred yards to the access road which extends eastward from Highway 87 to the river. The area not covered by the farmyard has been under cultivation for many years. No one has ever found relics of any nature indicating that a battle was fought here, and none of the returning soldiers in later years claimed that this was the place. The writer covered the area along the bank westward from the ranch house but found nothing. It is safe to say that neither skirmish line was in this vicinity.

The theory advanced by Fred Dustin is closer to the truth, and is based mainly upon evidence given at the Reno Court of Inquiry and upon statements of soldiers who returned to the scene of the action on the fiftieth anniversary of the battle in 1926.[5] While there was some confusion among the returning soldiers caused by changes in the terrain, they generally agreed that the right of the first skirmish line, after it had advanced about one hundred yards, extended from near the point of woods southwest of the most westerly bend of the river bottom, now known as Garryowen Bend, westerly and a little south across the prairie towards the bluffs for two hundred or two hundred fifty yards. However, they found so many changes that it was impossible to locate definitely the point of woods; these woods may have been

[5] Fred Dustin, *Echoes from the Little Big Horn: Reno's Positions in the Valley.*

removed to make way for the modern highway, which runs immediately west of the bend, and the railroad tracks, right-of-way,
and siding adjacent to the highway. A plowed field extended
westward from the railroad to the bluffs. Since the early days,
a small grocery store, known as the old Garryowen Store, stood
near the southwest side of the bend along the highway, while
five hundred feet south a monument had been erected where the
remains of a soldier were buried. Mr. Dustin assumed that the
led horses were in the woods in the Garryowen Bend, and in
explaining the second skirmish line (after the advance to the
north) he claimed that the men simply moved eastward by the
right flank and took position along the south bank of Garryowen
Bend, firing at Indians coming from the north and west. The line
then went down into the bottom when outflanked again, all the
action taking place in and around Garryowen Bend.

Mr. Dustin was of the opinion that the river had eroded four
hundred feet westward so that there was little, if any, bend at all
in 1876, but one observing the large trees and level area at the
bottom of the bend can see where the riverbed has shifted and
cut into the bank, and the distance is not over one hundred feet
towards the west. In 1923, the Chicago, Burlington and Quincy
Railroad Company, to prevent encroachment upon its right-of-
way, built a dike in the river so that it was diverted northward
along the bluffs, although flood waters continued to fill the old
channels. Joe Blummer, an old-timer who operated the old Garryowen store for many years, told the writer that Garryowen Bend
is about as it was when he first saw it in 1904. The western portion
of the bend appears the same now as it was in the United States
Geological Survey of 1891, shown in the edition of 1908, although
the course of the river to the east was much different than it is
today and was in 1876. While the Maguire map does not show
Garryowen Bend, it does show the loop extending southward
from the southeast portion of the present location of the bend,

which was the actual riverbed in 1891 but was the old riverbed in 1876. It is apparent that the western portion of Garryowen Bend in 1876 was the same as it is today except that the old course was one hundred feet farther east, after allowing for the erosion.

Since the fiftieth anniversary in 1926, the highway has been widened and the old store and monument torn down, while the western portion of the point of timber was undoubtedly removed when the railroad and highway were built. The testimony at the Reno Court of Inquiry was to the effect that the east end of the skirmish line was from seventy-five yards to two hundred yards from the river; some said it rested near the point of timber; while Sergeant O'Neill said the right rested near the brush.[6] Others said the right of the line was near the monument. Joe Blummer told the writer that shells, relics, and other indications of the battle had never been found around his store, but that a few expended .45–70 Springfield cartridges of the type used by the soldiers had been picked up from time to time in the railroad right-of-way west of his store and out into the field where some had been turned up during the course of farming operations. The western edge of Garryowen Bend is now 350 feet from the railroad tracks, or 450 feet from the site of the bend in 1876, so the right of the line rested on the west side of the highway extending over the railroad right-of-way and out into the field.

Sam Denny, a rancher who lives on the bluff west of the bend, told the writer that during the twenty-six years that he had operated the ranch, he had found in the plowed ground five or six expended .45–70 military cartridges from about the middle of his field to the railroad right-of-way, and on a line with the old store. Mr. Denny also said that military cartridges had been found along the railroad right-of-way from the passenger station, which is opposite the middle of the bend, northward for one hundred yards to the freight depot.

[6] E. A. Brininstool, *Troopers with Custer*, 130.

In letters to the writer dated October 8, 1965, and November 14, 1965, Roy Nagashima, who lived for many years in the house north of Garryowen Bend where the new store is now situated, said, "Yes, we did live at Garryowen and found a great many cartridges of that [army] description. We also found a pair of army spurs, an army rifle and many shells." In a sketch of the area, he indicated that the relics were found on the bench north of the bend in the vicinity of the house and in the bottom-land where the Indian village was located along the river. The cartridges found on the right-of-way and the relics north of the loop were probably used by the Arikara scouts who charged ahead of the line and, after firing into the tipis from the bench, beat a hasty retreat to avoid being cut off. The shells found in the village were possibly fired by the Indians at the scouts on the bench. This area is several hundred yards from, and north of, the first skirmish line as indicated by the soldiers, so the relics must have been from the weapons of the scouts or the hostile Indians, who also had a few .45-caliber Springfield carbines which they had captured at the Rosebud fight eight days before.[7]

Several years ago, while digging an irrigation ditch at the foot of the bluff just north of his house, Mr. Denny found two more military cartridge cases close together. As the skirmish line did not extend this far west, it might be speculated that they were fired by Sergeant Bob-Tailed Bull, the Arikara scout who valiantly held his ground on the extreme left until cut off by the enemy and killed.[8]

It is certain that many shots were fired by the soldiers on the first skirmish line, because some of them used up their fifty rounds during the fight in the valley, but few were used on the second skirmish line. Cartridges which had been fired on the first line

[7] T. B. MacMillan, *Chicago InterOcean* (June 24, 1876).

[8] Orin Grant Libby (ed.), *The Arikara Narrative of the Campaign Against the Hostile Dakotas, 1876, North Dakota Historical Collections*, Vol. VI, pp. 11, 96, 97, and 102.

probably rest now in the graded-up highway and railroad embankment, or deep in the plowed field to the west. The only conclusion one can reach concerning the location of the first line is that it covered an area from east to west of about 250 yards from the highway opposite the old Garryowen store westward out into the plowed field of Mr. Denny on a line with his ranch house, and southward five hundred feet to the old monument site. This depth in the line of five hundred feet would allow for normal movement while advancing and retreating and during the rearguard action in the retreat.

Our search for relics commenced at the site of the old Garryowen store, and the areas along the highway and eastward in the strip of timber along the south side of the bend were covered. Nothing was found, casting doubt on Dustin's theory about the location of the second line. The bank along the south side ends abruptly on the east, descending to the bottomland below, the end also forming the north terminus of the bank of an old riverbed coming up from the south, which likewise descends sharply into the bend. The two banks coming together form a right angle which rises a little higher than the adjoining prairie level. Three expended .45–70 military cartridges were found on the little rise. Since this point, which is now used as a horse corral, was found to be the extreme north end of the second skirmish line, the surrounding area will be described in detail. A Crow Indian named Albert Caplett owns the farm and lives with his family in their house about one hundred yards east of Highway 87, thirty yards south of Garryowen Bend, and twenty yards southwest of the horse corral. Mr. Caplett, who owns a two-hundred-acre allotment, gave permission to work on his place, and here were found all the second skirmish line, the timber where the unmounted horses were kept, and part of Reno's line of retreat. This house and farmland have been occupied for many years, a Japanese farmer having lived here earlier.

On the north of the point where the three cartridges were found, one can look down into Garryowen Bend twenty-five or thirty feet below, the bank being so steep that it cannot be scaled. To the east is the timber in the bottomland twenty to twenty-five feet below, while southward extends the bank above the old river-bed for about two hundred yards. Here the bank is not so steep but is covered with trees and a dense growth of underbrush. At the bottom of the bend running southward behind the Caplett house rushes grow in a band of swampland, while in the middle is a flat hay meadow of about five acres. Sixty yards south of the point a road leads easterly down into the bottom, and this road is the only feasible means of access from the bank. The old river channel makes a bend towards the north about one hundred yards east of the bank, and all the area north of the road from the bank to the old river channel is covered with trees and brush. It is believed that Reno's led horses were brought down this road, which was probably at that time a buffalo trail, and kept in the woods and adjoining flat during the fight, as this is the only accessible bottomland timber in the area. The bend behind the Caplett house describes an arc towards the east at its south end and returns northward to the vicinity of the river bend, thus enclosing the meadow on three sides.

Recalling that the soldiers said they fired a few rounds lying down behind the brow of a hill, with an old riverbed at their backs,[9] we decided that the bank behind the Indian's house must be the line on which they fought, so I started working southward along the edge with a metal detector. The work went rather slowly because many of the metallic objects which we dug up were parts from farm machinery, obviously not connected with the battle. The area had been used as a horse corral and barnyard

[9] Brininstool, *Troopers with Custer*, 130–31; testimony of Fred F. Gerard, Graham, *Official Record of a Court of Inquiry*, 85; in the latter volume see also the testimony of Sergeant Ferdinand A. Culbertson, 321, and the testimony of Captain Myles Moylan, 186.

for many years, and the working conditions were something less than ideal. Thirty yards south of the point was found a Springfield .50–70 expended cartridge flattened out, probably having been stepped on by a horse. This could have been fired by one of Reno's scouts who had arms of various calibers, or possibly by one of the hostile Indians firing from the bank at the retreating soldiers. At the north side of the road leading down to the bottom was found an expended .45–70 cartridge, while in the middle of the road, very deep, was a loaded .45–70 which had misfired, the faint print of the firing pin being still visible in the center. Nearby in the road was an expended .50–70 Springfield cartridge of commercial manufacture which had apparently been reloaded, as it had shattered upon firing. At the south edge of the road was another expended .45–70 cartridge, while at the place where the road reached the bottom were found a soldier's uniform blouse button, a stirrup hook, a snaffle bit, bit buckle, a horseshoe, and other cavalry equipment pronounced by Lieutenant Colonel E. L. Nye, U.S. Army, Retired, who for many years served as veterinarian with cavalry troops, to be genuine army equipment dating back to 1876.

South of the road and along the bank was plowed ground, so it was fortunate that three more expended .45–70 military cartridges, a horseshoe nail of the period, and the copper shield from the cantle of an army saddle with the legend "11 inch seat" stamped on it were found. This skirmish line was 160 yards long from the point at the north end to the place where the last shell was found. The bend now extends fifty yards farther south, but it is probable that the place where the last shell was found was the extreme south end of the bend in 1876, the last fifty yards appearing to be of more recent origin. It seemed clear that this was Reno's second skirmish line.

Although no tangible evidence had been found to locate the first line, the position of the second confirmed the assumption concerning the first one, for the latter was nearer the bluffs, and the men had fallen back closer to the river in the retreat. Each line confirms the other. In reconstructing the action, the men retreated by the right flank along or close to the south edge of Garryowen Bend, and upon arriving at the bank over the old riverbed, they turned to the right flank again and went along the bank where the relics were found. Here they faced the enemy who were approaching from the west. This maneuver explains Fred Gerard's statement that the line looked like it had swung around as if on a pivot so that the former left flank became the right flank.[10] He also at another time made the statement that when he saw the soldiers, after putting his horse in the bottom, they were in the line along the brow of a hill about six feet apart.[11] The men on the bank had only fired a few shots when the Indians outflanked them again, from the south and rear,[12] when Reno gave his order, "Men, to your horses. There are Indians in our rear." The line scrambled down the bank, and each man tried to find his horse and take his place in the three columns of companies being hastily formed by Reno in the bottom at the edge of the timber. When some Indians fired a volley at short range from the thickets, killing Bloody Knife at Reno's side, the latter gave the order to mount and charge, and the partially formed companies dashed eastward into the thickets in order to get up the bank onto the prairie level. Sergeant O'Neill said the soldiers rode out of the thickets in column of twos,[13] while Major Reno claimed they advanced in a column of fours.[14]

Fred Gerard, Charlie Reynolds, and Lieutenant Varnum had taken position at the rise on the north end of the second line and

---

[10] Testimony of Fred F. Gerard, Graham, *ibid.*, 74.

[11] Libby, *Arikara Narrative*, 171–75.

[12] Testimony of Fred F. Gerard, Graham, *Official Record of a Court of Inquiry*, 85, 173; and Brininstool, *Troopers with Custer*, 106, 131.

[13] Brininstool, *ibid.*, 131.

[14] Graham, *Official Record of a Court of Inquiry*, 685.

after firing a few shots, retired into the bottom, being in rear of the troops and farthest from the horses.[15] They were among the last to get out of the bottom, and Gerard told of seeing Reynolds ride up the bank behind the soldiers and being cut off and killed by the Indians when he was rendered helpless after his horse fell on him.[16] Gerard claimed that he was cut off by the enemy and barely made it back to the safety of the underbrush.[17] Lieutenant Varnum had a Kentucky thoroughbred and soon overtook the retreating men. Some of the troops under Lieutenant McIntosh, who were in line along the river protecting the led horses, did not hear the command to retreat, some of them staying in the timber, while Lieutenant McIntosh, late in coming out of the bottom, was killed in the field south of the bend of the bank west of the Pitsch house fifty yards north of the present access road. A marker was placed here but was moved in the early days to an inconspicuous site at the corner where the lane turns northward to the Pitsch buildings.

In searching for evidence of Reno's line of retreat in the bottom, the writer went along the little road from the line on the bank, eastward to the bend of the river channel, which is still full of water, the overflow from the live river to the east. Along the road were found a soldier's uniform button and a picket pin which had been driven deep into the ground a long time ago. It was impossible to say if it was of the army type because the head had been knocked off and the top flattened out by repeated blows, but it may have been driven there during the fight. It was in this area that the led horses were kept. Despite covering the entire river bank, the writer was unable to find any trace of the soldier line along the river guarding the led horses. At this bend, the river channel comes down from the north after describing a

---

[15] Testimony of Fred F. Gerard, *ibid.*, 79, 173–74.

[16] *Ibid.*

[17] *Ibid.*

wide, sweeping arc from the east and south which originates at the sharp bend at the foot of the steep bank at the Pitsch house. Within this wide arc bounded by the river channel on the north is a large hay meadow which extends southward to a slough at the foot of the bank partially covered with water and an extremely heavy growth of trees and underbrush. The slough commences in the vicinity of the river bend and extends eastward for about five hundred yards where it terminates at an open incline leading up onto the prairie level, which is in the form of a tongue of land jutting northward out into the meadow with an old river bank curving eastward to the river bend at the Pitsch buildings.

According to the 1891 survey, the river at that time flowed westward at the foot of this bank, from the Pitsch buildings, then northward around the tongue of land and westward along the bench to the loop south of Garryowen Bend. After following around the loop the river came into Garryowen Bend, where it flowed around the bend and thence northward. The soil along the Big Horn River is of such light consistency that during the floods, water runs over the banks and washes out new bends, often abandoning old channels. Mr. Blummer told the writer that one year at flood stage the river was one mile wide, covering the bottomland with mud and debris. As the river receded, some water remained in the lower areas and bends, making it difficult to say which was the river and which were the old channels during the spring and summer. Since 1908 the settlers probably changed the channel back to its original course so that more land could be farmed. The present channel is about where it was in 1876, as indicated in Maguire's map, although even then there was a slough at the foot of the bench caused by drainage from the long ravine to the south.

Reno's men, riding eastward at the foot of the bench, probably found the underbrush and thickets impassable except at several openings where they could get through to climb up the bank to the prairie level. It will be remembered that Reno had a hard time riding through the thickets and lost his hat and carbine. The men were strung out all the way from the woods to the river with Company A on the right and a little ahead, Company G next on the left, and Company M bringing up the rear, and it might be speculated that Reno with Company A turned south into the first opening in the thicket, while Company G, rather than waiting patiently in the line, dashed on ahead to the next opening, while the rear company may have gone up the incline farther to the east. It seems unlikely that the men would have all used the same path because their slow progress through the thickets would have left the rear of the column exposed to the Indian fire which was coming in from all directions.

When the Indians saw the soldiers commence to ride eastward up the bottom, they hurried along the prairie to the south to head them off as they came up onto the level. "They [the Indians] had come out of the woods or brush, and out of an old swale to the south, making a flank movement on us in order to cut off our retreat."[18]

When the soldiers came up the bank out of the brush, they had to run through the gantlet of Indians who were waiting for them on both sides, most of the warriors being on the south side, presumably to head the soldiers off from their line of retreat to the first ford crossing.[19]

Nothing was found in the slough, but on the tongue of land bordering it on the east were a few prairie dog mounds, and here were located with the detector two horse bells which Indians and some horsemen used to attach to harness around the withers of their horses, flattened out by a large piece of lead bullet nearby, together with an army halter buckle, and a flat sheet of steel used

[18] Letter dated February 28, 1898, from John E. Hammon to Charles E. DeLand, printed in Charles E. DeLand, "The Sioux Wars," *South Dakota Historical Collections*, 482–85.

[19] Brininstool, *Troopers with Custer*, 132–33.

General Crook's forces crossing the west fork of Goose Creek the
day before the Battle of the Rosebud, June 18, 1876.

Crook's infantry in the Black Hills, 1876. From a photograph by
S. J. Morrow.

Ravine from Calhoun Hill to Little Big Horn River. E Company troops fell at intervals along the ravine, while twenty-eight perished near the river.

Roahen Photos
Billings, Montana

Reno's second line looking north. Garryowen Bend is at left beyond the horse corral.

Photograph by the author

Looking northeast towards Custer Monument. E Company ravine is in the foreground, while troopers of E and C Companies fell where markers ascend the hill to the monument.

Roahen Photos
Billings, Montana

The Little Big Horn Battlefield as sketched by a correspondent
of *The Graphic*.

The Buckskin Lodge at Slim Buttes.

Horse travois carrying casualty after Battle of Slim Buttes.

on the hooves of lame horses. This was probably one of the escape routes used by some of Reno's men, and since the relics were both army and Indian, and being found at a prairie dog village, I speculated that this may have been the place where the horse of Isaiah Dorman was shot and fell on him, leaving the rider at the mercy of his pursuers.[20]

The slough was caused by an old ditch leading down from the south which collected flood and rain water and deposited it in low places at the foot of the bank where it collected, not draining into the river. In earlier times this ditch was lined with trees and brush, beginning some distance south of the access road, but thrifty farmers have in recent years removed the trees and brush up to the point where the ditch descends to the bottom in the form of a small ravine. While the slough and ravine are not shown on Maguire's map, they are shown on the 1908 edition of the 1891 survey map. They were undoubtedly there at the time of the battle because many of the soldiers spoke of the "thickets," while the Harmon account refers to "an old swale to the south."[21] This may have been the ravine which Lieutenant Varnum's horse (never known to jump before) cleared so handily during the headlong retreat.[22] This is also the ravine from which the Indians were believed to have emerged in Dr. Kuhlman's reconstruction of the action.

The marker honoring Charlie Reynolds, Custer's friend and chief scout, stands along the east side of the ditch and about thirty yards south of the slough, where he had been cut off and killed while coming up the bank out of the bottom in the wake of the soldiers. The marker was erected by George G. Osten on the spot pointed out to him by the returning soldiers, and on each Memorial Day he places a wreath on the marker to honor the

[20] See Stewart, *Custer's Luck*, 361, for a discussion of this incident.

[21] Letter dated February 28, 1898, from Hammon to DeLand, *op. cit.*

[22] Colonel E. L. Nye, "Cavalry Horse," *Montana: The Magazine of Western History*, Vol. 7, No. 2 (Spring, 1957), 40.

memory of the scout. North of the marker, at the edge of the slough, the writer found a horseshoe about one foot deep. Colonel Nye, who examined the shoe, proclaimed it to be a genuine cavalry shoe dating back to 1876. Since it had been bent and the nails were still protruding at various angles, he concluded that it had been thrown off by a running horse.

West of the slough is a tongue of land extending northward, but nothing was found here; the land has been under cultivation for many years and was probably not in the path of the retreating soldiers. Adjoining this strip of land on the west is the bend in which the led horses were kept, and along the west side of the strip the second skirmish line was located. The prairie at the south end of the bend was carefully examined, but nothing was found. A search of the southern extension of the second skirmish line was unavailing, probably because of the intensive cultivation of the land for many years. From this minute examination of the area, it appeared that there had been only a running fight from the second skirmish line eastward to the river, while the actual fighting occurred only in the vicinity of the two bends where the skirmish lines were located. There has been but little change in this immediate area since 1876, and although the two bends are each about one hundred feet longer because of deposits from the flooding river, this change has had little effect upon our conclusions.

When the retreating soldiers came up onto the bench, their route was eastward but south of the Pitsch ranch house. Here they were confronted with a low dry slough lying across their path, extending from the river on the north southward almost to the present access road and eastward to the next river bend. This low place was one hundred yards across and lay about fifteen feet to twenty feet below the prairie. The soldiers had either to go down into this swamp or detour around it to the south, where the Indians were waiting for them.

162

Roy Nayumatso, who lived from 1920 to 1946 in the Pitsch ranch house, in his letters of September 12 and December 6, 1965, to the author, wrote that all their fields and pasture were the battle area, and that they found "gun barrels, bullets, spurs and many other things. . . . We have found a bullet mold but have never found a gun intact just the rusty barrels." In his sketch accompanying the first letter it was indicated that most of the relics were found in the low slough, while some had been found in the next bend and in the one farthest east around and north of the ford of retreat, where the Hodgson marker is situated. This indicated that some of the soldiers went down into the low slough and retreated eastward across the two bends, crossing the river three times. It is probable that Gerard, William Jackson, Lieutenant De Rudio, and Sergeant O'Neill were among those who went down into the swamp and later found their way to Reno's hill position.[23] That part of the retreat route was across these river bends is supported by Blummer's story that Frank Bethune, who settled in this area in 1878, pointed out to him where seven or eight soldiers had been buried on the east side of the bend after having been caught upon a sandbar in the river east of the low slough. The soldiers had placed tree branches over the bodies and piled dirt on top. Bethune claimed he discovered the bodies when his horse broke through the enclosure. Blummer and Bethune's theory was that these men had been killed at the Reno retreat ford and that their bodies had floated around the two river bends until they were caught on the sandbar. It is difficult to believe that the bodies would all float around the two bends; it seems more likely that the bodies would have been stopped along the bank at the first bend. The soldiers probably were killed while crossing the river at the sandbar from the low slough.

The main line of retreat, however, was on the prairie south of the low slough. While Mr. Nayumatso said few relics were

[23] James Willard Schultz, *William Jackson, Indian Scout*, 136–54.

found south of the access road to the ford, which is in the direct line of the retreat, it should be remembered that in a running fight there is less firing, and the cartridges would be scattered over a wide area. It is probable that relics along here have either been plowed under or have been picked up by early settlers.

The writer and some friends have made an intensive search of the areas on both sides of the Hodgson ford and the river banks where most of the men crossed in retreat but have found nothing, probably because the flooding river over a period of years has covered everything in the vicinity along its course with dirt and debris. In the bend north of this ford were found remains of old campsites but nothing from the battle.

It should be pointed out that the difficulty in locating the skirmish lines was caused by the deficiencies in the revised map of Lieutenant Maguire used at the Reno Court of Inquiry in 1879. The Lieutenant and his assistant, Sergeant Becker, were misinformed concerning the location of the bend in the river from which the first skirmish line was formed, and their testimony on this point is what led Dr. Kuhlman into error. Many of the witnesses testified that the map did not correctly represent the terrain with respect to the valley fight.[24] Several witnesses indicated correctly that the first line extended from the bend farthest west, while General Gibbon said that the map was faulty in that it showed woods where there was actually a river bend and failed to show all the loops in the river.[25] He thus explained the difficulty, because Maguire had only one loop or bend at the west end when there were three. The loop in the old riverbed with the five-acre open space in the center is shown, but Garryowen Bend and the one north of it do not appear. In place of these is a large mass of timber extending northward for some distance. The course of the

[24] Testimony of George B. Herendeen, Graham, *Official Record of a Court of Inquiry*; in this volume see also the testimony of Fred F. Gerard, 79, and testimony of Lieutenant George D. Wallace, 42.

[25] Testimony of General John Gibbon, *ibid.*, 495–98.

river running northward all the way to the mouth of Medicine Tail Coulee is also incorrect. Although most witnesses said the Indians swarmed from a ravine two or three hundred yards in their front, no effort was made to show this ravine on the Maguire map. The makers, in the belief that the action occurred at the second bend from the east, did not bother to indicate Garryowen Bend nor to show accurately the area north of it. However, it should be borne in mind that an accurate sketch of this area would have been difficult to make even had its importance been known. There were only three days in which to draw the whole field of the Little Big Horn engagement.

When the burial party of Lieutenant Colonel Michael V. Sheridan came to the field in July, 1877, to rebury the soldiers and locate and remove the remains of the officers, a correspondent of the *New York Graphic* was present. His sketch of the battlefield appeared in the issue of August 13, 1877, and was later reproduced in Graham's, *The Custer Myth*, on page 373. The sketch confirms the existence in 1877 of the two bends, the locations of the two skirmish lines, and shows the ravine or bend from which the Indians emerged at the beginning of the fight. The sketch shows Garryowen Bend with the first position of the troops at G′,[26] while at the east end of the bend the loop comes up from the south forming the right angle, with G″ marking the second skirmish line. The Caplett house would be in the right angle where the two bends come together, while the old Garryowen store would be located near G′, for the bend lengthened westward over the years, probably widening also. From the sketch it appears that the river flowed east from Garryowen Bend and made an abrupt turn back to the west, where it again returned to the east, thus forming another bend north of and similar to Garry-

[26] Testimony of Fred F. Gerard, *ibid.*, 83. Here Gerard gives an accurate description of Garryowen Bend as viewed from his position at the north end of the second skirmish line. The sketch and this testimony confirm each other concerning the existence and extent of the bend in 1876.

owen Bend. The new Garryowen store is located in the open space between the two bends and about fifty yards back from the highway. Although the course of the river channel has been changed since 1876, one can still see the old bed coming westward north of the new store almost to the highway, running close to and parallel with it for more than one hundred yards. There are several ravines along here coming up from the bottomland, and since they are north of and about the right distance from Reno's first line, this could be the place where the warriors swarmed up onto the prairie from the low land where their village was located.

Sam Denny and the writer checked the accuracy of the sketch, especially with reference to the scene of the fighting, and found that the artist stood on one of the bluffs north of Shoulderblade Creek (the one north of Denny Bluff), and as we viewed the field from that angle, every feature of the terrain fell into place. The row of trees and brush in the right middle ground still mark the course of the creek, and the old riverbeds are still visible. While one cannot rely too strongly on an unknown artist, the sketch tends to confirm all the other evidence and points up the existence of the Indian's ravine, which is still substantiated by visible evidence on the site.

In conclusion, it is believed that the tangible evidence set forth in this study, supported by the statements of returning soldiers at the fiftieth anniversary and the testimony at the Reno Court of Inquiry have enabled the writer to reconstruct the location of the fight in the valley which has long plagued students of the battle.

6

The Burning of Heck Reel's Wagon Train[1]

ᒣᒣᒣᒣᒣᒣᒣᒣᒣᒣᒣᒣᒣᒣᒣᒣᒣᒣᒣᒣᒣ

AFTER THE DEFEAT OF GENERAL CUSTER at the Little Big Horn on June 25, 1876, the Sioux and Cheyenne Indians were free to continue their depredations on the white settlements. During the summer small bands of them, well armed with .45–70 Springfield carbines taken from the dead troopers, ranged far and wide along the frontier. Numerous raids were made on isolated ranches along the North Platte River, and many settlers were killed, their herds of horses and mules stolen. Travelers and freight outfits were in constant fear of the marauders. This is the story of an attack by a band of these Indians upon a wagon train on the old Oregon Trail ten miles west of the present site of Glendo, Wyoming.

Fort Laramie and Fort Fetterman were the two army posts in this area which protected the emigrants and settlers; but since the two posts were not on a railroad line, supplies had to be laboriously freighted in from Cheyenne by large covered wagons hauled by oxen. A. H. Reel, of Cheyenne, popularly called "Heck," was a widely known freighter and cattleman who operated one of these freight outfits under contract with the army.

[1] The late L. C. Bishop, of Cheyenne, Wyoming, collaborated in the writing of this chapter, and two previously published articles have been most helpful: J. C. Shaw, "Indian Story of Sylvester Sherman," *Annals of Wyoming*, Vol. 3, No. 3, 177–78; and Joe Weppner, "Burning of the Heck Reel Wagon Train," *Annals of Wyoming*, Vol. 28, No. 1, p. 48–54.

He had been a member of the territorial assembly in 1875 and in later years was to become a state senator and mayor of Cheyenne.[2]

The headquarters for his supply train was at Camp Carlin, located two miles northwest of Cheyenne beside Crow Creek. Camp Carlin was the supply depot for a number of the Western army posts and consisted of warehouses, blacksmith shops, wheelright shops, carpenter shops, saddle and harness shops, wagon sheds, stables, corrals, and bunkhouses. As a result of his long experience in the freighting business, Heck Reel had organized his freight wagons into units of three wagons each, drawn by twelve to fourteen yoke of oxen. The front wagon carried upwards of fifteen thousand pounds of freight; the second one carried nine thousand pounds; and the rear one, cooking utensils, tents, and food for the trip. The tongues of the second and third wagons were cut off short and chained to the axle of the wagon in front.[3]

The wagon boss in charge of the train was George Throstle, who had been in Reel's employ for nine years. He was about thirty-five years old, faithful, industrious, and temperate. He had many friends and was brave almost to rashness. Sylvester "Ves" Sherman, the second boss, had been working for Heck Reel for several years. He was described as a "fine Western character, a good shot, and he usually had his firearms where they could be reached in a second."[4] Sherman, in his later years, ranched on Rawhide Creek, where he died in 1925.

In 1876, as we have seen, Fort Fetterman was the springboard for expeditions under General Crook against the Sioux. During the summer the army was sending supplies to the fort destined for the use of Crook's army, then encamped on Little Goose Creek in northern Wyoming. Heck Reel was one of the freighters

2 "Biography of A. H. Reel," *Annals of Wyoming*, Vol. 5, No. 3, p. 71.
3 "Camp Carlin," *Annals of Wyoming*, Vol. 5, No. 3, p. 25.
4 Shaw, "Indian Story of Sylvester Sherman," *Annals of Wyoming*, Vol. 3, No. 3, p. 177.

with a contract to haul flour, bacon, and other supplies to the fort during the month of July. Reel overhauled his wagons and gave them a coat of bright red paint. He then began loading with government freight and hiring men for the expedition. Since good bullwhackers were hard to find, a few Mexicans and "long-haired Missourians" were included in the crew of sixteen. Reel told Throstle to furnish every man with a good .45-caliber sixshooter and a .44-caliber Winchester. Most of the guns furnished were the new 1873 Model .44 Winchesters, although there were a few .50-caliber Spencers. The guns were to be carried in the jocky box at the front of the wagon. Because Indian signs had been seen along the North Platte, the men were instructed to be on the lookout for Indians and at all times to be careful.

While only three units of three wagons each are specifically mentioned in the accounts, it is probable that there were more wagons in the train because of the large crew of sixteen men. The front units were loaded with flour, groceries, whisky, and drygoods, while the rear unit carried ten thousand pounds of bacon packed in the first two wagons, and forty barrels of beer in the last one.

One morning in the latter part of July, the caravan broke camp and traveled the old road from Cheyenne to the Black Hills.[5] One mile from camp they passed Fort D. A. Russell and then headed northward across the treeless hills. Several days later they came to the ranch of Portugee Phillips on the Chugwater, and following down the stream they reached Bordeaux, a ranch operated by John Hunton, sixty-six miles north of Cheyenne. Hunton had served all through the Civil War in the Confederate Army. He had been a captain in the Virginia Cavalry and was wounded at Gettysburg. After the war he headed West, acquiring the ranch from James Bordeaux, who had operated a trading post there.

[5] See Spring, *Stage Routes*.

The road divided at Bordeaux, one branch continuing northeast twenty-seven miles to Fort Laramie, while the other swung to the northwest, forming the "cutoff" to Fort Fetterman. Taking the latter route, the supply train arrived at Cottonwood Creek a short distance west of the present crossing of Highway 87. Just north of the creek they struck the south branch of the Oregon Trail coming in from the east. Instead of following this main-traveled road towards the northwest, the supply train continued northward along a cutoff running west of Highway 87 for four miles, and then angled northeast parallel to the present site of the highway for four miles. Turning to the right, the caravan soon struck the north branch of the main Oregon Trail near Bull's Bend, a favorite camping place within a bend of the North Platte. The route which Throstle followed was known as the "Bull's Bend-Cottonwood Road." While it has not been explored, it is plotted on the U.S. Geological Survey Contour Maps of the area. It is easy to see from the maps why Throstle took this cutoff. The road followed a valley where there were no steep grades and but few ravines to cross. It also led to Bull's Bend, where there was plenty of water to refresh the men and stock. The wagon train probably camped here on the night of July 30, because the next evening's camp was made on Elkhorn Creek, one of the best camping places along the Oregon Trail, being well supplied with plenty of wood, water, and grass.

Early the next morning, Tuesday, August 1, the men started the strenuous task of getting the wagons up the long, hard hill north of Elkhorn Creek. Throstle and Sherman stayed behind to supervise the ascent of the heavily laden wagons. They probably had to unchain the trail wagons and drag each one up separately. Finally, all were up on the divide, but soon the train came to the valley of Coffee Creek. Here was another long, hard hill, and by the time all the wagons had gotten up on the divide late afternoon had arrived. The course was now northwestward along the

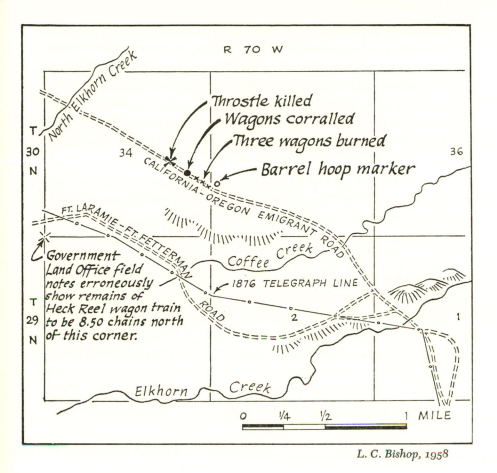

L. C. Bishop, 1958

The Burning of Heck Reel's Wagon Train

divide with the creeks they had just crossed lying to their left, and a few draws lay on their right and ahead. Towards the southwest the wooded slopes of Laramie Peak loomed against the sky.

Throstle and Sherman rode three hundred yards ahead of the lead team, resuming their usual position in advance so they could look over the road. Sherman was on the right side and a little in the lead. The experienced men were driving the lead teams, while one of the Mexicans was driving the unit next to the rear. A "long-haired Missourian" was driving the rear team. Bullwhackers walked alongside the ox teams and tried to make up for lost time by lashing the plodding animals with their stinging bullwhips. Their camp for the night on La Bonte Creek still lay ten miles ahead. The day was hot and dry, and the long lines of oxen churned up huge clouds of dust along the trail.

At about four o'clock, as Throstle and Sherman approached a little ridge running southward across the trail in front of them, about thirty Indians jumped from a deep draw north of the road and started shooting. Passing near Sherman, three bullets struck Throstle, who threw up both hands and exclaimed, "Oh, My God," and fell dead from his horse. One bullet struck the fork of Sherman's saddle. The Indians yelled and made a dash to cut him off from the wagon train. It was a close race as the Indians, whipping, shooting and yelling, caused both horses to circle toward the south instead of running straight. Sherman had no time to fire during this wild rush, because he kept both feet and hands busy whipping his horse. As he drew closer to the wagon train, the Indians pulled away but kept up a constant fire at the men running up and down the teams. Irish Pete was shot through the leg, and yelled out as loud as he could, "Corral the wagons, Ves, or they will kill every one of us." Sherman then called to the lead man to corral, and since all the good men were driving the lead teams and knew what to do, the wagons were corralled in a short time just south of the road. During this time the men were shooting at the Indians with six shooters as they rode closer.

The Mexican driving the next to the last unit deserted his post at the first of the fighting and crawled in among the dry-goods in one of the lead wagons. The Missourian in the rear, seeing that there was no chance to get his team in, left it, taking charge of the Mexican's wagon and whacking it on in. It looked for a while as if the Indians would get him, but he shot with one hand and whacked the bulls with the other.

When Sherman called for the rifles, there was only one man who knew where they were, and he jumped on a wagon and began to throw out flour. The guns had five thousand pounds of flour on top of them. The sacks of flour were used to build breast-works, behind which the men took position with their rifles. The Indians, from the gullies and ravines just below the edge of the divide about two hundred yards south of the wagons, opened up a brisk fire. Believing that the freighters had nothing but pistols, some of the Indians rode up close to the wagons, splitting the air with their war cries. Running at full speed on their war ponies, the Indians fired from under the horses' necks, while keeping themselves concealed by lying down on the ponies' sides. The Indians were armed with .45–70 Springfield carbines and .50–70 Springfield rifles and had plenty of ammunition. While they did not kill any more of the freighters, they killed and injured a number of the work cattle and the saddle horses in the train. After the freighters got in a few good rounds with their rifles, the Indians fell back and waited for night to come.

The Mexican had a little dog that he seemed to love very much, but the dog was gun shy and would run out of camp at the sight of a gun, and as we lay looking through our port holes, Irish Pete and I side by side, we saw something crawling toward us. Irish Pete whispered, "It is an Indian, we will both shoot, but let me shoot first as I feel sure I can hit him."

We both fired and a dog howled out, and a shrill voice cried,
"You killed my dog, you killed my dog!"[6]

The men held their positions in the corral the rest of the day.
As night came on, the Indians raided the rear wagon which had
been left about three hundred yards to the east, throwing off
the beer and rolling the kegs down the long hill toward the creek.
The ten thousand pounds of bacon were set afire, and the blaze
seemed to reach two hundred feet in height. The men could see
well enough to have picked up a pin in the corral. They knew that
if the Indians could see the situation they were in, they would
charge the wagons after dark. They felt sure their scalps were
gone. However, the Indians seemed to be afraid and did not
even fire into the camp.

The next morning the Indians were gone. The oxen were
unyoked and driven back to the creek for water, while some of
the men surveyed the damage from the attack. Wagon Boss
Throstle had been killed. Irish Pete had been shot in the leg,
and Sherman was injured by the shot which had struck the fork
of his saddle. Ten oxen and four horses had been killed, and the
rear unit of three wagons had been destroyed by the fire. The
wheel oxen of the rear unit had been burned to death, while the
next team had pulled the front wheels off the wagon in its blind
panic to escape the fire. Five teams were found quietly grazing
around still hitched together.

When the train resumed its journey about eleven o'clock in
the morning, Throstle was found lying where he had fallen. The
Indians had stripped and scalped him, cutting out his heart. He
was laid on a tarpaulin on top of some groceries in the lead wagon.

When we went on up the road we met two cowpunchers,
and after talking to them a minute we asked if they had seen
any Indians. They laughed and said no that they did not be-

[6] Shaw, "Indian Story of Sylvester Sherman," *Annals of Wyoming*, Vol. 3,
No. 3, p. 178.

lieve there were any Indians in the country. They said they had been on La Prele Creek for two years and had not as much as seen a moccasin track. I told them we had had a fight with them the day before. They laughed again and said show them the signs. I handed one of them my bridle reins, and stepped up on the brake and pulled the tarp back and let them see Throstle's body. They turned my horse loose and turned and rode for Ft. Fetterman, and the last we saw of them they were riding like jockeys on the last quarter in a mile race.[7]

Early that morning, August 2, a hay train left Fort Fetterman under George Powell, the hay contractor for the post, traveling eastward on the Fort Laramie road. The hay train learned of the tragedy some time during the day, probably after meeting the two cowpunchers on the trail. Powell and Groves started back to Fort Fetterman to alarm the garrison of the hostile Indians and arrived there about 9:30 P.M. John Hunton, who was at the fort, sent a telegram that night to Mr. Reel in Cheyenne informing him of the attack:

FORT LARAMIE, Aug 2

The Indians attacked your train near Elkhorn, yesterday about four o'clock. They killed and scalped Geo. Throstle, wounded a teamster, killed four horses, ten oxen, and burned three wagons.

Sam Graves and Geo. Powell brought Throstle's body into this fort tonight. Your train is on the Labonte to-night.

JOHN HUNTON[8]

Reel telegraphed instructions to have the body sent to Medicine Bow, where he would meet it with a coffin and bring it to Cheyenne for burial.[9]

[7] *Ibid.*
[8] "Doings of Devils," *Cheyenne Daily Leader* (August 3, 1876), reprinted in *Annals of Wyoming*, Vol. 28, No. 1, p. 54.
[9] *Ibid.*

Early on Thursday, August 3, George Powell set out with a party of men from Fort Fetterman to get Throstle's body and bring in the wounded. After they had left, Corporal Ward came into the fort with two men, reporting that he had come up with the ox train which had been attacked while carrying supplies to the fort. Ward had been sent out several days previously with a party as escort to Captain Hanton, who was bound for Fort Laramie. Ward's party had been relieved at Twin Springs. On its way back to Fetterman, on the east side of Horse Shoe Creek, Ward and Privates Mulcay of Company I and Williams of Company C went hunting mounted on their horses, while Privates Duncan and Troper of Companies I and C of the Fourth Infantry continued on towards the fort in the ambulance. Upon returning from the hunt, Ward, not finding any trace of the ambulance and men, started on towards Fort Fetterman. He overtook the ox train which had been attacked but passed it and came on to the fort. Since the men in the ambulance had not arrived there, they were believed to have been killed by Indians, and Ward was promptly thrown into the guard house for leaving his men.[10]

About noon Powell and his party returned to the post with Throstle's body and with Irish Pete. Throstle's body was buried later in the day in the post cemetery without any ceremony.[11] Powell then disbanded his hay party because of fear of Indian attacks. In the afternoon Sergeant Webber and four men were sent out to find the ambulance and the missing men. After they had gone, the men and the ambulance all returned safely to the post, apparently without meeting Sergeant Webber's party. That evening, because Indians were reported in the vicinity of Fort Fetterman, extra pickets were put out, and all attached men and citizen employees were armed.

On Friday, August 4, Sergeant Webber and his party re-

[10] *War Department Journal of Fort Fetterman* (August 3, 1876).
[11] *Ibid.*; and L. G. Flannery, *John Hunton's Diary*, II, 132.

turned to the post but were sent back again to escort the supply train which was still on the road to the fort. On the afternoon of Saturday, August 5, the supply train finally arrived, escorted by Sergeant Webber and his men.[12]

It had taken the supply train two and one-half days to go from La Bonte Creek to Fort Fetterman, a distance of twenty-four miles. It is difficult to understand why such slow progress was made when everyone must have been anxious to get to the fort where he would be safe from Indian attacks. Ten oxen and four horses had been killed, but there were three fewer wagons to be pulled. The oxen which had pulled the front wheels off the rear wagon were badly burned, and it is probable that some of the stock had been crippled by the gunfire. One thing is certain: all were glad to reach the safety of the fort after their harrowing experience.

The attack on the wagon train was duly reported in the August 3 edition of the Denver *Rocky Mountain News*:

Cheyenne August 2–Geo. Powell, hay contractor at Fetterman, arrived here tonight and brings the following: yesterday evening about thirty Indians attacked the wagon train of A. H. Reel, loaded with government stores for that post, killed and scalped the wagon master, Geo. Throstle, who was riding ahead, and wounded a teamster; killed four horses, ten cattle, and burned three wagons with their contents, consisting of flour and bacon. It is thought the Indians will be very troublesome on the road the rest of the season. Friday last forty-four head of horses were run off by Indians near Horse and Cottonwood Creeks.

Back on the trail remained the metal parts and the charred remnants of the burnt wagons. Animal bones and other debris lay scattered for about one-half mile along the trail. As it was a main-traveled road, supply trains, emigrants' wagons, and sol-

[12] *War Department Journal of Fort Fetterman* (August 5, 1876).

diers carried off souvenirs and everything else of value. Soon there was nothing left to indicate the incident had occurred, and in later years the exact spot had been forgotten. The bone fragments and pieces of barrel hoops remaining above ground were not accepted as conclusive evidence of the location. Until recently there were three different sites variously believed to be the place where the wagons were burned. At the first of these, where the barrel hoops were found, Bob Peterson placed a marker inscribed, "Oregon Trail. Barrel Hoop Site." Ves Sherman had told Mr. Ed Foy, the owner of the land, that this was where the action had occurred. The second site was one mile to the west at a point where the old telegraph line came up from the southeast and joined the Fort Laramie–Fort Fetterman Road. The survey notes of the General Land Office show that the remains of the A. H. Reel train were located 8.50 chains north of the southwest corner of Section 34, Township 30 North, Range 70 West, as surveyed by Jack Cole.[13] Within a few hundred feet of this location a sheepherder found a burnt wagon wheel, and Fred Dilts, the owner of this land, found a burnt wagon hub. L. C. Bishop found near here a few 8B cut nails and a staple of the kind used to hold the bows on wagon boxes. Bows were semi-circular pieces of thin oak wood which were bent so as to support the canvas covering the wagons. This site was considered authentic by some because it checked with the old road and telegraph line as shown by the Land Office plats and field notes. A marker was placed here showing that this was the site of the wagon burning. The third site was on top of the steep hill north of Elkhorn Creek, but nothing was ever found here.

In order to pinpoint the exact location of the burnt wagons and of the attack, a party which included the writers made a thorough check of all three areas with a metal detector in 1957. We went over the government-survey site first and found nothing

[13] See the U.S. Geological Contour Survey Maps of the area.

178

but one 8D cut nail. It was obvious that nothing had occurred here. We concluded that the oxen which had pulled the front wheels off the rear wagon had dragged them to this vicinity, probably with a fragment of the wagonbed, and that the government surveyor, seeing these, assumed that the wagons had been burned here.

At the barrel-hoop site we found many pieces of barrel hoops on the surface and some from two inches to five inches below the surface. Within one hundred feet south and east of the marker, on lower ground, were located three .50–70 Springfield center-fire inside-primed empty cartridge cases of the type commonly used by the Indians at that time. These may have been cartridges fired at the animals or at the Missourian as he whacked the Mexican's bulls to the corral. Nothing else was found within one hundred feet of the marker. We decided that this was the spot where the forty barrels of beer had been pushed from the rear trail wagon. While many of the barrels had been rolled down the hill, some, apparently, had been opened here. One wonders if the failure of the Indians to continue their attack that night and the next day could be attributed to their fondness for the contents of the barrels.[14]

Working northwestward, we found fifteen pieces of barrel hoop in and along the old trail beneath the surface, while some were still on top of the ground. Fifty yards west of the marker metal wagons parts were found. At 110 yards from the marker were located a band from a wagon hub eleven and one-fourth inches in diameter, one and three-fourth inches wide, and one-fourth inch thick, just south of the old trail. Within thirty feet of this band to the northwest were found seven pieces of oak wood. Probably all the wood had been burned, but only two still

---

[14] One wonders if the "Narrative" of American Horse, Tablet 16 of the Ricker Interviews in the custody of the Nebraska State Historical Society, describes the burning of this wagon train from the Indian point of view.

had charcoal on the ends, and one had red paint on the down side. Other wagon parts found beneath the surface were five miscellaneous pieces of iron; one piece of a strip from the top of a wagon box eight inches long; one brace iron from the outside of a wagon box ten inches long with two one-fourth-inch rivets through the flat part and a five-eighth-inch nut on the round end; one 20D cut nail; one 10D cut nail; one flattened iron band two and one-fourth inches wide and six inches long as flattened with two one-fourth-inch holes. The latter may have been used around a splice of a broken coupling pole or wagon tongue. One iron staple from the side of a wagon box for holding a bow, and one circular metal disc about the size of a silver dollar and in the shape of the back of a watch case were also found. All these items were found scattered along the trail for seventy yards, commencing fifty yards west of the barrel-hoop marker. This is where the three wagons were actually burned, although it is possible that they were first set afire near the barrel-hoop marker. The Indians undoubtedly removed the beer before firing the wagons. Since the three wagons were not more than seventy yards long, the frantic oxen must have plunged forward when the blaze started in an attempt to escape the fire, carrying the wagons to the 110-yard mark where the front wheels came loose and the hub band fell off. The oxen probably continued forward with the front wheels to the government-survey site, leaving the burning wagons in their rear. No empty cartridge cases were found near this place, but many old bone fragments were seen scattered along the trail, mostly on the south side.

From here the vicinity of the trail westward was explored for three hundred yards (410 yards northwest of the marker), but nothing was found except animal bones. At this point and just south of the trail was found a wagon hub band eight and one-fourth inches in diameter, four inches wide, and one-fourth inch thick, with a notch for a lynch pin. About forty feet northwest of the hub-band iron was found a lynch pin two and one-half inches long by one inch wide and one-fourth inch thick with a one-fourth-inch hole near the small end. In the north track of the trail opposite the hub band was found a loaded .50-caliber Spencer cartridge, and within twenty-five feet southeast of the hub band were found two .44–.40 center-fire empty shells which had probably been fired in a Model 1873 Winchester rifle. Within a short distance a .50-caliber Spencer empty cartridge case was dug up. Within an area of about sixty feet were found one five-eighth-inch nut; one bow staple; one four-inch strip from the top of a wagon box; one piece of one-eighth-inch iron plate four inches by five inches; one piece of one-fourth-inch thick iron with three-eighth-inch hole and one five-sixteenth-inch nut. The evidence showed that this was the place where the wagons were corralled and where the attack was made.

Since the freighters had fired their pistols in the early part of the fight, we were surprised that empty pistol cartridges were not found. Their absence can be explained by the fact that the firing was from the wagons, and the empty cartridges were probably ejected in the wagons. If the shells were outside primed, the men may have saved them for reloading.

No evidence of burning was found here except for the presence of the wagon parts, which were buried about four inches deep, indicating that they had been there as long as the empty .44–.40 Winchester cartridges. All the accounts state that it was the three wagons forming the rear unit which was burned; none say that the corralled wagons were burned. But if no wagons burned here, how can the presence of the wagon parts be explained? It is improbable that these were shot off or otherwise dislodged from the corralled wagons by the attacking Indians. After the oxen had torn the two front wheels from the wagon, they continued their stampede along the trail to the corral site where the hub band and other parts came off. Perhaps a freighter tried to stop them and they swerved, so that the careening wheels were upset or sideswiped the corral wagons, causing the parts to fall off. The wheel oxen, which were burned to death, and the next pair which were burned slightly must have done a lot of rearing and plunging in their frantic attempts to escape the flames. Their mad dash probably continued until they reached the government-survey site three-fourths of a mile farther on.

About two hundred yards south of the corral site were found two .45–70 Model 1873 Springfield inside-primed empty cartridge cases of the type used by the army at this time, and one hundred yards to the west were found two more. All four were just over the crest of the hill or divide from where the wagons were corralled and are probably from the carbines of the Indians. A short distance west of the shells we found a pile of rocks which had been there many years. The pile was of a type similar to those built by Indians in marking the location of incidents which were important to them. After every battle, it was their custom to return to the scene and mark by such monuments the spots where some white man or Indian had been killed, or where some particularly impressive feat of bravery had been performed. These are found on nearly all Indian battlefields, and this one may mark the spot where a brave was killed.

After exploring this area thoroughly and finding nothing more than old animal bones, we continued westward along the trail for two hundred yards where two broken horseshoes were found on the south side. From this point, which was on the northwest crest of a hill, we continued westward to a large draw about two hundred yards farther on, finding nothing. At this point a little ridge runs southward across the road and was probably where the Indians fired on Throstle and Sherman on the hill crest two hundred yards to the east where we found the horseshoes.

Believing the material already found sufficient to locate the sites, we made no attempt to explore the area by an exhaustive foot-by-foot search with the metal detector. The relics mentioned have been donated to the Pioneer Museum at Douglas, Wyoming, where they are on display. Most of the animal bones and all surface barrel hoops were left where they were found. The wagon parts have been identified by L. C. Bishop, Albert Sims, and Russell Thorp, all of whom grew up near Fort Fetterman and Cheyenne and are familiar with all aspects of the early-day freighting operations. We feel that the barrel-hoop marker should be maintained where it is and that the marker at the government-survey site be altered so as to show only that this was the place where the old telegraph line reached the road. It is hoped that an appropriate marker will be placed at the 110-yard site to indicate the exact location where the wagons burned, and another in the center of the corral site where the attack was made. The valiant stand made by this gallant little band of freighters on the old Oregon Trail should be marked accurately.

7
The Buckskin Lodge at Slim Buttes

ᒥᒧᒥᒧᒥᒧᒥᒧᒥᒧᒥᒧᒥᒧᒥᒧᒥᒧᒥᒧᒥᒧᒥᒧ

AFTER GENERAL CUSTER MET DISASTER on June 25, 1876, at the Little Big Horn, the Indians scattered, having exhausted their supplies and ammunition. Generals Crook and Terry launched an expedition from the Rosebud Valley in Montana in pursuit of the elusive hostiles. Crook's command soon separated from Terry's forces and followed the trail of a band of them into the barren country of the Dakota Territory and southward into present South Dakota. The scanty rations carried on the pack mules failed to last during the "Starvation March," and the jaded cavalry horses were shot to provide food for the men. The situation became so critical that Captain Anson Mills of the Third Cavalry was sent ahead with 150 picked men and horses of his regiment, together with fifty pack mules under Thomas Moore, the chief packer, under orders to hurry south to Deadwood City, in the Black Hills, to bring back supplies.

On September 8, the next afternoon after the party left, their scout, Frank Grouard, signaled a halt, saying they were nearing an Indian village. The Brulé Sioux village lay in several ravines surrounded by the steep Slim Buttes on the north, west, and south. The men, hiding about one mile and a half away from the village beneath the banks and cottonwood trees of a little stream, were drenched with cold rain. At three in the morning, the pack mules were left under the guard of Lieutenant John W. Bubb with twenty-five men, while the rest of the command moved

184

through the mud and early-morning mists as close to the village as possible. Lieutenant Schwatka was to charge through the village with twenty-five mounted men and drive the Indian ponies away, while Lieutenants Crawford and Von Luettwitz would attack on the right and left with fifty dismounted men each. Unfortunately, the ponies scented the soldiers and stampeded through the tipis, closely pursued by Schwatka's men. Crawford and Von Luettwitz, advancing through the drizzling rain, drove the Indians pell-mell from their lodges up into the rocks. The Indians kept up a steady fire on the troops; but Captain Mills, after entrenching his line, managed to hold the village until the main body under General Crook came up at about eleven-thirty that morning. At the beginning of the fight Lieutenant Von Luettwitz was shot as he stood on a little knoll, Captain Mills catching him as he fell. The chief of the band, American Horse Number Two, or Iron Shield, was mortally wounded in the abdomen and took refuge in a cave in a ravine with some of his followers, mostly women and children. After fierce resistance, they were persuaded to surrender upon promise of immunity. The surgeons tried to replace his intestines, but the chief died about midnight.

The Brulé Sioux village consisted of thirty-seven lodges and the frameworks of four more. The tipis were well stocked with meat, supplies, and robes for the winter. It was evident that this band had been at Little Big Horn because one of Custer's guidons was found attached to the outside of the tipi of Chief American Horse. A gauntlet which had belonged to Captain Myles Keogh, a corporal's overcoat, cavalry saddles and equipment, and several horses with the Seventh Cavalry brand were captured.

While most of the tipis and supplies were destroyed, one lodge was moved to a little ravine near the stream for the use of the wounded. Captain Mills was permitted to keep this lodge as a trophy, and he carried it along with him the rest of the march.

Two photographs were taken of "Buckskin Lodge" with Custer's guidon fastened to the tipi. One of these, taken by Stanley J. Morrow, the eminent frontier photographer, is in the Morrow Collection of the State University of South Dakota.[1] The Indian captives are shown lined up in front of the lodge with Frank Grouard on the left and Lieutenant Schwatka on the right. On the back of the photograph appear the words, "Prisoners captured at the Battle of Slim Buttes, with Captors Custers Battle flag and Buckskin Lodge as trophies." The other photograph of Buckskin Lodge is in the National Archives, Record Group III, Records of the Office of the Chief Signal Officer, and is numbered CN–1425. This is the one most widely known, appearing on page 110 of Anson Mills's *My Story* (see following page 160 of the present work). This picture is the same as the one with the Indian captives except that in place of the Indians are three men standing behind four men seated. On the back is written, "Buckskin Lodge, Sioux prisoners, and General Custer's battle flag; captured at the Battle of Slim Buttes. Officers in command of the charge. Lodge at Slim Buttes, 1876."

The men in this photograph are not named, but it is possible to identify some of them from the photograph numbered SC–90633 in the National Archives entitled, "Officers of 3rd Cavalry (less Cos. 'H' and 'K') in camp near Crook City, North [sic] Dakota, Sept. 1876, during Black Hills and Yellowstone Expedition." Here the officers are seated on the face of a large rock formation, with their names given on the back. This picture was evidently taken after the tipi picture, because the officers appearing in both photos had shaved and trimmed their beards and mustaches before the second was made.

Since no photographer accompanied the troops,[2] these photo-

---

[1] See Wesley R. Hurt and William R. Lass, *Frontier Photographer: Stanley J. Morrow's Dakota Years.*

[2] John F. Finerty, *Warpath and Bivouac*, 241–42.

graphs could not have been taken at Slim Buttes. In the opinion of Wesley R. Hurt, museum director and custodian of the Morrow Collection, all the pictures were taken by Morrow, who came out from Deadwood City with the supply train and joined the troops on Friday, September 13, while the soldiers were encamped on Whitewood Creek, near Crook City.[3] There are many photographs in the National Archives that were taken by Morrow but which are not in the Morrow Collection. One might speculate that he sold what photographs he could to the soldiers, and that these are the photos which later appeared in the files of the Signal Corps.

The seven men appearing in the Buckskin Lodge photograph of the National Archives rode in the charge that captured the village, and since they were familiar figures in their day, it seems fitting that their identities should be preserved. The tall man in the buckskin suit standing at the left of the picture is General Crook's head scout, Frank Grouard. He had been enlisted by General Crook, together with many other scouts, in the fall of 1875, but in the campaign to Powder River in March, 1876, he became recognized as the head scout because of his superior knowledge of the country and of the Indians' traits and habits. He served as head scout in the summer expedition that culminated in the Battle of the Rosebud on June 17, 1876, and in November of that year accompanied Crook's campaign which resulted in the destruction of the Dull Knife Village in the Big Horn Mountains of Wyoming by General Mackenzie. After the Indian Wars he was employed as army scout at Fort McKinney, becoming a familiar figure in Sheridan, Wyoming. Positive identification of Grouard in the photograph has been made by the late Tom Colsen, a long-time resident of Sheridan.

Prior to his enlistment, Grouard had lived in the camps of Sitting Bull and Crazy Horse. Here he had learned the Sioux

3 *Ibid.*, 281; and Hurt and Lass, *Frontier Photographer*, 104.

language and Indian habits and ways. He explained his dark complexion by saying that he had been born on an island in the Paumotu Group in the South Pacific.[4] At first there was a disposition to doubt his loyalty to the army because of his life among the hostile Sioux, but after the Rosebud campaign, during which he proved himself invaluable, his loyalty was never questioned. General Crook is said to have remarked that he had rather lose one-third of his command than lose the services of Grouard. Whatever may have been his early history, it is certain that he was one of the most valuable scouts during the Indian Wars. His biography has been published under the title *Life and Adventures of Frank Grouard*, by Joe DeBarthe, a newspaper correspondent who preserved in shorthand many of Grouard's own words.

The soldier in the center, standing rigidly at attention in the presence of the regimental brass, is Private W. J. McClinton, of Company C, Third Cavalry. He was honored by being included in the picture because during the charge through the village he discovered the guidon of the ill-fated Custer command fastened to the lodge of American Horse, secured the trophy, and presented it to Captain Mills. It was eventually acquired by the Seventh Cavalry and is now in the museum of the Custer Battlefield National Monument. McClinton was very proud of this feat, and on his discharge from the army received a document inscribed in red ink, with a statement of the fact that he had captured the flag in the battle of Slim Buttes.[5] After leaving the army, McClinton moved to Sheridan, Wyoming, where he became a successful businessman. Positive identification of McClinton has been made by his old friend, Tom Colsen, who has written the

[4] See DeBarthe, *Life and Adventures of Frank Grouard, xvii*; J. W. Vaughn, *With Crook at the Rosebud*, 28–29; and John S. Gray, "Frank Grouard: Kanaka Scout or Mulatto Renegade?" Chicago *Westerners Brand Book* (October, 1959), 57–64.
[5] DeBarthe, *Life and Adventures of Frank Grouard*, 155.

author that he had heard McClinton tell many times of jumping from his horse to pick up the Custer guidon, and of seeing American Horse come out of the bloody ravine clamping a stick between his teeth and carrying his intestines in his hands.

The man standing on the right with the broad-brimmed hat and the light-colored kerchief around his neck is Lieutenant Frederick Schwatka, Third Cavalry, the only West Pointer in the group. One of the most unusual individuals ever to serve in the army, Schwatka was born in Galena, Illinois, on September 29, 1849, moving with his family to Salem, Oregon, when he was ten years old. Here he worked as a printer and attended Willamette University. On his graduation from West Point in the class of 1871, he was assigned to the Third Cavalry. While serving at various army posts, he studied law and medicine and was admitted to the Nebraska bar in 1875, receiving his medical degree from Bellevue Hospital Medical College at New York City in 1876. He accompanied General Crook's summer expedition against the Sioux, serving in Company E, Third Cavalry, under Captain Alexander Sutorius. His identification is obtained from the Third Cavalry group photograph where he appears in the same clothing but minus the straggly beard.

While in the army Schwatka became interested in reports brought from the Arctic region by Captain Thomas F. Barry concerning the fate of the famous expedition of Sir John Franklin. For thirty years after the loss of the expedition British and American explorers sought the bodies or papers of this party. Schwatka persuaded the American Geographical Society to organize a new search in the Arctic. This expedition, commanded by Schwatka, who had obtained a leave of absence from the army, and William Henry Gelder, of the *New York Herald*, sailed from New York City on June 19, 1878, in the ship *Eothen*.

They were gone two years. During their search in King William's Land in 1879–80, the party performed the longest sledge journey on record, being absent from their base of supplies for eleven months and twenty days, and traversing 2,819 geographical, or 3,251 statute, miles. Schwatka discovered the wreckage of the one untraced ship of the Franklin party, located many of their graves, and gave other remains decent burial. The expedition brought back various relics of the region and established beyond doubt that Franklin's records were lost. Schwatka's search, described by Gelder in the *New York Herald*, became a popular subject, and his discoveries were hailed as a triumph of Arctic exploration. Ironically, after spending two years in the frozen north, Schwatka slipped on the ice on a sidewalk in New York City and broke his leg.

In 1885, he resigned his army commission and devoted himself to writing and lecturing. He explored the Yukon River and described his experiences in his books, *Along Alaska's Great River* (1885), and *Nimrod in the North* (1885). He commanded another Alaskan expedition, launched by the *New York Times*, in 1886, and published a book on the trip, *The Children of the Cold*, the same year.

After exploring northern Mexico, he wrote about the Tarahumari Indians of Chihuahua in a volume published after his death, *In the Land of Cave and Cliff Dweller* (1893).

His spectacular expeditions appealed to the public imagination and established that white men could exist in the Arctic if they conformed to native habits. During the last years of his life he suffered from a stomach disorder and died in Portland, Oregon, on November 2, 1892, from an overdose of laudanum. The explorer had set out on his last journey.[6]

The officer with the white hair and beard seated at the extreme left is believed to be Lieutenant Colonel William B. Royall, temporarily in command of the Third Cavalry Regiment while

[6] Information on Lieutenant Schwatka was obtained from the *Dictionary of American Biography*, XVI, 481–82.

Colonel Joseph J. Reynolds was under arrest at Fort D. A. Russell awaiting court-martial trial for alleged misconduct in the fight at the Indian village on Powder River the preceding March 17. It is impossible to make a positive identification because of the heavy growth of whiskers and the hat jammed down over his eyes. However it would seem to be the same officer as that designated as Royall in the Third Cavalry group photograph, although in the latter the beard is trimmed. The clothes and posture are the same except that at the tipi the officer was wearing a black hat. This identification is confirmed by the picture of Royall in Finerty, *Warpath and Bivouac*, facing page 44 in the original edition, although obviously taken several years after Slim Buttes. While Royall was not mentioned as being in the charge, it is possible that while in the vicinity he was asked to sit in the picture as a matter of courtesy. During the campaign he was in command of a brigade of cavalry that included his own Third Cavalry companies. He was described by Finerty as a tall, handsome man of about fifty, with a full gray mustache, dark eyebrows, blue eyes, and a high forehead.[7]

When the Civil War broke out, Royall was appointed to the army from Missouri and served all through that conflict, being breveted for gallant services at Hanover Court House, Virginia, and in the cavalry fight at Old Church, Virginia. In the latter action, Royall, armed with a revolver, with two troops of the Fifth Cavalry, charged General Jeb Stuart's advance under Captain Latane, who was armed with a saber. Royall and Latane met in a headlong charge. Latane was killed, but Royall charged through the enemy and rejoined his command with six saber wounds, several of which left scars visible through his cropped hair at the apex of his forehead.[8] This encounter received widespread publicity because of the controversy in the army con-

---

[7] Finerty, *Warpath and Bivouac*, 50.
[8] *Ibid.*; see also *United States Cavalry Journal*, V, 47.

cerning whether cavalry should be armed with sabers or revolvers, and had much to do with the army's decision to dispense
with sabers and use only pistols during the Indian Wars.

After the Civil War, Royall continued to serve in the Fifth
Cavalry under General Eugene Asa Carr until he was transferred
to the Third Cavalry. His name appears many times in the records
of Indian skirmishes. He commanded the cavalry forces at the
Battle of the Rosebud on June 17, 1876, where, after hard fighting, he was able to cut his way through to the main command
after having been isolated with four companies after the cavalry
charge on the left flank.[9]

After the Indian Wars, Royall had a long and honorable career in the army, attaining the rank of colonel with the duties of
an inspector. He was one of the important leaders in the army
during the post-Civil War period, although as a colonel he did
not receive wide publicity.

The officer with the long gray beard, seated second from the
left, is Captain William H. Andrews, Third Cavalry. He appears
the same here as in the group photograph, although in the latter
he has trimmed his beard so that it comes to a point. He served
with distinction in the Battle of the Rosebud, where he commanded one of the companies under Lieutenant Colonel Royall
that had charged too far to the left and was isolated from the
main command. During this charge, Andrews gallantly led one
platoon along a ridge to the west all the way to Andrews Point
(a prominent bluff named after him), while Lieutenant James
E. H. Foster advanced along a parallel ridge to the south with
the other platoon. Both detachments, nearly cut off by the Indians, were forced to retire to join the other four companies, which
were formed along the ridge known as Royall's first position.

Andrews had been appointed to the army from New York as

[9] For the Rosebud campaign and battle see Vaughn, *With Crook at the
Rosebud*.

192

captain of the Tenth New York Infantry. After serving all through the Civil War, he was transferred to the Twelfth Infantry and later to the Thirtieth Infantry. In 1870 he was assigned as first lieutenant in the Third Cavalry, later attaining the rank of captain which he held until his death. Captain Andrews had suffered from inflammatory rheumatism for years, the result of many years of campaigning, but the immediate cause of his death in June, 1880, was pneumonia.[10] One of the work horses of the frontier army, Andrews had worn himself out in the service of his country.

The officer who commanded the detachment that charged the village at Slim Buttes was Captain Anson Mills, who is seated below Custer's guidon. In the group picture his black beard has been trimmed and shaved down to the mustache and goatee that he usually wore in the style of the period. He was a strikingly handsome man with black hair and black eyes. In his manner he was very nervous and abrupt, and his superiors must have found him very trying because he was ever ready to criticize and offer advice.

Mills was a Texan who served in the U.S. Infantry during the Civil War and was breveted for bravery in the battles of Murfreesboro, Chickamauga, and Nashville. He played a prominent part in the attack on the Indian village on Powder River, March 17, 1876, being leader of a cavalry battalion. At the Rosebud he commanded a cavalry battalion and led several cavalry charges against the Sioux and Cheyennes. In later years he rose to the rank of a general officer and traveled extensively. He became famous for designing articles of military equipment that were used in World War I and which bore his name.

In 1918 General Mills published his autobiography under the title, *My Story*, privately printed in Washington, D.C. Dealing extensively with his experiences and describing the Indian battles

[10] *Army and Navy Journal* (June 26, 1880), 963.

in which he participated, the book is an important contribution to the literature of army life on the frontier. The story of his ideal family life runs through the narrative, the saga of one of the lesser known line officers during the Indian Wars.

Seated at the extreme right of the photograph is one of the most interesting men who ever served in the cavalry. Lieutenant Joseph Lawson was known as a "character" throughout the Third Cavalry, and his fellow officers spent much of their leisure time in badgering him. He took it all good-naturedly but would retaliate by yawning loudly during the recitals of their deeds of heroism around the campfires. He was about six feet in height with a slim, wiry build; and his red, straggly beard was generally covered with tobacco juice. Born in Ireland, he moved to Kentucky near the Ohio border, where he operated a grocery store until the Civil War broke out. Although he was forty years of age and had a wife and four or five children, he entered the service as a second lieutenant in the Eleventh Kentucky Cavalry and was soon commissioned captain. After the war he was commissioned second lieutenant in the Third Cavalry but was later promoted to first lieutenant. He served with General Crook in the Powder River campaign of March, 1876, but did not see action with Reynolds at the Indian village because he was assigned to remain with Crook and the pack train. He displayed dauntless courage at the Battle of the Rosebud and was promoted to captain the following September 25. In September, 1879, he distinguished himself in the Thornburg fight with the Ute Indians at Milk River in Colorado. Lawson was in every way a good fellow, a trusted and honest soldier. Although older than the other officers of his grade, he asked no odds of younger men, and there were few whom he could not tire out in the saddle.

Captain Lawson died on a Sunday night, January 30, 1881, at Fort Fred Steele, Wyoming, of paralysis, at the age of fifty-nine.[11] Like Captain Andrews, he had worn himself out serving in the frontier army.

This completes the identification of the men clustered in front of Buckskin Lodge. Lieutenant Emmet Crawford, Third Cavalry, who led one of the detachments during the charge through the village, does not appear in the photograph; it may be assumed that his duties kept him elsewhere. Crawford had served during the Rosebud campaign. In 1886 he led a force into Old Mexico in pursuit of Geronimo. While trying to call a peace parley, he was shot and killed by irregular Mexican troops as he stood on a high rock waving a white flag of truce.

Lieutenant Adolphus H. Von Luettwitz also is absent from the picture. After being shot in the knee, he was placed in one of the lodges with the other wounded and was made as comfortable as possible. His knee cap had been shot off, the bullet lodging in the joint. About four o'clock in the afternoon of the battle, he was laid on the grass while the surgeons knelt beside him and amputated his leg above the knee. While Dr. Valentine McGillicuddy was sawing on the bone, the Indians made an attack from the bluffs, but the surgeons completed the amputation while the attack was being repulsed. Von Luettwitz was carried along with the column in a litter swung between two mules. Dr. McGillicuddy reported that on the first day's march, the lieutenant, being in great pain, kept exclaiming, "Goddamity, Goddamity." The lieutenant was exhausted and in constant pain, and he insistently demanded that the column "shtop" so that he could rest. Since the surgeons were in charge of the wounded-train, however, he could not find anyone to take his orders.[12]

Von Luettwitz was a Prussian who had been a professional soldier ever since his graduation from the Artillery and Engineer

---

[11] Finerty, *Warpath and Bivouac*, 200; and *ibid.* (February 5, 1881), 543.
[12] Julia B. McGillicuddy, *McGillicuddy, Agent*, 58–61.

School in Berlin at the age of seventeen. He had enlisted in the Austrian and Prussian armies, had fought at Montebollo, Magenta, Solferino, and all through the Italian campaign of 1859. He served with the New York Volunteers during the American Civil War and distinguished himself at Gettysburg and other major battles, escaping comparatively unscathed.[13] Yet his hour had come, and his brilliant career was ended in the rain and mud of Slim Buttes. He was retired from the army on a pension and lived in Washington, D.C.

[13] Finerty, *Warpath and Bivouac,* 251.

Appendices

⎍⎍⎍⎍⎍⎍⎍⎍⎍⎍

APPENDIX A
from Carrington, *Wyoming Reopened, 1866*
pp. 33–42
EXPLANATION OF CONGRESSIONAL DELAY
FOR TWENTY YEARS

In the publication of General Carrington's full History of Indian Operations on the Plains, in 1866, culminating in the loss of Fetterman's Detachment, December 21, 1866.

On the 5th day of April, 1887, at the 1st session of the 50th Congress, the United States Senate called upon the Secretary of the Interior, for:

"COPY OF THE HISTORY OF INDIAN OPERATIONS ON THE PLAINS, FURNISHED BY COLONEL HENRY B. CARRINGTON TO THE SPECIAL COMMISSION AT FORT MCPHERSON, IN THE SPRING OF 1867."

After long delay, Secretary Hoke Smith, furnished the same, made up, as he reports to the Senate, in nearly 146 typewritten pages. Secretary Hoke Smith, in advising me of the finding of the original papers wrote me as follows:

"These papers were found, after long search, among waste rubbish in the basement of the building."

They appear as Senate Document No. 33, 1st Session, 50th Congress.

They are the complete evidence, upon which the Special

197

Commission of Four Generals and two civilians, made Report and fully exonerated Col. Carrington, as per Senate, Document No. 13, 40th Congress, 1st Session, 1867.

That Commission, broke up and formed Special *Sub-Commissions*, after having disposed finally of the Fetterman Disaster.

One of the civilians of that Commission, was John F. Kinney the Sutler at Fort Phil Kearney, at the time of the massacre, who had in vain tried to have Col. Carrington recognize some claims he had made against soldiers of the garrison, in connection with his sutlership.

When the Commission dissolved, said Kinney was detailed to visit Fort Phil Kearney and meet the Crow Indians, in the interest of peace and permanent friendship, with no regard whatever for the subject-matter for which the original Commission was organized.

While at that Post, "under the" official heading of the Original Commission, as if it were still in operation, "he took an *Ex-Parte Affidavit*, of Captain James Powell, in which he induced said Powell to testify that the soldiers, without interference, were allowed to plunder his store, as well as the Commissary supplies, at will, and "without punishment" that "the chief business of the mounted Infantry was horse-racing and gambling," that "he, Powell, was Executive Officer on the day of the massacre, at Col. Carrington's request"; that *he*, (Powell), *put the garrison under arms, sent out reinforcements, fired howitzers*, and *had charge of all action to relieve Fetterman and bring in the bodies*, "and that, otherwise, the *discipline was all chaotic*," etc. . . , etc.

The foregoing affidavit made up wholly of self-assertion of acts done entirely by myself, and policy falsehoods, most of which were absurdly impossible as facts, was responsive to leading questions and leading suggestions by said Kinney, who had been a lawyer and judge in Utah before securing the sutlership at Fort Phil Kearney, but it was never noticed by said Kinney in his Official Report to Washington of his visit to Fort Phil Kearney at the time the affidavit was taken.

But, it was sent by said Kinney to the Secretary of the Interior for reference to General Grant and Secretary Stanton, and was in their possession at the time of the receipt of my own Official Report. This was a deliberate attempt of said Kinney to forestall the arrival at Washington of the Report of the Special Indian Commission of which he had been a sworn member.

Mr. Browning, Secretary of the Interior, who had known me in Indiana during the war and had been my personal advisor in military affairs while I commanded that military district in 1862–1865, promptly sent me a copy of said affidavit to which I replied with full details, and the affidavit was treated by him as the affidavit of an insane man, or as procured through some extraordinary pressure expressly designed to prejudice my own Report. I not only filed the response but called in person upon Secretary Stanton and General Grant requesting that they publish my Report in full as *prima-facie* conclusive, eminating as it did from the Commanding Officer of the Rocky Mountain District. Secretary Stanton referred me to General Grant, and upon my insistant demand that it was my right to have it published in view of the false telegrams sent throughout the country Christmas week, 1866, he still declined unless sanctioned by General Grant.

I called upon General Grant immediately, never having met him before, repeated my request as a reference from Secretary Stanton, and he referred me back to Mr. Stanton, declining to take action without instructions from him. I then stated unequivocally to General Grant that the affidavit of Bvt. Maj. Powell sent to Secretary Browning was procured by John Kinney, late of the Indian Commission, to defeat recognition of the Report of said Commission of which he had been a member; that "the affidavit was gross perjury and false in all its leading particulars."

To this statement General Grant very seriously replied "that is a very serious charge sir." In response I said: "The Official Report of the Special Indian Commission which had before them statements of said affidavit; that I pledged my Commission and character as officer and General upon the truth of my statement," and that, if he desired I would prefer charges against the affiant Powell, and that my visit as advised by Secretary Stanton had for its purpose the immediate publication of my Report, which would give to the country, (already excited by false reports as to the disaster of Fetterman's command, Dec. 21, 1866), the truth, and render the exposure of said Powell, who was an uneducated man taken from the old Army Ranks, unnecessary, and save him and the Army from the discredit attached to his affidavit.

I dropped the subject at that moment, but before leaving stated that "an old pupil of mine by the name of Adam C. Badeau was Colonel on his staff, and if present, I would like to renew acquaintance." He replied, "there is no person of that name on my staff, unless you refer to General Adam Badeau." He then called Gen. Badeau into the office, who instantly recognized his old instructor and "would be glad to call upon me after office hours at my boarding place." He did so in the evening, and we had frequent interviews afterwards, reminiscent of his school days at the Irving Institute at Tarrytown, N.Y., where I was an instructor, during the years 1846–7 (afterwards at London in 1875, Gen. Badeau, then Consul-General of London, was very polite in his attentions, as ever afterwards while he lived). I was painfully impressed by the interview with General Grant with the conviction that he believed the affidavit to so compromise my Report that he honestly believed that it ought not to be published, perhaps for my own sake, as well as the protection of said Powell. I did not know at that time and did not know until twenty years later that General Grant had a copy of my Report in his possession, forwarded by Maj. Gen. Phillip St. George Cooke, Commanding Department of the Platte, under whom I served while commanding the Rocky Mountain District on which, in transmission of the same to Washington he had made an endorsement from a private letter to one of his staff at his Omaha Headquarters from Bvt. Maj. James Powell, which endorsement was in substance that of said Powell's affidavit taken by said Kinney. Said endorsement even denied his own telegrams to me, the originals of which were before the Commission, and were endorsed by that Commission as genuine and truthful. On the night of Dec. 22, 1866 I secured a messenger by the name of Phillips, who volunteered to start that night for Fort Laramie with dispatch both to General Cooke and General Grant the receipt of which was immediately made public; sent to Congress and published in the Senate Document No. 13, P. 26, First Session Fortieth Congress. But at the time, July 13th, 1867, when the material for said Document No. 13 was sent to the Senate my Official Report, of which said telegram was a preliminary abstract, was in possession of the War Department, and said Report, although called for by the United States Senate upon motion of Senator John Sherman by the unanimous consent of said Senate, March 29, 1867, as it appears on Page 430 of the Congressional Globe, for that Session was not furnished in response to said call of the Senate. Its publication at that time would have summarily disposed of all errors of fact which for many years passed, officially uncorrected.

My Official Report was dated Jan. 3, 1867, and Powell's letter was dated Jan. 4, 1867, so that both went with special mail that I sent as soon as I could do so to Fort Laramie to follow up in detail the telegram taken by my special messenger Phillips.

It was not until Feb. 19, 1887, responsive to another Senate demand of Feb. 11, 1887, that Gen. Cooke's endorsement of my Report which he forwarded to Washington Jan. 22, 1867, through

Gen. Sherman was published as Senate Document #97, Second Session of the Forty-Nineth Congress. In that endorsement Gen. Cooke contradicts a statement of my Report as follows: "No reinforcements for 'assured' to Col. C. failed to be sent." In the testimony given before the Special Indian Commission, and, later, before a Court of Inquiry I produced an original telegram from Gen. Cooke, stating, that, "A regiment of Infantry had been ordered to leave St. Louis to my support." When Bvt. Maj. Chambers questioned the integrity of the telegram I produced before the Commission a manuscript copy of the same signed by said Chambers as a correct copy of said telegram. On the 29th of January, 1867, General Sherman in the transmission of General P. St. George Cooke's communication says "I have to request that, if any remedial measures are deemed necessary, the investigation of the matter be left entirely with Bvt. Maj. Gen. Augur, the Department Commander, who is, by law, vested with authority to order general Court-Martials whenever necessary."

General Cooke had been already displaced in the command of the Department by General Augur, General Sherman commending as afterwards appeared in testimony with my conduct in the Expedition and Campaign. It conformed fully to his own written instructions to myself, sent during its progress while I was in command of the Rocky Mountain District.

At the time of my interview with Secretary Stanton and General Grant, already referred to, I did not know that Powell's name had already been sent to the Senate for an additional Brevet as Lieutenant Colonel because of his successful defense behind wagon beds of a wood-party, against the combined forces of Sioux Indians, being for the second time under command of Red Cloud in person during the summer succeeding the Fetterman Disaster. Upon consultation with General Sherman, who had written to Mrs. Carrington that my Report was correct in all details and it was her privilege to publish the same in the second edition of her book entitled "AB–SA–RA–KA," The Home of The Crows, I took no further action, until later, when the history had been so publicly falsified that I again went to the Senate for relief.

At the complete investigation of the Special Indian Commission which lasted for thirty days at my house at Fort Mc-Phearson, all books, letters, telegrams, and records were examined and both officers and orderlies who were at Fort Phil Kearney at the time of the Disaster were at the disposal of the Commission and its findings as reported to the Government by General Sanborn were accepted as conclusive. . . .

A Military Court of Inquiry also took my evidence and upon the basis that no additional testimony other than my Official Report and the action of the Indian Commission was needed in explanation of the Fetterman Disaster, and the events of that Campaign for the opening of the Wagon Route to Montana around the Big Horn Mountains, Gen. Sherman dissolved the Court *sine die.* . . .

Several years after my own retirement from active service, and during my detail as Military Professor at Wabash College, Indiana, upon learning that Powell, also retired, was living near Peoria, Ill., I visited him having learned that he had been in poor health, was pleasantly received, and without going into details, mentioned the fact that Judge Kinney after having acted as a member of the Indian Commission had visited Fort Phil Kearney and had charged him with having given a version of events that occurred during the few weeks after his (Powell's) arrival at Fort Phil Kearney, up to the date of Fetterman's Disaster, quite contrary to my Official Report. This was his reply: "It is so long ago that I do not recollect anything about his visit, except that it was something about his sutler's account against the Government to get a settlement for articles stolen from his sutler's stock by soldiers while he was sutler there." "I do not recollect at all what Kinney did write down, only, that he wanted some evidence to support his claim." He added before parting "I had the time of my life afterwards in fighting with Red Cloud and his Red Devils when they attacked a wood-train, which was in my charge, and have always wondered we were not all butchered before Fetterman himself was surprised and killed with his whole command." Powell seemed to enjoy my call, saying, "It was enough to craze anybody to hold that Fort when there was everlasting danger with neither men nor ammunition enough to hold our own and save the Post."

Powell's manner was kindly and showed so plainly that he had in fact forgotten all else with regard to his affidavit, that I parted from him with the conviction that his testimony furnished Judge Kinney was under a mental condition thoroughly unsound, and for which, with his temperament he was hardly responsible.

On account of the existence of the affidavit on the files of the Interior Department, and the tacit credit given to Powell's defense behind the wagon beds, the year after he had led several historical writers to off-set that against my administration in 1866, and to its discredit, I therefore, submitted the affidavit itself to all surviving officers, viz, Captain Ten Eyck, who was next to myself in command, Quartermaster Wands, and my chief Surgeon, Samuel M. Horton, (Now living retired as Colonel) of whom the last named was afterwards surgeon until the post was finally abandoned, shortly after the "Wagon Bed Fight." Each of these officers furnished written statements that Captain (Brevet Major) Powell was certainly "out of his head," and that there was no excuse whatever for the statements made to Judge Kinney, and that, "there was no plausible foundation whatever for any discredit to my Official Report."

During the winter of 1889–90 I visited Gen. Cooke and showed him Senate Executive Document #97, before referred to, he seemed deeply pained that his hasty action caused me so much worry, and said "I was in haste to forward your report as the country was greatly excited, and the Government very urgent, so that I endorsed the papers for transmission as prepared by one of my staff but do not remember which." I replied, "The endorsement by whomsoever written was a false one as to facts, which the Report itself, and those for the previous six months would have shown. Had I seen this document when the events were fresh in the public mind, I should have preferred charges of a very grave nature." To this he replied, "I can do nothing more now than to express my deep pain at what transpired. My memory recalls nothing of the details, except that in the end you were fully vindicated."

When on duty at Wabash College I was invited by Congressman Godlove S. Orth to take part with himself and Governor Morton of Indiana in a reception at his house (Lafayette, Indiana), tendered to Ex-President Grant, then visiting the City, and at a banquet given in his honor. The section of artillery of the students of Wabash College under my training accompanied me to Lafayette, and fired appropriate salutes in honor of the distinguished visitor. I had never met General Grant before, except at the interview at Washington already noticed, when I urged the publication of my Official Report. On this occasion after Governor Morton had spoken of my service in Indiana during the war, and on the Plains, General Grant gave me his hand with the simple remark, "you are doing a good work here with these young men, and Governor Morton does not say too much as to your service in Indiana, while absent from field service with your Regiment. The work done by Indiana in the support and protection of her advance troops was a notable factor in our success." He then added, "I regret that I did not know more of you during the war."

When Dr. Cyrus Townsend Brady was preparing his book

entitled "Indian Fights and Fighters" he visited me at Hyde Park, Mass., and had access to all my records, including the action of Judge Kinney, and the affidavit of Powell, but as he designed to make Powell's Wagon Bed Defense a speciality of a desperate and successful resistance by a small number of men in the use of modern repeating rifles, he did not deem it advisable to enlarge upon the methods by which the Government had been induced to delay publication of my report of operations in 1866, believing that the country at large gave full recognition to my service in opening the present State of Wyoming for settlement by white men through the expedition under my command during 1866.

A quite recent volume of a series entitled "American Commonwealth" has so fully misrepresented that expedition in respect to its chief tragedy that this record has legitimate value, and especially in the fact that it relieves the delay in the publication of my Official Report from the imputation of having been a deliberate act of injustice.

Appendix B
from Carrington, *Wyoming Reopened, 1866*
pp. 63–77

General H. B. Carrington's response to letter of Secretary of the Interior, Mr. Browning, transmitting for his information an affidavit of Captain James Powell concerning the administration of military affairs at Fort Phil Kearney in 1866, which affidavit had been procured by John F. Kinney, Sutler of said Post, who was one of the Commissioners to investigate the cause of Fetterman's Disaster, Dec. 21, 1866; said affidavit having been procured by said Kinney shortly after the full Commission fully vindicated Col. Carrington's administration and adjourned sine die as a Commission, and having also made a final solution of a matter submitted to said Commission respecting said military disaster.

In the matter of the Phil Kearney Massacre.

Henry B. Carrington, Col. 18th U.S. Infantry, upon honor, and under oath, (additional evidence given before the Special Indian Commission, at Fort McPherson, Nebraska,) having read the testimony of Bvt. Maj. Powell, furnishes the following facts, omitted by Major Powell, to make his evidence truthful and complete.

1st.—Bvt. Major Powell states that "the discipline of the enlisted men to be chaotic, owing to a want of proper support, officially and personally by company commanders from the Commanding Officer."

REMARKS: Col. Carrington personally superintended all important garrison details,—nightly visited the sentries no matter who was Officer of the Day, and, invariably supported his officers, each and all, who conformed to Order, No. 38, before given in evidence, the Regulations of the Army, and the Rules and Articles of War, Order No. 38 was enforced, although not according to the acceptance of Bt. Maj. Powell and Capt. Bisbee, and said order illustrated Col. Carrington's system of government of men.

Bvt. Maj. Powell's exception to the detail of his Lieutenant, Maj. Grummond, to command the mounted Infantry, (As Major Powell alone had a spare officer) was over-ruled.

His refusal to take up public property left by Lieut. Adair was over-ruled.

His application for return to his company, of its proportion of mounted men was refused:—the last two items applying also to Company A. Bvt. Lt. Col. Fetterman.

Officers were always supported when they were humane, just as well as exact, and conformed to the orders of their Commanding Officer. No others complained of this discipline. Striking, cursing, and other such modes of brutal departure from Order No. 38 were not supported, but reprehended, and Bvt. Maj. Powell's theory was most obnoxious to the spirit of that Order; while another officer, when absent, boasted that he "broke out a soldier's teeth with the heel of his boot"—out of pure respect for Carrington's discipline. "That officer had been the recipient of special compliments from his Colonel."

2nd.—Bvt. Maj. Powell states, that "Mounted Infantry formed a detachment from the different companies, which Detachment had no direct or immediate Commander."

REMARKS: When Bvt. Maj. Powell came to the Post, Lieut. J. J. Adair commanded the Mounted Infantry, Lieut. G. W. Grummond, assigned to same company (Powell's) and formerly a Field Officer of Volunteers, was assigned to relieve Adair in command of the Mounted Infantry and was detached from his company (Powell's) by a written order received by Maj. Powell. The Mounted Infantry were separately quartered, near their horses and never were without a direct immediate Commander. The Mounted Infantry were organized and officered and according to General Pope's Order, and as appears from Col. Carrington's evidence, were mounted at a time when they composed, within twenty, all there was of the Battalion. The desire of Maj. Powell to have a full company and a Lieut. (alone of all others) does not explain a statement which he knew to be without foundation.

3rd.—Bvt. Maj. Powell states,—that—"The parolled prisoners, being without guard, seemed to exercise their pleasure, if such it could be called, of breaking into the Commissary and stealing provisions, and also breaking into the sutler's store, which facts came under his official notice."

REMARKS: Bvt. Maj. Powell omits the fact that the prisoners

were not parolled until the day of the massacre, to make all men available for some duty;—also, that of four previously parolled, two, from the 5th U.S. Volunteers were not under charges and their regiment had been mustered out, and of the other two, both experts, one as engineer and one as a sawyer, at the mills, one came under the terms of the Executive pardon, the other within a few days of it, and both were signally industrious and faithful;— also, that the General Court Martial was ordered by the Department Commander:—and that the Commanding Officer exercised his discretion without consulting Bvt. Maj. Powell.

Also, omits the fact that neither of the parolled prisoners was ever charged with or suspected of the thefts referred to.

Also, omits the fact that there was but one robbery at the Sutler's, when the East Store Room door was left open by the carpenter, close by where the prisoners were under a tarpaulin, where they had to remain during the erection of the guard-house and then there were no signs of breaking in.

Also, omits the fact that the Colonel first notified the sutler and examined into the matter, and that Bvt. Maj. Powell, neither as Officer of the Day, or otherwise claimed to have detected the offenders:—neither did he officially, or otherwise make them known to his Commanding Officer or prefer charges.

Also, omits the fact that a special sentinel was always at the Commissary Building, day and night, even in the severest weather:—that an extra sentinel was posted in cases of reported theft, that Quarter Master Sergeant and clerk were sometimes required to sleep inside with arms, ordered to shoot whoever attempted to enter, and that with the exception of a few cans of blackberries and some syrup the thefts at the Commissary were small and rare.

Also, omits the fact that Bvt. Maj. Powell did not disclose the names of such trespassers or affords the Commanding Officer the opportunity to punish.

Also, omits the fact that with competent staff officers and Captain Ten Eyck senior to Bvt. Maj. Powell at the Post, he (Powell) could not be expected to know the plans or purposes of the Commanding Officer except as they related to his company or duties, neither did he.

4th.—Bvt. Maj. Powell states "That the Mounted Detachment amused themselves principally with card-playing, horse-racing, and getting drunk"—and, "the rest of the garrison performed their accustomed details in a very loose manner; viz, guard duties, fatigue duties in the Quarter Masters and Commissary Departments wood-trains."

REMARKS: Bvt. Maj. Powell omits the fact that when two officers playfully tested their horses on the plain below the fort, and the Colonel found that high betting took place among the enlisted men, an Order was promptly issued forbidding all racing and betting:—notwithstanding such action was deemed by some, —not excepting Maj. Powell as being an unwarrantable interference and affecting moral questions beyond the Colonel's control.

Also, omits the fact, that there was the only show of a horse-race;—that mounted infantry never used their horses more than to go a few rods to water unless in pursuit of Indians or on duty as mail carriers or otherwise.

Also, omits the fact that while there were a few incorrigables who would get dumb when they got liquor the Colonel declined his (Powell's) request to transfer such to his company for application of the discipline he proposed and that there was almost no liquor of any kind attainable soon after his arrival, since the hospital could only secure a half barrel at the sutlers when it became necessary for its use.

Also, omits the fact, that the Colonel arrested two officers one day, for undue use of stimulants even in extreme weather and made it the occasion to reprimand such use in an Order read at public parade.

Also, omits these facts,—that, often guards were changed half-hourly,—that all half-hours were called at night—that men could not, all, have two consecutive nights in bed, that all posts were carefully maintained and were visited in all weathers by the Colonel, whoever was Officer of the Day, and that Captain Bisbee, who was Post Adjutant nearly all the year, inspected and formed the Guard, made the Roster of Duty, and never reported that he was deficient, or otherwise made it apparent in the guard-system in force.

Also, omits the fact, that such was the system of preparation and watchfulness, that, at night, upon a false alarm, purposely given by the Colonel, the whole garrison was dressed and formed in line by seven minutes—was despatched to its loop-holes and positions of defense ordered—and that, not only every company but every citizen, and the sutler's clerks had their written orders as to duty, upon a general alarm, even as early as in October.

5th.—Bvt. Major Powell states, that,—"There seemed to be a system of volunteering,—officers going out in charge of men from the number of about forty to about sixty, which custom seemed to be tolerated by the Post Commander."

REMARKS: Bvt. Maj. Powell omits the fact, that a mounted detachment was kept subject to the order of the Quarter Master, who often had to go out to see about his herds:—and also the fact that the Officer of the Day was expected at once to act, upon a sudden alarm so that no time should be lost.

Also, omits the fact that Bvt. Maj. Powell, himself did not participate in volunteering and that Captain Ten Eyck, Lieut. Wands, Lieut. Adair, Captain (then Lieut.) Brown, Lieut. Matson, and Lieut. Arnold were the only officers who ever volunteered a movement toward Indian aggression, except the case of Bvt. Lieut. Col. Fetterman, Dec. 21st, 1866.

Also, omits the fact that when, on the 6th of December, in the field, I sent for Bvt. Maj. Powell to bring out reinforcements and ambulance, Lieut. Arnold took his place.

Also, omits the fact, that, in October, and a month before his arrival, the number of horses of Mounted Infantry had been reduced to 37, some of which were always on Mail duty, and that the numbers 40 and 60, are imaginary or bad recollection.

6th.—Bvt. Maj. Powell states, that,—"Indians were seldom pursued, exceeding eight or nine miles by cavalry, and the Detachment of Mounted Infantry as a general thing, Lieut. H. S. Bingham usually in charge of the cavalry and Capt. F. H. Brown, Post Quar. Mast. in charge of the Mounted Infantry."

REMARKS: Bvt. Maj. Powell omits to state, that twice, Lieut. Adair, then commanding the Mounted Infantry accompanied by Quar. Mas. Brown, pursued Indians more than twenty miles, returning so late as to occasion alarm;—that twice Colonel Carrington went to the source of Rock Creek and forks of Goose Creek, returning at night:—that several times, Capt. Ten Eyck and Lieut. Wands made pursuit until after dark, and, that all had general instructions to avoid rash pursuit as soon as the first wear of horses indicated that further pursuit would be fruitless.

Also, omits the fact, that soon after Lieut. Bingham's arrival in November, he was sent with half his company 91 miles to Fort C. F. Smith to await completion of the Post Returns for November and left there December 1st, arriving just in time to go out Dec. 6th, where he lost his life, and, that Lieut. Bingham never did go out more than once, in pursuit of Indians.

Also, omits the fact, as before intimated, that Captain Brown never did command the Mounted Infantry:—but only such details as with his employees, were permitted to aid in execution of his duties.

7th.—Bvt. Maj. Powell states, that, "The Indians were Cheyennes that between the 6th and 21st of December no additional measures were adopted at the Post, to provide against Indians:—that the line was less safe than when the Post was established:—that, on the 19th of December he had 140 men:—that the effective force for the field was 40 to a company, (140 giving him nearly the whole garrison that day not allowing for those with the train he was sent to relieve); and that, on said 19th of December, he occupied a point, a mile and a half from the Pinery, inaccessible to horses where he ordered the train to join him."

REMARKS: Bvt. Maj. Powell omits to state, that Bridger and all messengers from the Crow Indians, stated that the hostile Indians were not Cheyennes, and that he (Powell) never visited the Indians or had any intercourse with them.

Also, omits to state, that, not only Post teams but all the ex-teams of citizens were hired to complete the corral:—that work on guard-house and hospital were prosecuted even on the Sabbath twice;—and that the measures taken were so effective that only the incidental loss of the campaign preceded that of December 21st;—and, that then, the wood-party went to the woods on the 20th for their timber and worked amid snow to hasten the work.

Also, omits to state, the Colonel's trip on the 20th of December the day after he now states that he was threatened by 2500 Indians, reported by him then, at from 300 to 500.

Also, omits to state, that the line was less safe, because of a first year's occupation of a hostile region with a small force and not from failure to complete the fort and prosecute work to success.

Also, omits to state, that there is no point on the Sullivant

Hills which the road follows to the Pinery, where ambulances have not safely carried ladies or where mounted pickets or details have not often been.

Also, omits the fact that there was no time before December 21st except December 6th, when one half of 140 men went forth under any command whatever.

Also, omits the fact, that the increase of guard-detail, December 21st, was by detail upon the respective companies, his included.

8th.—Bvt. Maj. Powell makes certain statements as to the Phil Kearney Massacre,—omitting items which complete those statements.

REMARKS: Bvt. Maj. Powell omits the fact that, on the 20th, the Colonel suspended the train for the 21st and did not conclude to send it out until quite late in the morning. This omission is explained by the fact that, each night, for months, the Colonel made up a Bill for the Quarter Master of timber of different kinds to be hauled, to keep all work in progress and that the number of available wagons was reported daily and these were sent by the Colonel, first finding out whether any companies required more urgently than others. It is also explained by the fact that the Colonel occasionally consulted Bvt. Maj. Powell as to the loads required to finish his cabin;—but not as to general details. Hence, Bvt. Maj. Powell's omission as to time on the 21st of December.

9th.—Bvt. Maj. Powell states that, "Colonel Carrington commanding the Post ordered the guns of the garrison to be got in readiness 'and' during that time he sent his Adjutant to Col. Fetterman, telling him that he would furnish him a detail to go to the relief of the wood train."

REMARKS: Bvt. Maj. Powell *omits* the fact, that Col. Carrington in person assigned him (Powell) to relieve the wood-train, and later, Co. C 2nd Cavalry which he commanded, and, that Fetterman, then present, claimed the command as Powell's senior:—that the Adjutant did not detail Fetterman:—that when Fetterman asked to take Infantry, it was granted and Powell went to his own Company to send a detail to join Co. A—Fetterman's.

Also, omits the fact, that, then, and there, in his presence Lieut. Grummond received permission to go out.—Bvt. Maj. Powell not urging any claim, or desire to go.

10th.—Bvt. Maj. Powell states that "he saw Col. Carrington in conversation with Col. Fetterman, but observed that Col. Fetterman's command, in place of going to the relief of the wood-train, filed to the right and went on the Big Horn road."

REMARKS: Did Bvt. Maj. Powell hear the Order to relieve the wood-train?

Bvt. Maj. Powell omits the fact that Col. Fetterman followed the usual course to the Creek; but did not follow the Big Horn Road proper which crosses it, and turned left up the Creek, a very natural course to cut off the Indians, it being supposed the train would hold its own: but could not prosecute its work, unsupported.

11th.—Bvt. Maj. Powell states that "he (using the term) endeavored to drive the Indians from their flanks and front by shelling them, which he (I) succeeded in doing."

REMARKS:—Bvt. Maj. Powell *omits* the fact that only three caseshot were sent; that the fuses were cut and the direction given by the Colonel, while he, with a few men assisted in handling the piece and moving it to the front after recoil.

Also, omits, that he made publicly and repeatedly the remark "that last shot of the Colonel's was as good as he ever saw."

12th.—Bvt. Maj. Powell states that "he (Powell) requested

Col. Carrington to arm all employees at the Post and at once send some person to the relief of Col. Fetterman with ammunition and wagons"—that "Col. Carrington gave his consent to his request and asked his opinion, etc," that, "he armed these men, had the wagons prepared, organized the detachment, consisting of employees and soldiers, Col. Carrington ordering Capt. Ten Eyck to take command."

Bvt. Maj. Powell *omits* the fact, that nothing of the kind was done by him and that, with Capt. Ten Eyck the Colonel inspected as well as organized his command which consisted solely of soldiers, and Bvt. Maj. Powell was not present; that the Colonel called upon him to help inspect the old arms issued to teamsters, as they came out of the Magazine and those had been sent for by the Colonel through either Lieut. Wands or an Orderly before he (the Colonel) left the lookout, and that Guide Williams, acting Master of Transportation, in Hill's absence received his instructions at the Colonel's house and from him alone.

Bvt. Maj. Powell also *omits* to state, that "The Colonel had ordered the ASSEMBLY to be sounded upon the first shot, and everything started before he left the house, even to sending Orders to Capt. Ten Eyck to report and command a supporting party."

Also omits to state the fact that Adjt. Arnold obtained reports from all Companies and Quarters, as ordered by the Colonel and reported in writing at 12 o'clock A.M. that there were but 119 men at the Post.

13th.—Bvt. Maj. Powell gives statements as to conversations with his Commanding Officer and that he was practically executive Officer of the Post; without saying whether he took Lieut. Grummond's sash or otherwise was Officer of the Day; or stating that any officer, or Company received orders from or through him other than the remaining men of his Company;—and *omits* to state that when his Company took its place, he was with it at its loopholes for instructions and that every other Company acted equally under its own officer without any responsibility to him.

Bvt. Maj. Powell also *omits* the fact that the Colonel's clock was Post Time, placed by him in the Adjutant's tent; and that the messenger from Capt. Ten Eyck, was the Colonel's own mounted orderly sent out with Captain Ten Eyck, and that he returned to the Fort just after 1 o'clock.

Also, omits to state that the Orderly reported directly to the Colonel at his house, received his written instructions from the house and returned to Capt. Ten Eyck,—AND—that Bvt. Maj. Powell never saw those instructions nor was consulted about them—and, his statement as to their purport does not agree with those sent, a copy of which retained at the time is in Colonel Carrington's Original evidence.

Also, omits to state, that Capt. Ten Eyck left within the shortest possible time after firing began;—and had nearly reached the hill overlooking the scene of action when firing ceased.

14th.—Bvt. Maj. Powell stated, that "Col. Carrington told him that he thought, that he (Powell) had better take charge of the whole thing, or something to that effect;—that he (Powell) immediately did so, stopped all work and prepared the men for action.

Bvt. Maj. Powell may have had in mind the fact that "I" Colonel Carrington, afterwards detailed him to organize the unarmed men into squads for the howitzers, but *omits* the fact that it was found on the second night that the four guns were before his own door and that the detail was sleeping in a cabin close by his own bedroom;—and so remained until they were changed to tents by the Colonel's order.

Also, omits the fact that this having been done early, the Colonel, in forming Capt. Ten Eyck's party, verbally but distinctly called to arms such companies as he wished without a word to or from Bvt. Maj. Powell.

Also, omits the fact that the Colonel did not know of his "many years' experience among Indians" except from Bvt. Maj. Powell's sufficiently elaborate account of his adventures while an enlisted man in the Army.

Also, omits the fact that himself and Bvt. Lt. Col. Fetterman had shortly before been required to draw 2,000 rounds of additional ammunition for their respective Companies, to keep up their complement, as they seemed to be deficient upon inspection by the Colonel.

15th.—Bvt. Maj. Powell states that Dr. Hines was sent out twice.

REMARK: Bvt. Maj. Powell *omits* to state that Dr. Hines was sent out but once and with the Colonel's Orderly and that both came back just in time to accompany Capt. Ten Eyck.

16th.—Bvt. Maj. Powell states,—"It was nearly an hour after heavy firing was heard" before certain conversations were had with the Colonel, and during that time, no steps to his knowledge were taken to send relief;—but that half an hour after Captain Ten Eyck left.

REMARK: It was not more than an hour, hardly quite an hour after the first shot was fired before Cap. Ten Eyck sent back his messenger. Twelve o'clock sounded just after the sound of fire began, and no time was lost. Ten Eyck's men went on the run so that they straggled on the ascending slope, from the speed they made.

17th.—Bvt. Maj. Powell states that nearly all this time, the Commanding Officer was sitting on the top of his house listening to the firing;—that Dr. Hines went out about nine o'clock and

218

returned about half past ten o'clock; he soon started out again and returned about half past eleven.

REMARKS: The Memorandum note sent to order the train to the woods was not sent to the Quarter Master until nearly 10 o'clock, and Fetterman left just about 11 o'clock.

THESE FACTS ARE CERTAIN:—but are *omitted* by Bvt. Maj. Powell, as he had nothing to do with them and his surmises should not be as given under oath.

Bvt. Maj. Powell also *omits* all orders given by the Colonel from the lookout.

Also, omits who "expressed fears about Fetterman when he started," though stating that they were entertained;—but, that still, he told the Colonel, after the firing, that he thought, Fetterman was safe."

Also, omits mention of the fact that the train went safely to the woods and cut its load, so that if Fetterman had been with it, or had simply crossed the line of the retreating Indians, all the anxiety expressed would have been superfluous.

18th.—Bvt. Maj. Powell states that "Col. Carrington certainly saw him throw a shell."

REMARKS: Bvt. Maj. Powell *omits* to state that the time he (Powell) was throwing shell was some days afterward when at the Colonel's order he practiced his squad in ranges;—and that, on the 21st of December he did nothing of the kind.

19th.—Bvt. Maj. Powell states, that there were 30 bodies brought in the night of the 21st.

REMARKS: Bvt. Maj. Powell *omits* the fact that the Commanding Officer was equally desirous with him to recognize the dead;—that the circumstances would naturally induce him to look over the bodies to find Fetterman who built quarters with him, occupied the next room and went in his place to the field;—

and, that it was desirable to find how many were still missing;—and that, not 30 but 49 bodies were examined by the Colonel, Capt. Ten Eyck, and the Surgeon that evening, instead of 30.

Also, omits the fact that he was not the senior Captain at the Post, next the Colonel even after Bvt. Lt. Col. Fetterman's death;—that he had not been recognized by the Colonel as in any sense the superior of other Captains;—but had repeatedly subjected himself to the kind but positive rebuke of the Colonel for his scoffing at the Chaplain, Lieut. Adair, and religion generally, his style of treating soldiers and general methods, with the men.

20th.—Bvt. Maj. Powell, having omitted all allusions to the personal labors of his Commanding Officer, does, incidentally confirm his (the Colonel's) Report of January 3, 1867, which Report was approved by Capt. Ten Eyck, Lieut. Wands, Lieut. Matson, Dr. Horton, by every officer who saw it, when he (Powell) states July 24th, 1867, that no expedition had been made, neither could there be.

Bvt. Maj. Powell *omits* the fact, that five companies reinforced Fort Phil Kearney in January, and does not explain how Colonel Carrington could do with two-fifths the numbers, what the five-fifths could not do, after the fort had been completed and fatigue duty was less.

But, Maj. Powell does state that Colonel Carrington, Captain Ten Eyck and Lieut. Matson, with eighty or ninety men went out for the rest of the bodies.

Bvt. Maj. Powell *omits* the fact that at an interview of all the officers with the Colonel on the morning of the 22nd December, he, Bvt. Maj. Powell pronounced it unsafe to venture their rescue and that therefore, Colonel Carrington took Captain Ten Eyck with himself, for reasons given in Report of January 3d, 1867, leaving Bvt. Maj. Powell in the least exposed position, at the Post.

But, Maj. Powell *omits* the fact that at the same interview he

(Powell) recommended abandonment of the stockade (a perfect defense) and, that each Company Officer should resort to his own quarters upon an alarm and there fire upon the foe. This plan left the MAGAZINE in the center of the parade ground—abandoned the HOSPITALS, ware-houses and family quarters—gave the loop-holes to the foes, and left uncertain the effect of fire from four buildings, facing each other, two and two.

Bvt. Maj. Powell *omits* the fact that the suggestion had no supporters;—that the Colonel never, on any occasion, took instructions from his officers;—but, after the interview made his detail, recovered the dead, and that night gave to Bvt. Maj. Powell one flank to guard with his Company as well as the general superintendance of the squad with the guns.

In the scarcety of officers, all were used, but none presumed to dictate, and none was more subservient to a superior than Bvt. Maj. Powell. . . .

No explanation is offered as to Bvt. Maj. Powell's testimony, other than to supply the omission of facts.

From the last day on which after his arrival he was the guest of his Colonel at the family table until he arranged for his private Mess,—not even to say goodbye when his former host and hostess started eastward on a stormy winter's day of uncertain risk and exposure, did Bvt. Maj. Powell visit Colonel Carrington's house socially, either on INVITATION, or on his own promptings. He attended one officers' meeting, December 22nd. He reported for orders when Officer of the Day. He was never consulted or entrusted with instructions except as the incidents of duty made it proper, and the fore-going facts leave for solution the explanation of his testimony under oath, if explanation can be made.

There was no prejudice of the Colonel against Bvt. Maj. Powell for the Colonel telegraphed that he and Fetterman might be hurried forward.

His (Bvt. Maj. Powell's) illiterateness, profanity and coarseness were over-looked on account of his antecedents as a soldier, and those mistakes which made mirth for others were never repeated, or harshly judged by his Colonel. Twice he was officially mentioned with credit.

When he arrived with Bvt. Lt. Col. Fetterman, knowing that the 2nd Batallion had become the 27th Infantry, they expected the respective commands of Fort C. F. Smith and Fort Phil Kearney.

The impressions with which they came are not to be traced in this correction of Bvt. Maj. Powell's testimony.

Those corrections are due Colonel Carrington then the Commanding Officer of Fort Phil Kearney;—are due to the Record of that massacre—and no less due, for the sake of all in the Army who are struggling for honor, without prestige, and have character at stake.

Without such a full statement as an example, some would take Bvt. Maj. Powell's evidence as truthful;—and would not see how it is possible in the color of a successful skirmish of June 1867, a year later, to acquire such confidence as to revive the massacre of 1866, and make a history such as never transpired, thereby assuming laurels never won.

The testimony of Bvt. Maj. Powell was taken by one of the Commissioners after the six members had together declined to take other testimony, then at Fort McPherson, where the Commission remained for over a month, "having sufficient." My testimony in chief, names those witnesses and the substance of their proof. One was the Orderly who accompanied Dr. Hines and Captain Ten Eyck.

The (my) Report of January 3d, is the true version of the Phil Kearney Massacre.

This evidence is added, in the hope that the confirmation of that Report will give it the usual credit accorded to Reports of

Commanding Officers, which as a rule of the profession in Europe and the old Army is taken as true, in the first instance, upon their character and honor.

HENRY B. CARRINGTON, *Col. 18th U.S. Infy.*

Appendix C
Official Report of Colonel Henry B. Carrington
of January 3, 1867
(50 Cong., 1 sess., Sen. Exec. Doc. 33, pp. 39–41)
HEADQUARTERS POST,
FORT PHILIP KEARNY, DAK., January 3, 1867
ASSISTANT ADJUTANT-GENERAL, DEPARTMENT OF THE PLATTE,
Omaha, Nebr.

SIR: I respectfully state the facts of fight with Indians on the 21st ultimo. This disaster had the effect to confirm my judgment as to the hostility of Indians, and solemnly declares by its roll of dead and the number engaged that my declaration, from my arrival at Laramie, in June, was not idle conjecture, but true.

It also declares that in Indian warfare there must be perfect coolness, steadiness, and judgment. This contest is in their best and almost last hunting-grounds. They can not be whipped or punished by some little dash after a handful, nor by mere resistance of offensive movements. They must be subjected and made to respect and fear the whites.

It also declares with equal plainness that my letter from Fort Laramie as to the absolute failure of the treaty, so far as relates to my command, was true.

It also vindicates every report from my pen and every measure I have taken to secure defensive and tenable posts on this line.

It vindicates my administration of the Mountain District, Department of the Platte, and asserts that the confidence reposed in me by Lieutenant-General Sherman has been fully met.

It vindicates my application so often made for reinforcements, and demonstrates the fact that if I had received those assured to me by telegraph and letter I could have kept up communications and opened a safe route for emigrants next spring.

It proves correct my report of 1,500 lodges of hostile Indians on Tongue River not many hours' ride from the post.

It no less declares that while there has been partial success in impromptu dashes, the Indian, now desperate and bitter, looks upon the rash white man as a sure victim, no less than he does a coward, and that the United States must come to the deliberate resolve to send an army equal to a fight with the Indians of the Northwest.

Better to have the expense at once than to have a lingering, provoking war for years. It must be met, and the time is just now. I respectfully refer to my official reports and correspondence from Department headquarters for verification of the foregoing propositions, and proceed to the details of Fetterman's massacre.

On the morning of the 21st ultimo at about 11 o'clock A.M. my picket on Pilot Hill reported the wood train corralled and threatened by Indians on Sullivant Hills, a mile and a half from the fort. A few shots were heard; Indians also appeared in the brush at the crossing of Pinery by the Virginia City road. Upon tendering to Brevet Major Powell the command of Company C, Second U.S. Cavalry, then without an officer, but which he had been drilling, Brevet Lieutenant-Colonel Fetterman claimed by rank to go out. I acquiesced, giving him the men of his own company that were for duty and a portion of Company C, Second Battalion, Eighteenth U.S. Infantry.

Lieut. G. W. Grummond, who had commanded the mounted infantry, requested to take out the cavalry. He did so. In the previous skirmish Lieutenant Grummond was barely saved from the disaster that befell Lieutenant Bingham by timely aid.

Brevet Lieutenant-Colonel Fetterman also was admonished,

as well as myself, that we were fighting brave and desperate enemies who sought to make up by cunning and deceit all the advantage which the white man gains by intelligence and better arms.

My instructions were therefore preemptory and explicit. I knew the ambition of each to win honor, but being unprepared for large aggressive action through want of force (now fully demonstrated), I looked to continuance of timber supplies to prepare for more troops as the one practicable duty. Hence two days before Major Powell, sent out to cover the train under similar circumstances, simply did that duty when he could have had a fight to any extent.

The day before, viz, the 20th ultimo, I went myself to the Pinery and built a bridge of 45 feet span to expedite the passage of wagons from the woods into open ground.

Hence my instruction to Brevet Lieutenant-Colonel Fetterman, viz, "Support the wood train, relieve it, and report to me. Do not engage or pursue Indians at its expense. Under no circumstances pursue over the ridge, viz, Lodge Trail Ridge, as per map in your possession."

To Lieutenant Grummond I gave orders to report to Brevet Lieutenant-Colonel Fetterman, implicitly obey orders, and not leave him.

Before the command left I instructed Lieut. A. H. Wands, my regimental quartermaster and acting adjutant, to repeat these orders. He did so. Fearing still that the spirit of ambition might override prudence (as my refusal to permit 60 mounted men and 40 citizens to go for several days down Tongue River Valley after villages had been unfavorably regarded by Brevet Lieutenant-Colonel Fetterman and Captain Brown), I crossed the parade and from a sentry platform halted the cavalry and again repeated my precise orders.

I knew that the Indians had for several days returned, each

time with increased numbers, to feel our strength and decoy detachments to their sacrifice, and believed to foil their purpose was actual victory until reinforcement should arrive and my preparations were complete. I was right. Just as the command left, 5 Indians reappeared at the crossing. The glass revealed others in the thicket, having the apparent object of determining the watchfulness of the garrison or cutting off any small party that should move out. A case-shot dismounted 1 and developed nearly 30 more, who broke for the hills and ravines to the north.

In half an hour the picket reported that the wood train had broken corral and moved on to the Pinery. No report came from the detachment. It was composed of 81 officers and men, including 2 citizens, all well armed, the cavalry having new carbines, while the detachment of infantry was of choice men, the pride of their companies.

At 12 o'clock firing was heard toward Peno Creek, beyond Lodge Trail Ridge. A few shots were followed by constant shots, not to be counted. Captain Ten Eyck was immediately dispatched with infantry and the remaining cavalry and 2 wagons and orders to join Colonel Fetterman at all hazards.

The men moved promptly and on the run, but within little more than half an hour from the first shot, and just as the supporting party reached the hill overlooking the scene of action, all firing ceased.

Captain Ten Eyck sent a mounted orderly back with the report that he could see and hear nothing of Fetterman, but that a body of Indians on the road below him were challenging him to come down, while larger bodies were in all the valleys for several miles around. Moving cautiously forward with the wagons—evidently supposed by the enemy to be guns, as mounted men were in advance—he rescued from the spot where the enemy had been nearest 49 bodies, including those of Brevet Lieutenant-Colonel Fetterman and Capt. F. H. Brown. The latter went out without my consent or knowledge, fearless to fight Indians with any adverse odds, and determined to kill one at least before joining his company.

Captain Ten Eyck fell back slowly, but not pressed by the enemy, reaching the fort without loss. The following morning, finding general doubt as to the success of an attempt to recover other bodies, but believing that failure to rescue them would dishearten the command and encourage the Indians, who are so particular in this regard, I took 80 men and went to the scene of action, leaving a picket to advise me of any movement in the rear and to keep signal communication with the garrison. The scene of action told its story. The road on the little ridge where the final stand took place was strewn with arrowheads, scalp poles, and broken shafts of spears. The arrows that were spent harmlessly from all directions show that the command was suddenly overwhelmed, surrounded, and cut off while in retreat. Not an officer or man survived. A few bodies were found at the north end of the divide, over which the road runs, just below Lodge Trail Ridge.

Nearly all were heaped near four rocks at the point nearest the fort, these rocks, including a space about 6 feet square, having been the last refuge for defense. Here were also a few unexpended rounds of Spencer cartridges.

Fetterman and Brown had each a revolver shot in the left temple. As Brown always declared he would reserve a shot for himself as a last resort, so I am convinced that these two brave men fell each by the other's hand rather than undergo the slow torture inflicted upon others.

Lieutenant Grummond's body was on the road between the two extremes with a few others. This was not far from 5 miles from the fort and nearly as far from the wood train. Neither its own guard nor the detachment could by any possibility have helped each other, and the train was incidentally saved by the fierceness of the fight in the brave but rash impulse of pursuit.

The officers who fell believed that no Indian force could overwhelm that number of troops well held in hand.

Their terrible massacre bore marks of great valor, and has demonstrated the force and character of the foe; but no valor could have saved them.

Pools of blood on the road and sloping sides of the narrow divide showed where Indians bled fatally, but their bodies were carried off. I counted 65 such pools in the space of an acre, and 3 within 10 feet of Lieutenant Grummond's body.

Eleven American horses and 9 Indian ponies were on the road or near the line of bodies; others crippled were in the valleys. At the northwest or farther point, between two rocks and apparently where the command first fell back from the valley, realizing their danger, I found citizen James S. Wheatley and Isaac Fisher, of Blue Springs, Neb., who with "Henry rifles" felt invincible, but fell, one having 105 arrows in his naked body. The widow and family of Wheatley are here. The cartridge shells about him told how well they fought.

Before closing this report, I wish to say that every man— officer, soldier, or citizen—received burial with such record as to identify each. Fetterman, Brown, and Grummond lie in one grave. The remainder also share one tomb, buried as they fought, together, but the cases in which they were laid are duly placed and numbered.

I asked the general commanding to give my report, in absence of division commander, an access to the eye and ear of the general-in-chief. The department commander must have more troops, and I declare this my judgment solemnly and for the general public good, without one spark of personal ambition other than to do my duty daily as it comes, and whether I seem to speak too plainly or not, ever with the purpose to declare the whole truth, and with proper respect to my superior officers, who are entitled to the facts as to scenes remote from their own immediate notice.

I was asked to send all the bad news; I do it so far as I can. I give some of the facts as to my men, whose bodies I found just at dark, resolved to bring all in, viz: Mutilations: Eyes torn out and laid on the rocks; noses cut off; ears cut off; chins hewn off; teeth chopped out; joints of fingers; brains taken out and placed on rocks with other members of the body; entrails taken out and exposed; hands cut off; feet cut off; arms taken out from sockets; private parts severed and indecently placed on the person; eyes, ears, mouth, and arms penetrated with spearheads, sticks, and arrows; ribs slashed to separation with knives; skulls severed in every form, from chin to crown; muscles of calves, thighs, stomach, breast, back, arms, and cheek taken out.

Punctures upon every sensitive part of the body, even to the soles of the feet and palms of the hand.

All this only approximates to the whole truth.

Every medical officer was faithfully aided by a large force of men, and all were not buried until Wednesday after the fight.

The great real fact is that these Indians take alive when possible, and slowly torture. It is the opinion of D.S.M. Horton, post surgeon, that not more than six were killed by balls. Of course the whole arrows, hundreds of which were removed from naked bodies, were all used after removal of the clothing.

I have said enough. It is a hard but absolute duty. In the establishment of this post I designed to put it where it fell the heaviest upon the Indian and, therefore, the better for the emigrant. My duty will be done when I leave, as ordered to my new regiment headquarters, Fort Casper.

I submit herewith list of casualties, marked A. I shall also, as soon as practicable, make full report for the year 1866 of operations in the establishment of this new line.

I am, very respectfully, your obedient servant,

HENRY B. CARRINGTON
Colonel Eighteenth Infantry, Commanding

Appendix D
Memorial Address of General H. B. Carrington, Delivered at the
Monument on Massacre Hill, Sheridan County, Wyoming
on July 3rd, 1908

Fort Phil Kearney had been finished, with a strong stockade enclosure; winter had set in, and we still needed logs from the head of Piney Creek for our saw mills, and to finish our hospital.

My Official Report, shows that on the 19th I sent Captain Powell, who had recently arrived at the Fort, to relieve a threatened wood train. He reported that "he saw two or three hundred Indians," as he estimated the number, but "declined to force an engagement because of my positive orders to the contrary." It is just to him that I repeat the record made so public on the 3rd of January 1866, to his credit, as it was the first and only case in which he was out of the stockade after his arrival, and my Report also shows that on the 20th of December, the day before the great disaster, now celebrated, I went in person, with a large force, to feel the position he had reported as dangerous, and brought in a full wood train, although delayed to build a bridge to the island where the timber was cut. But on that day, no Indians appeared.

On the 21st of December, the wood train, as usual took the trail, just south of Sullivant Hill, as late as ten o'clock. The signal was soon given from Pilot Hill, that the party was threatened by Indians. I started Captain Bvt. Lt. Col. Fetterman with a strong detachment of troops to the relief of the train with positive orders twice repeated, to "relieve the wood train, escort it back in safety but not to pursue Indians, under any conditions," and especially not to cross Lodge Trail Ridge, north of the Fort.

He disappeared from sight, apparently having taken the right direction around Sullivant Hill to the north, so as to cut the Indians off from retreat over Lodge Trail Ridge.

The wood party went on, unmolested, brought home forty wagon loads of logs, two on each wagon, and some of them eighteen inches to two feet in thickness, without having had a fight, or having heard a shot, or knowledge that there had been a fight.

Fetterman, gallant through the entire Civil War from the time he joined my regiment in 1861, was impatient, and wanted a fight. He said, "I can take eighty men and go to Tongue River." To this boast, my Chief Guide, the veteran James Bridger, replied, in my presence: "Your men who fought down South, are crazy! They don't know anything about fighting Indians."

I had supposed that Fetterman was with the wood train. All at once, I heard two or three successive shots; but in the wrong direction, far over Lodge Trail Ridge. Hardly a minute passed when a few scattering shots were succeeded, three times, by something like a volley.

In sixteen minutes, shots began to *drop, drop, drop, drop,* then came dead silence. At the first shot, I went to the balcony lookout, on my building, and instantly ordered the sentry in front to fire his piece, and had the Assembly sounded. I inspected every man and his piece, and in seventeen minutes both the Infantry and a few mounted men to guard their wagons, were out of the Fort and moving at a double-quick pace for the crossing, toward the scene of conflict. Just as they crossed the Creek, the firing ceased. I said to my orderly and officers at my side, "that means that Fetterman has killed or repulsed them all, or they are accummulating for a rush." We could not imagine the real facts; but the suspense was simply stunning.

Ten Eyck, after crossing the Creek, had gone to the nearest high hill, and in sight from the Fort, to get the bearing of the Fetterman party, and sent back my Orderly, Sample, who went with him to tell me that "the Valley was full of Indians, challenging him to come down, but he could see nothing of Fetterman." I sent the Orderly back, followed by reinforcements, with this written order, "I send you forty men and ten thousand rounds of ammunition. Join Fetterman at all hazards! Keep cool! You would have saved two miles today, if you had gone as I directed over Lodge Trail Ridge." This was not a reprimand, at all, but suggestive as to the location of the enemy, as he could not otherwise know, after the firing had ceased, and he could not judge as I could, on my lookout, of the locality in peril.

As a fact, Ten Eyck obeyed my order. He pressed on, kept his men in hand, rescued forty-nine dead bodies, brought them home in safety without the loss of a man. The whole firing was over and the last man was killed inside of twenty-one minutes, and as already stated it took me fifty to come from the site of the Fort today.

Appendix E

Official Report of Captain William J. Fetterman

Dated December 7, 1866.

(40 Cong., 1 sess., *Sen. Exec. Doc. 13*, pp. 37–38)

FORT PHILIP KEARNEY, DAKOTA TERRITORY,

December 7, 1866

CAPTAIN: In compliance with your communication of to-day I have the honor to submit to the colonel commanding the post the following report of the operations of my party on the 6th instant, while in pursuit of Indians who had attacked the wood party:

In obedience to the instructions of the colonel commanding, I took command of the cavalry, numbering about thirty men, under the immediate command of Second Lieutenant H. S. Bingham, second United States cavalry, and proceeded to the wood train, about four miles from the post, which I found corralled and surrounded by Indians. There I was joined by Captain Fred. H. Brown, eighteenth United States infantry, and a couple of mounted infantry, who had already started for the relief of the train, and was overtaken by Second Lieutenant A. H. Wands, eighteenth United States infantry, and started in pursuit of the Indians, who retired before us for five miles, when, arriving in a valley through which passed the Big Horn road, the Indians offered us battle. In the most unaccountable manner the cavalry turned and commenced a retreat, which I, assisted by Captain Brown and Lieutenant Wands, used every exertion to check. The Indians, corralling and closing around us, it was plain the retreat, if continued, would be a rout and massacre. We, therefore, with the two mounted infantrymen who were with us, dismounted from our horses, and, continuing our exertions, succeeded in calling back a few of the cavalry, which swelled our number to about fourteen men, with which we turned and fought the enemy, who numbered about one hundred, surrounding us on both sides. While thus engaged, the mounted infantry which had started out on the Big Horn road, under the command of Colonel Carrington, came in sight, and passed along the road about half a mile to our right, with the purpose, I hoped, of getting to the rear of the enemy, who had a low ridge at their back. The Indians, seeing the approach of the mounted infantry, retired, we following; but finding that their rear was not attacked, a large number of them returned. After fighting about twenty minutes longer, they again retired, we in pursuit. Not being able to overtake them, I concluded to take the road and join Colonel Carrington's party, which we soon found on the road a short distance in advance. I cannot speak too highly of the conduct of Captain Brown and Lieutenant Wands, without whose assistance I fear we must have suffered serious disaster. Lieutenant Bingham, while retiring with the major part of the cavalry, encountered the mounted infantry as they were descending the road, and joined them, leaving my party of about fourteen men to oppose a hundred Indians. I cannot account for this movement on the part of an officer of such unquestionable gallantry as Lieutenant Bingham; but is it presumed that being unable to check the retreat of his men, he deemed it most prudent to hold his men in hand as much as possible, and fall back on the mounted infantry who were expected down the road.

Our casualties at this time were one man wounded, two horses wounded, and one killed.

Three Indians were shot, and two men were seen carried from the field.

I am, sir, very respectfully, your obedient servant,

WM. J. FETTERMAN

Capt. Eighteenth U. S. Infantry, Brevet Lieut. Col. U. S. A.
Brevet Captain Wm. H. Bisbie,

Eighteenth Infantry, Post Adjutant Fort Philip Kearney, D. T.
Official:

Appendix F
Annual Record of the Twenty-seventh Infantry, 1867

August 1 [1867]. A party of nineteen (19) soldiers of the 27th Infantry, commanded by 2nd Lieut. Sigismund Sternberg, 27th Infantry, on duty guarding haymakers procuring hay for the Government, about 4 miles from Fort C. F. Smith, M. T., were attacked by Indians estimated to be five hundred (500) strong. The troops were partially protected by a corral made of green brush; this small party with twelve (12) citizens defended themselves against this fearful odds for eight hours until relief reached them from the Post. Bvt. Major Burrowes, Captain 27th Infantry, with Cos. G and H and one piece of artillery, was sent to their relief; upon the arrival of this reinforcement, the Indians withdrew. The Indians made frequent attempts to charge into the enclosure, but were repulsed with great loss. The new arms, handled with great coolness, saved the party from massacre. The extent of the loss of the Indians cannot be correctly stated, but was evidently severe, as they were seen to carry off large numbers of killed and wounded, while some of their dead were left on the field. Our loss in the engagement was 2nd Lieut. S. Sternberg, Private Thomas Navin of H Co., and one citizen killed. Sergeant James Norton, Co. I and Private H. C. Vincent, Co. G, severely wounded. Lieut. Sternberg joined his company only a few days previous to the engagement. Unused to Indian warfare, he is spoken of by the men, who fought under him in this engagement, as having acted with great coolness and gallantry, in the face of such overwhelming numbers. He was killed in one of the desperate charges of the enemy, by a musket ball through the head.

Appendix G
Post Return of Fort C. F. Smith, M.T., For August, 1867
Record of Events

On the 1st inst a party of nineteen soldiers and six citizens under command of 2nd Lieut. S. Sternburg 27th Inf who were guarding a party cutting hay were attacked by a force of Indians variously estimated at from 500 to 800. The troops were partly protected by a brush and log corral and fought heroically three or four hours until relieved by troops sent from the Post. The Indians were severely punished and sustained a heavy loss estimated at eight killed and thirty wounded. With the exception of one they carried off all their killed and wounded. Our loss was Lieut Sternburg, one private and one citizen killed and one Sergeant and two privates wounded.

Since that time the troops have been engaged in performing the usual garrison duties building quarters guarding hay and wood parties and escorting supply trains between this Post and Fort Reno, D. T.

L. P. Bradley
Lieut Col 27th Inf Bvt Brig Gen U.S.A.
Commanding the Post

Appendix H

The Hayfield Fight

Ricker Interviews, Interview with Baptiste (Big Bat) Pourière,
Tablet 15, p. 110 ff.

Bat does not know when Fort C. F. Smith was built, but he
and John Richaud Jr reached the fort about one or two days after
the fight took place in the hayfield. John Richaud Jr then took
the contract to finish the haying. The Indians attacked the haying
party which was out a mile from the fort, the attack being made
about daylight. This was done by Red Cloud's Indians. The fight
lasted until about noon. Something like two or three white men
were killed, and some wounded. The Indians were trying to dislodge the whites who had their wagons coralled, and had limbs
of timber and brush put upon the inside so as to conceal themselves from view. The Indians set fire to the hay and tried to burn
the whites out. Some of the wagons were burnt up; the brush got
on fire, and the smoke and heat were intense which made the
situation of the whites extremely critical; for they had to remain
inside, as to go outside was sure death from the shots of the
enemy. There was a small military guard there from the fort.
At last a white man volunteered to go to the fort for help. He
mounted a horse and dashed among the Indians, but succeeded
in getting thru them without a scratch, and reached the fort.
A company started from the fort but was driven back by the
Indians. The Indians at length withdrew about noon. There must
have been, Bat says, judging from what the Indians say themselves 7 or 8 Indians killed and quite a number wounded. After
this the hay party moved to the fort. Next day John Richaud
came and took the hay contract off the hands of the contractor
who had lost a part of his horses and was otherwise crippled in
his outfit. Following the completion of the hay contract John
Richaud Jr took the wood contract and Bat worked for him all

winter as a hunter for the outfit to keep the men supplied with meat.

Appendix I
Official Report of Lieutenant Colonel Luther P. Bradley

FT. C. F. SMITH

August 5 1867

LIEUTENANT:

I have the honor to report for the information of the General Comdg. that matters are progressing as favorably at this post as can be expected with the means at hand. The saw mill is nearly completed and we expect to cut timber this week. I am working large details cutting and hauling timber and guarding and escorting hay parties and trains. Grass is not as good as represented by Bridger and much lighter than it was last year, as I am informed by the officers at the post. I have scouted for a circuit of ten miles around the post and find very little good hay ground. I think it will trouble us to get in the five or six hundred tons needed for this post, as the Indians are burning grass all around us and will still do it I suppose as fast as it ripens. My hay party, consisting of Lieut. Sternberg, 20 enlisted men and six citizens, was attacked on the 1st inst. by a large force of Indians, numbering I think, 500 at least. After a sharp fight of over four hours, the Indians were driven off with a heavy loss. I regret to report that Mr. Sternberg, Private Nevin of "H" and John G. Hollister, Citizen, were killed, and Serg. Norton of "I" and Private Vinson of "G" and Law of "E" severely wounded in the engagement. Nineteen mules out of 22 were shot, four of which died the same day: the balance will probably recover in time. These mules were owned by Citizen Contractors.

The Indians left *one* of their dead on the ground and several dead and wounded ponies. I am satisfied the Indians were severely punished: they carried off *eight* dead beyond any doubt,

237

and I think from the best information I can get that their killed and wounded numbered *twenty five.*

Our men fought behind a light stockade, and the Indians charged it several times both mounted and on foot, coming up within 20 paces of it in considerable numbers, while others were circling around at a little distance. They showed a good deal of pluck and were determined to take the stockade. Nothing but the coolness of our men in reserving their fire for close shots saved them. The hay grounds are 2½ miles from the fort and entirely hidden from view by high bluffs. I did not know of the fight until it had been going on some hours, very little firing was heard, and not a large body of Indians were seen, though a few rode near the post, and threatened the timber train, which was out in an opposite direction. Wishing to send out the train of hay wagons in the afternoon I directed 20 mounted men under Mr. Shurley to go in advance and reconnoiter. They developed a large number of Indians and were obliged to fall back. I then sent Maj Burroughs with Companies "G" and "H" and a howitzer when the Indians were driven back and the party at the stockade relieved. Maj. Burroughs fired a couple of case shot into their mounted parties and scattered them. He thinks that but for the howitzer, he would have had all the fighting he wanted before he got back, and that the Indians had about 800 warriors within reach when he got to the stockade.

I am having a strong stockade built at the hay grounds and shall keep a company of men and howitzer there as permanent guard. I do not think a less force than this will secure the hay.

I enclose Maj. Burroughs' report.

I return by the ox train *two* deserters from Maj. Gordon's Co who were arrested here two days ago after he left, disguised as civilians, also one horse, saddle, bridle and carbine. The six deserters reported in my last have been arrested and are now in custody. I respectfully request that a General Court Martial may be convened as soon as possible for the trial of deserters.

I have to report that Sergeant Garrett "E" Co, detailed as principal musician in Gen Order 12, deserted from this post on the 30th July. He has been tracked some distance on the road south, and I am inclined to think that he has gone to Ft Phil Kearny to fill this detail. He did not take his rifle and accouterments, but he will not need them as principal musician. The breech loading arms have not come up by the ox train. I don't understand the delay, they cannot be more needed anywhere than at this post. I send Co. "E" down with the train and I particularly request of the Genl Comdg. that he will arm them with the new rifle before they return.

I am satisfied from information gleaned from Crow Chiefs, when they were here, that my men were shot in the late fight with "treaty" powder got at Phil Kearny. I might not be able to prove this to a lawyer, or a judge, but I can prove it to any candid man, and I ask the Genl Comdg to give this his consideration, and to make such use of the information as he thinks proper. The Indians in this attack had but about *one* rifle to ten bows but they used the arrow with great effect.

Reports due to this date will be forwarded by this mail.

L. P. BRADLEY
Lt Col 27th Inf
Comdg Post

Lt Brown
A. A. A. G.
Mountain Dist.

Head Quarters Mountain Dist.
Ft Phil Kearny. I. T. Aug 12th, 1867

Official Copy
A. H. BROWN
1st Lieutenant 27th Inf. A. A. A. Gen.

Bibliography

ⅬⅬⅬⅬⅬⅬⅬⅬⅬ

(major sources only)

Army and Navy Journal.

Banta, R. E. "General Carrington's Hoosier Debacle," New York *Westerners Brand Book*, Vol. IV, No. 3 (1957).

Bent, George. "Letters to George E. Hyde," Yale University Library, New Haven.

"Biography of A. H. Reel," *Annals of Wyoming*, Vol. V, No. 3, p. 71.

Bisbee, William H. *Through Four American Wars*. Boston, 1931.

Bourke, John G. "Diary." U.S. Military Academy Library, West Point, N.Y.

Brininstool, E. A. *Troopers With Custer*. Harrisburg, 1952.

Brown, Dee. *Fort Phil Kearny: An American Saga*. New York, 1962.

Brown, Jesse, and A. M. Willard. *The Black Hills Trails*. Rapid City, S.D., 1924.

"Camp Carlin," *Annals of Wyoming*, Vol. V, No. 2, p. 25.

Carrington, Frances C. *My Army Life*. Philadelphia, 1911.

Carrington, Margaret Irvin. *Ab-Sa-Ra-Ka, Land of Massacre*. London, 1878.

Coutant, George C. *History of Wyoming*. Laramie, 1899.

Crawford, Lewis F. *Rekindling Campfires*. Bismarck, N.D., 1926.

David, Robert B. *Finn Burnett, Frontiersman: The Life and Adventures of an Indian Fighter*. Glendale, 1937.

DeBarthe, Joe. *Life and Adventures of Frank Grouard.* Ed. and with an introduction by Edgar I. Stewart. Norman, 1958.

Dictionary of American Biography. New York, 1935.

"Doings of Devils," *Cheyenne Daily Leader* (August 3, 1876).

Dustin, Fred. *Echoes from the Little Big Horn: Reno's Position in the Valley.* Saginaw, Mich., 1953.

Finerty, John F. *Warpath and Bivouac; or, the Conquest of the Sioux.* New York, 1890.

Frazer, Robert W. *Forts of the West.* Norman, 1965.

Gluckman, Col. Arcadi. *United States Muskets, Rifles, and Carbines.* Reprint edition. Harrisburg, 1959.

Graham, William A., ed. *The Official Record of a Court of Inquiry Convened by the President of the United States at Chicago, Illinois, January 13, 1879 by Request of Major Marcus A. Reno, to Investigate His Conduct at the Battle of the Little Big Horn, June 25–26, 1876.* Pacific Palisades, Calif., 1951.

Gray, John S. "Frank Grouard: Kanaka Scout or Mulatto Renegade?" Chicago *Westerners Brand Book* (October, 1959).

Grinnell, George Bird. *The Fighting Cheyennes.* Introduction by Stanley Vestal. Norman, 1956.

Guthrie, John. "The Fetterman Massacre," *Winners of the West* (September, 1939).

Hebard, Grace Raymond, and E. A. Brininstool. *The Bozeman Trail.* 2 vols. Reprint edition. Glendale, 1960.

Henry, Guy V. "Wounded in an Indian Fight," *Collections of the Wyoming Historical Society,* 1897.

Menry, Maude W. [Mrs. Will M.]. "Brown Springs Station," *Annals of Wyoming,* Vol. XXXVI, No. 1 (April, 1964).

Hunton, John. *John Hunton's Diary, 1876–'77.* Ed. by L. G. Flannery. Lingle, Wyo., 1958.

Hurt, Wesley R., and William R. Lass. *Frontier Photographer: Stanley J. Morrow's Dakota Years.* Lincoln, Neb., 1956.

Hyde, George E. *Red Cloud's Folk: A History of the Oglala Sioux Indians*. Norman, 1937.

Kelly, Fanny. *Narrative of My Captivity Among the Sioux Indians*. Philadelphia, 1872.

Klement, Frank L. "Carrington and the Golden Circle Legend in Indiana During the Civil War," *Indiana Magazine of History*, Vol. LXI (March, 1965).

Kuhlman, Charles. *Legend Into History: The Custer Mystery*. Harrisburg, 1951.

Lockwood, James D. *Life and Adventures of a Drummer Boy; or, Seven Years a Soldier*. Albany, N.Y., 1893.

McFarling, Lloyd. *Exploring the Northern Plains*. Caldwell, Idaho, 1955.

McGillicuddy, Julia B. *McGillicuddy, Agent*. Stanford University, 1941.

MacMillan, T. B. "On the Warpath," *The Chicago InterOcean* (June 24, 1876).

Marquis, Thomas B. *A Warrior Who Fought Custer*. Minneapolis, 1931.

Mills, Anson. *My Story*. Washington, D.C., 1918.

Murphy, William. "The Forgotten Battalion," *Winners of the West* (May 30 and June 30, 1928).

North Dakota Historical Collections, Vol. VI, Bismarck, N.D., 1920.

Nye, Col. E. L. "Cavalry Horse," *Montana: The Magazine of Western History*, Vol. VII, No. 2 (Spring, 1957).

O'Brien, Timothy. Letter to the editor, *Winners of the West* (March 30, 1933).

Ostrander, Alson B. *An Army Boy of the Sixties*. Yonkers, N.Y., 1924.

Ricker, Eli S., Interviews of. Tablets 15 and 16, Nebraska State Historical Society, Lincoln, 1906, 1907.

Schultz, James Willard. *William Jackson, Indian Scout.* Cambridge, Mass., 1926.

Shaw, J. C. "Burning of the Heck Reel Wagon Train," *Annals of Wyoming*, Vol. III, No. 3 (January, 1926), 177–80.

———. "Indian Story of Sylvester Sherman," *Annals of Wyoming*, Vol. III, No. 3 (January, 1926), 177–80.

South Dakota Historical Collections, Vol. XXV, Pierre, S.D.

Spring, Agnes Wright. *The Cheyenne and Black Hills Stage and Express Routes.* Glendale, 1949.

Stewart, Edgar I. *Custer's Luck.* Norman, 1955.

Straight, Michael. *Carrington.* New York, 1962.

———. "The Strange Testimony of Major Powell in the Fetterman Massacre Inquiry," New York *Westerners Brand Book*, Vol. VII, No. 1 (1960).

United States Cavalry Journal, Vol. V, p. 47.

Trenholme, Virginia Cole. *Footprints on the Frontier.* Douglas, Wyo., 1945.

Vaughn, J. W. *The Reynolds Campaign on Powder River.* Norman, 1961.

———. *With Crook at the Rosebud.* Harrisburg, 1956.

Watson, Elmo Scott. "The Bravery of Our Bugler is Much Spoken Of," *Old Travois Trails*, Vol. I, No. 6 (1941).

Weppner, Joe. "Burning of the Heck Reel Wagon Train," *Annals of Wyoming*, Vol. XXVIII, No. 1 (April, 1956), 48–54.

Index

┌┐┌┐┌┐┌┐┌┐┌┐┌┐

245

The type face selected for *Indian Fights* is 11-point Caledonia, a distinguished face designed by the late W. A. Dwiggins, the eminent American graphic artist. It is set on the Linotype with three points of space between lines for added legibility. The paper on which the book is printed bears the watermark of the University of Oklahoma Press and has an effective life of at least three hundred years.

Vaughn, Jesse Wendell, 1903–
    Indian fights; new facts on seven encounters, by J. W.
Vaughn. ₁1st ed.₁ Norman, University of Oklahoma Press
₁1966₁

    xv, 250 p. Illus., maps. 23 cm.

    Bibliography : p. 240-243.

    1. Indians of North America—Wars, 1862-1865. 2. Indians of North
America—Wars, 1866-1895. 3. Indians of North America—The West.
ɪ. Title.

E83.866.V29   978.02   66–13416

        Library of Congress   ₁5₁